to Jason —

keep it coming,

fellow Emersonian —

EMERSON AND SELF-RELIANCE

G.

MODERNITY AND
POLITICAL THOUGHT

Series Editor: Morton Schoolman
State University of New York at Albany

This unique collection of orginal studies of the great figures in the history of political and social thought critically examines their contributions to our understanding of modernity, its constitution, and the promise and problems latent within it. These works are written by some of the finest theorists of our time for scholars and students of the social sciences and humanities.

EMERSON AND SELF-RELIANCE

GEORGE KATEB

Modernity and Political Thought
VOLUME 8

SAGE Publications
International Educational and Professional Publisher
Thousand Oaks   London   New Delhi

For information address:

SAGE Publications, Inc.
2455 Teller Road
Thousand Oaks, California 91320

SAGE Publications Ltd.
6 Bonhill Street
London EC2A 4PU
United Kingdom

SAGE Publications India Pvt. Ltd.
M-32 Market
Greater Kailash I
New Delhi 110048 India

Printed in the United States of America

Library of Congress Cataloging-in-Publication Data

Kateb, George.
    Emerson and self-reliance/George Kateb.
      p. cm—(Modernity and political thought: 8)
    Includes bibliographical references and index.
    ISBN 0-8039-3866-7.—ISBN 0-8039-3867-5 (pbk.)
     1. Emerson, Ralph Waldo, 1803-1882—Political and social views.
   2. Literature and society—United States—History—19th century.
   3. Emerson, Ralph Waldo, 1803-1882. Self-reliance. 4. Self—
reliance in literature. 5. Individualism in literature.
I. Title. II. Series: Modernity and political thought; vol. 8.
PS1642.S58K38 1995
814'.3—dc20   94-22959

95 96 97 98 10 9 8 7 6 5 4 3 2 1

Sage Production Editor: Diana E. Axelsen

To Amy Gutmann

Contents

Series Editor's Introduction

George Kateb's *Emerson and Self-Reliance* is the eighth volume to appear in the Sage Series **Modernity and Political Thought.** Kateb's work coincides with the publication of Jane Bennett's *Thoreau's Nature: Ethics, Politics, and the Wild,* and follows the Spring 1994 publication of Stephen White's *Edmund Burke: Modernity, Politics and Aesthetics* and Tracy Strong's *Jean-Jacques Rousseau: The Politics of the Ordinary* (volumes 5 and 6, respectively). The series was inaugurated in 1993 with the publication of William Connolly's *The Augustinian Imperative: A Reflection on the Politics of Morality*; Richard Flathman's *Thomas Hobbes: Skepticism, Individuality, and Chastened Politics*; Fred Dallmayr's *G.W.F. Hegel: Modernity and Politics*; and Michael Shapiro's *Reading "Adam Smith": Desire, History, and Value* (volumes 1 through 4). The series will conclude with books on selected past political thinkers by leading contemporary political theorists. These will include studies of Michel Foucault by Thomas Dumm, Hannah Arendt by Seyla Benhabib, Sigmund Freud by Jean Elshtain, and Friedrich Nietzsche by Benjamin

Barber. As those who are familiar with the previous works of these authors will expect, the Sage studies adopt a variety of approaches and pose importantly different questions. As contributors to **Modernity and Political Thought,** however, their efforts also are commonly devoted to critically examining the contributions that major political theorists have made to our understanding of modernity—its constitution, and the problems, promises and dangers that are latent within it.

From its conceptual origins in the nineteenth century, individualism has been the object of sustained criticism and contestation. During the past two centuries, very few important philosophers and social theorists and the schools of thought that formed around their teachings have abstained from taking individualism to task in whole or in part. Marx, Marxists, and neo-Marxists may have been the most prominent of individualism's critics. Several other forms of communitarianism, though, including versions of feminist theory, and philosophical thought largely inimical to communitarianism, notably forms of existentialism, contemporary liberalism and post-structuralism have mounted attacks on one or another feature of individualism. In light of all this attention, it must be considered, among other possibilities, that the concept of individualism may be required for the construction of its critics' theoretical frameworks and the body of thought they support. If so, then the debates between the proponents of individualism and its adversaries would be locked into an analytical relationship that imposes rather definite limits on the theoretical progress that each side could make. Further development of the theory and practice of both individualism and its critics beyond these limits would require that individualism be extricated from this adversarial structure. In effect, individualism would have to undergo a transformation that frees it from, or at least relaxes, the obligation to define and redefine its position in reference to its opponents' discontents. With that move the conceptual boundaries of individualism could be expanded beyond its prior restrictions and its theory and practice (as well as that of its critics) could be at least partially reconstituted.

Such a transformation has been undertaken by George Kateb in his work, *The Inner Ocean: Individualism and Democratic Culture.*[1] Refusing to adopt as his point of departure another defense of the individualism targeted by a history of deadlocked criticism (recently known as the individualism-communitarian debate), Kateb distinguishes his own efforts by pointing out that "the ferocious modern or recent onslaughts on the doctrine of the individual often pay no attention to the fact that there is such a thing as a doctrine of democratic individuality."[2] What is new here, in other words, is a theory built on the recognition that theorists have neglected an individualism that has a "democratic connection." As a consequence, they have confused democratic individuality with an "unqualified" individualism, an individualism "pure and simple," an individualism severed from democratic ties. To be sure, the theory of democratic individuality does not originate with Kateb. Indeed, he eagerly demonstrates the extent to which his own efforts can be traced to those of Whitman, Thoreau, and especially Emerson—the thinker whose work serves Kateb presently as the opportunity for further explicating and developing the theory of democratic individuality. Yet, as he restores the intellectual foundations for the idea of individuality, Kateb breaks new ground in several ways. His work reflects a deep commitment to enabling us to appreciate Whitman, Thoreau, and Emerson as "the theorists of democratic individuality." Kateb directs much of the force of his own argument to conveying how the aesthetic energy and strength of their writings are, themselves, sufficient to sensitize us to the most delicate and elusive as well as robust features of individuality. By recognizing in their writings an individuality that cannot be reduced to individualism pure and simple, he opens the theory of individuality to the possibility of new discoveries that rest upon that recognition. And, finally, Kateb offers us a provocative view of what discoveries await a reconstructed theory of individuality.

It is important not to interpret the democratic connection simply as a means of reconfiguring individuality. Even though the argument often appears to be driven by an exclusive interest in renewing the meaning of "individuality," Kateb's democratic individuality should be read as weighting equally "democratic" and "individuality." The great contribution that democracy makes to individuality reflects brightly on its own nature, on the life it inspires and instructs. Kateb expresses this quite eloquently by saying that "what is at issue is the doctrine of *democratic* individuality and the way in which democracy's most elevated justification lies in its encouragement of individuality."[3] And although it is democracy, specifically representative democracy, that contributes to the birth of a transformed individuality, in Kateb's estimation it is the American democratic experience that is responsible for its flowering. The singularity of the American contribution is set off by contrast to the protestant individuality of English society and the tenacious Germanic stress on individual uniqueness. They are not democratic, but rather aristocratic and even antisocial in their existential and moral expressions, although Kateb allows that these expressions may be democratically adapted. And, of course, it speaks powerfully to America's special claim on the theory of democratic individuality, which need not be peculiarly American, that its most articulate and imaginative theorists, Whitman, Thoreau, and Emerson, are American. When we have reviewed Kateb's explanation of the ways in which American democratic political institutions nurture individuality, it will be a simple matter to follow why he privileges America's role in the flourishing of democratic individuality.

By what alchemy is an individualism without qualification turned into democratic individualism? This question directs our attention to Kateb's mentors and to the teachings that lead him to propose the notion of a "culture of democratic individuality," which we shall take up below. As Kateb explains, although they do not thematize the electoral system in a sustained way, common to the background of Whitman, Thoreau, and Emerson is the "mere" fact of the electoral system—"that all political offices are filled by contested elections, and for a limited term, and in a way that both judges the past conduct of officeholders and provides general instruction for future ones, *is a strong dissolver of the mystique of authority, first in the public realm and, ineluctably, in all others as well.*"[4] Thus Kateb brings to the surface an insight shared by the theorists of democratic individuality. When it is joined to the electoral system, when it is regularly elected and reelected, that is, *created* and *recreated,* political authority undergoes a change. It is "desacralized or demystified," terms Kateb adopts but also cautions are really too clumsy to describe adequately the enormous alteration in authority that occurs. Despite their clumsiness, however, they nevertheless intimate the metamorphosis in authority that establishes the electoral system as one of two fundamental institutions of representative democracy. (The second, constitutional due process, will be considered shortly.) Representative government's electoral process constitutes a definite authority relation between the elected and the electorate. When authority is created and recreated in the minds of the elected and the electorate, it acquires definite characteristics.

Authority is softened, restrained, subdued, disciplined or, in Kateb's words, "representative democracy signifies a radical chastening of political authority."[5] Authority is *chastened* because the electoral opportunities instituted by a representative system, to either choose authority or to be an authority that is chosen or eligible to be chosen, teaches moral lessons to both of these parties to the electoral process, in effect to society, about the nature of authority. Representative government thus has a certain "moral distinctiveness"; by virtue of electoral practices distinctive moral phenomena enter the life of society.

"What, then," Kateb asks, "are these moral phenomena?"

> First of all, there is independence of spirit . . . the independence that ordinary people show in their extraordinary moments. . . .The chastening of political authority encourages individuals to be less fearful of authority, whether concentrated in particular figures of authority or impersonally present in given rules and conventions. The positive expression of independence in the face of personal and impersonal authority can be called autonomy. Autonomy is acting on one's own, making one's life one's own, freely making commitments, accepting conventions known to be conventions, and straining to construct the architecture of one's soul. . . .The negative expression of independence is the disposition to say no, to dissent, to engage in acts of principled or conscientious disobedience or resistance or rebelliousness, whether in acts of citizenship or in the rest of life.
>
> Second, the mere status of citizen which enables one to run for office and to vote in the contested elections for office is a continuous incitement to claim the status of citizen—or something analogous—in all nonpolitical relations of life. Indeed, the incitement is to politicize the nonpolitical relations of life and to democratize them. As we know, this politicization may invade the most intimate and domestic relations of life as well as the more formal relations inherent in institutions, organizations, and associations of every sort.
>
> The third moral phenomenon follows from the electoral system's partisan or factional basis. In a representative democracy, political authority is in essence partial (to leave aside the judiciary). A part—a party or faction or coalition—is temporarily allowed to stand for the whole. Parts take turns standing for the whole and giving it a temporary moral emphasis or coloration. The very association of authority and partisanship promotes a sense of moral indeterminacy. This should not be confused with skepticism or relativism. It is rather the belief that within a frame of settled commitments, a number of contrasting and competing responses to

morally tinged questions are to be expected and welcomed. . . . A struggle against those in authority understood as defenders of one possible right answer rather than the only possible right answer is thus encouraged. Disseminated into society, this notion not only intensifies the demand to democratize all relations but cultivates a general tolerance of, and even affection for, diversity: diversity in itself, and diversity as the source of regulated contest and competition.[6]

It is now clear why Kateb is willing to speak of the "enormous alteration" in political authority for which representative government is responsible. The alteration occurs not simply, and perhaps not always, as an actual reduction in power, command, or influence of authority. And it certainly does not occur simply, as Kateb already has cautioned, by divesting authority of its aura. Rather, the alteration occurs in the individual—in beliefs and understandings, attitudes and behavior. By being implicated in the electoral process, individuals receive instruction. They learn independence by participating in or witnessing or knowing of a political practice that encourages and relies upon independent expression. They lose some fear of authority, and thus are taught to consider its limits, because that independence can be expressed to invest or to revoke authority, or to refuse to comply with an authority once it is chosen. Learning that the independence formally guaranteed by citizenship fosters an independent character, the individual may resolve to expand her role as citizen and to insinuate that independence into private—personal, family, and professional—as well as public relations. And having learned that authority is limited by those who independently constitute it, individuals come to view the moral positions attached to authority and to those who contest it as limited and necessarily open to the practical reasoning that all participants in the electoral process may contribute.

Kateb supplements his reading of representative government by introducing a conceptual scheme that refines his interpretation of democracy's pedagogical virtues. To say that the electoral process teaches these moral lessons is to say that it *contains* values or has *intrinsic* value, and does so in three ways—by accommodating, embodying, and expressing values. Where we saw, for instance, that the electoral system instructs citizens about the moral limitations of positions articulated through the essentially partial character of the electoral process (campaigns, party platforms and caucuses, public opinion, pressure, and protest groups), intrinsic to this instruction is the *accommodation* of a plurality of contested values that provides the opportunity to have morally valuable experience. Where we encountered individuals learning that authority is constituted through the electoral capacities of citizenship, intrinsic to this instruction is the *embodiment* of the idea that the individual counts, counts only as one, and is owed an account. Finally,[where we discovered individuals taking the lessons of citizenship, the sum of accommodated and embodied values, out of public life and into their professional, domestic, and personal lives, intrinsic to this instruction is the insight that representative government expresses values that work on the imaginations of its participants and that "act as a continuously potent force of suggestiveness."]

The electoral process is not the only teacher of democratic individuality. Kateb allows for many institutions and practices of representative democracy that are morally distinctive. But in addition to the electoral system there are only constitutionally protected legal procedures, specifically due process, which in his view comprise the second of the two most important pedagogical components of representative government. By due process Kateb understands not only the minimal requirements of non-arbitrary rule of law, but "enlarged" due process, which includes the adversarial system.[7] As with the electoral process, due process accommodates, embodies, and expresses values that ground its intrinsic value by providing a range of individuals with the opportunity for certain types of valuable lessons. In this area, Kateb underscores the accommodation of the values of impartiality, deliberation, and the serious play of agonistic debate taught to judges, jurors, and lawyers constrained by the rules of due process.[The value of individual dignity is accommodated by due process through the respect it exhibits for the dignity of suspects, defendants, and prisoners who may have failed to respect the dignity of others.] Yet in Kateb's view the values embodied and expressed by due process outweigh in importance those accommodated. That the government is not permitted to treat any individual as having forfeited certain rights or as having a diminished status before the law regardless of crimes committed, or is forbidden to employ any expedient to achieve worthy outcomes but must strengthen its adversary with the means to ensure a good contest, are but a few examples of the ways in which due process embodies the paramount values of justice and fairness. And as with the electoral system, taking the procedures of due process as a whole would show how they express values by teaching the sum of its valuable lessons. Among other lessons, the values accommodated and embodied by due process teach restraint. Consequently, the individual is encouraged in his public and private roles to imitate governmental procedures by exercising and internalizing the self-doubt and self-correction indicative of restraint. It is precisely because self-doubt and self-correction are imitated that they are values expressed by due process.

Just as Kateb introduces the terms *accommodate, embody,* and *express* to clarify the meaning of the moral distinctiveness of constitutional representative government, he adopts two other conceptual schemes to represent different aspects and levels of individuality. These serve quite well not only to articulate the protean forms individuality assumes in a democratic society and to deepen our appreciation of the type of political system that sponsors their production. They also distinguish from one another the elements of individuality emphatically present in the work of the theorists of democratic individuality.

Positive individuality goes to the essence of the meaning of autonomy and its turns of mind. It refers to the beliefs and attitudes engendered by the chastening of authority that may dispose the individual to examine social conventions that partially constitute our personal identities. Implicit in this disposition is the aspiration to take responsibility for oneself by determining if such conventions provide adequate opportunities for praiseworthy conduct and valuable experience. Present in Whitman, Kateb points out, is precisely this sense of responsibility as the ambition to fully display and to take pride in one's self as one is. In Thoreau it appears as the courage to reveal one's self to oneself and to others. And Emerson gives voice to the idea that one takes responsibility for one's self as a project, forever unfinished and under construction. *Negative* individuality refers to the disposition to disobey unjustifiable conventions and unjust laws. Kateb turns to Thoreau's *Civil Disobedience* for an elaboration of this democratically inspired inclination. Those who have the capacity to disobey and to recognize the occasions when disobedience is appropriate and necessary must be prepared to disobey and be disposed to other forms of disobedience—heresy, dissent, unorthodoxy, no-saying. And presupposed by such democratic virtue is the ability to engage in moral self-scrutiny, another of the character traits that constitutional representative democracy helps to foster. While negative and positive individuality provide us with our most familiar experiences of individuality, *impersonal* individuality moves beyond the inclination to distinguish oneself from the ready-made identities available through social conventions, beyond the passion to make oneself over and in every instance to author the sum of experiences and relations with others. Impersonal individuality has nothing to do with reconstituting the boundaries of personal identity and everything to do with exceeding or, better, negating them. It is the love of the world for what it is and it is expressed through what Kateb provocatively describes as an "almost promiscuous acceptance of one thing after another, almost no matter what." Its art lies in nourishing that which is superior to an ever-changing individuality—the soul. Receptive without discrimination to all that it embraces, impersonal individuality forges a qualitatively different relation to experience, "which may be called either a philosophical or poetical relation to reality." [8]

Does impersonal individuality appear to be far too exceptional to be realistically descriptive of the lives of any but a privileged few members of democratic societies? It may seem so at first, for Kateb does stress that impersonal individuality incorporates individuality's finest but also rarest qualities. Accordingly, he explains that the philosophical and poetical relation to reality that differentiates impersonal individuality possesses three elements that place it at a considerable distance from even the exceptional positive and negative forms of individuality to which democratic life gives birth. Although the poetical relationship is vital and distinctive in the work of Emerson and Thoreau, it reaches its perfection, Kateb shows, with Whitman's *Song of Myself.* It is there that each of the elements appear to be best represented, in these ways. The aesthetic element of the poetical relation is "to see all persons as beautiful, even when by conventional definition they are not. . . . the aesthetic thus becomes indistinguishable from the moral." Then there is the *overtly moral* element, which is "to see all persons as human, as able to suffer, and to sympathize with them in their ardors and their travails."[9] Finally, there is an *existential* dimension that "pertains not only to how one should perceive and understand but also to how one should act. A belief in one's inviolability allows one to take chances, to transform dead seriousness into play," into experimentation. Uncommon as these forms of expression seem to be even in the most developed democratic societies, this is no claim against Kateb's argument. Kateb's belief is that democracy is not only morally distinctive for the forms of individuality that are palpable and more or less familiar. It is distinctive, as well, for laying the foundation, to play on Marx's words, for qualities that are of democratic society but not in democratic society. Kateb puts this well by saying that "the view of all three writers is that a democratic society is best justified as a preparation for this [impersonal] individuality and is indeed justifiable as the only society in which such individuality can exist as a possibility for all. It makes possible *what goes beyond it.*"[10] And what evidence for Kateb's argument might we find to support what appears to be such an eccentric view? It is not that the theorists of democratic individuality are also the architects of its most unusual qualities. It is not, in other words, that we must take their words for it. Rather, it is that Whitman, Thoreau, and Emerson, who themselves exemplify these qualities through their work, are also emanations of democratic society.

But we should not understand from Kateb's discussion of these most precious features of impersonal individuality and of those whose intellectual achievements best represent them, that for the democratic majority individuality lies *only* in a virtually unattainable realm of possibility. This would be to place the choicest fruits of democracy beyond the reach of the numbers whose morally distinctive education justifies a democratic way of life. Kateb's entire argument would have been constructed in bad faith. On the contrary, Kateb is careful to distinguish modes of individuality according to various levels, each of which are intended to represent its actual or expected—not unexpected—presence in a democracy. While not intending to affirm the possibility that impersonal individuality is merely a form of expression exclusive to the few, Kateb positions impersonal individuality as falling within a *transcendent* level of democratic achievement. This is entirely appropriate, for transcendence is not being used here to refer to that which surpasses the horizons of the many. Rather, it is meant to convey the idea that through impersonal individuality the egoistic sense that one is better or more valuable than anything that lies outside the self is discarded or overcome. And we can see how this highest level of individualist expression is actually the next step up from other, preparatory levels upon which it rests. As examples of an *extraordinary* level of democratic individuality Kateb includes self-reliance, independent thinking, and unexpected creativity as its positive forms; civil disobedience as its negative form; and the bestowal of sympathy and the effort to see beauty in everything as its impersonal form of individuality. Again, extraordinary refers less to the fact that it is confined to the few, which it is not or is only for a time, than to the episodic or occasional experience of these forms of individuality for the many.

Yet there is the third, so-called "normal" level that, of the three, appears to be the most attractive, but not simply because it is the most common or democratic in the ordinary sense. Indeed, is it necessary at this point in our discussion to indicate that for Kateb there is nothing ordinary about democracy? The normal level of democratic individuality is the most attractive because its common eloquence leaves no doubt that our everyday experiences of individuality are not impossibly removed or disconnected from less frequent and rare forms of democratic individuality. As positive expressions of normal individuality, Kateb argues, it is quite common for those living in democratic societies to think of themselves as individuals, to suspend or perhaps abandon their identities and to adopt new roles. It has become more and more common for those who are members of marginalized, victimized, or stigmatized groups to express their individuality "negatively" by saying no to their condition and insisting that each member of any group is an individual and not a mere member of a category. And individuals who discover within themselves the capacity to practice an all-forgiving tolerance practice an impersonal individuality that must only be different in degree and not in kind from its extraordinary and transcendent forms. It is not accidental that one of the loveliest passages in *The Inner Ocean* refers to the normal level of democratic individuality, as though the beauty of its ordinary qualities should be described in a way that foretells of its ever greater possibilities.

> Though democratic surfaces change with extreme quickness, individual expression may take place, to a great extent, within a range of small differences. . . .–An observer needs a sympathetic eye to notice many of the differences. The most desirable democratic diversity is that shown by each person in relation to himself or herself in the instant or over time, a self-overcoming driven as much by self-displeased honesty as by a taste for adventure.[11]

When considered as part of democratic individuality's wonderfully articulated chromaticism, the democratic surfaces of normal democratic individuality appear to run deep.

For what reason does Kateb go to the length of providing such an elaborately textured conceptualization of democratic individuality? Would it not be sufficient to describe simply the qualities of individuality that are either encouraged by constitutional representative democracy or envisioned by the theorists of democratic individuality, without the benefit of construing individuality in terms of its forms, elements, and levels of expression? A more conservative conceptual strategy certainly would be sufficient if it were Kateb's intention to leave us with the impression that each and every individual necessarily and without fail will be the beneficiary of the moral distinctiveness of representative democracy. Rather, in his view to say that the institutions and practices of constitutionalism and representative government create or encourage or nurture individuality is to say also that they create a "*culture* of democratic individuality"—a collection of opportunities and possibilities that await individuals who become more or less involved in a democratic form of life. Accordingly, it follows that no individual's experience of a democratic form of life could be like any other's. It would vary according to the widest variety of sociological or idiosyncratic factors. The lessons individuals are taught—even the instruction entailed by the "mere" fact of voting, in one sense the most elementary of lessons and in another the most miraculous for its transfiguration of authority—would be understood on different levels, expressed in different forms, inclusive of different elements. And the notion of a political culture internalized differently by different individuals is consistent with the spirit of democratic individuality. For would it not be contrary to the nature of individuality for it to appear uniformly throughout the society that engenders it? It is not enough to understand that by teaching moral lessons democracy "suggests" or "implies" or "intimates" values, beliefs, attitudes, perspectives, dispositions, and the like. Just by so doing, democratic society is at the same time suggesting, implying, and intimating individuality in its very being— namely, that each individual's individuality is contingent and indeterminate. Only through the idea of a "culture of democratic individuality" can we comprehend the expansiveness and indefiniteness of democratic society's moral distinctiveness.

It would be mistaken to conclude from this idea of a culture of democratic individuality, however, that Kateb means to strictly equate individuality with its inexhaustibly possible expressions. To say that individu-

ality indefinitely exceeds its productions would be to aestheticize democratic theory. It would be to encourage us to take delight in individuality
only for the beauty expressed as the sheer multiplicity of its forms. To be
sure, such an aesthetic experience of individuality would be cognitive as
well as sensuous. The display of individuality is pleasurable because it
discloses the essence of individuality's being. But although the aesthetic
dimension of Kateb's work is prominent, the aesthetic qualities of individuality derive from a more fundamental, "moral" source that the aesthetic of individuality must not obscure. As Kateb explains at the outset
of *The Inner Ocean,* his argument has a moral basis, the belief that respect
for individual rights is the best way of honoring human dignity. Individual
rights honor human dignity because only through the expression of rights
can the dignity of the individual—the infinity of individuality—be represented. Thus, we can understand why Kateb insists that to speak of
individualism is to speak of democracy's moral commitment. By encouraging, nurturing, in effect, creating individuality, constitutional representative democracy is committed to human dignity, the highest moral
standard. From this, we can understand, too, why Kateb privileges American constitutionalism and representative government. Its theory and practice of promoting and protecting the expression of individual rights
promotes and protects individuality—human dignity—writ large. Put
differently, the aesthetic of American democratic individuality is the
moral accomplishment that separates it from individualism pure and
simple.

The Inner Ocean is an important contribution to the theory of democratic individuality, only a very small part of which I have been able to
explore here. As is apparent from what I have touched on in this introduction, Kateb's work is occupied with elaborating the specific features of
the theory of democratic individuality. What is necessarily omitted from
my discussion, however, is an examination of the extent to which he also
is concerned with serious philosophical questions posed by contemporary
theoretical discourse and the unique ways in which the theory of democratic individuality is able to respond. In *The Inner Ocean* Kateb enlists
the assistance of Whitman, Thoreau, and Emerson to attain both of these
objectives. It is clear from Kateb's account that the idea of a theory of
democratic individuality, its general features and philosophical sophisti-
cation, originates with their work. And it is also clear that the further

development of the theory of democratic individuality could benefit from more concentrated studies of each of its principal architects. It is to this project that Kateb turned in the closing chapter of *The Inner Ocean*, entitled "Whitman and the Culture of Democracy," and that he now continues with *Emerson and Self-Reliance*.

Once again the editor and authors of **Modernity and Political Thought** wish to thank Sage Publications for the care it has devoted to our series, and we would like to express our special gratitude to Carrie Mullen and Diana Axelsen for helping the series to achieve its fullest potential.

—*Morton Schoolman*
State University of New York at Albany

Notes

1. George Kateb, *The Inner Ocean: Individualism and Democratic Culture*. Copyright © 1992 by Cornell University. Used by permission of the publisher, Cornell University Press, Ithaca, New York.

2. Ibid., p. 80.

3. Ibid., p.78.

4. Ibid., p. 85 (my italics).

5. Ibid., p.37 (my italics).

6. Ibid., pp. 39-40.

7. Kateb notes that, strictly speaking, his model of due process would also entail the rights and entitlements specified in amendments four to eight, generously interpreted and read to include the exclusionary rule. This is less important, though, than the understanding that what he means by due process is distinct from the continental civil-law tradition and refers to an enlarged due process procedure patterned after the "due process model" conceptualized by Herbert L. Packer in *The Limits of Criminal Sanction* (Stanford: Stanford University Press, 1968).

8. *The Inner Ocean*, p. 93.

9. Ibid., pp. 93-95.

10. Ibid., p. 96 (my italics).

11. Ibid., p. 31.

Acknowledgments

I am indebted to Morton Schoolman for asking me to write about Emerson for the Sage series on **Modernity and Political Thought** and for his insight on Emerson's work.

The chapters of this book were given as lectures at Amherst College in the fall of 1992 and spring of 1993, when I served as John Jay McCloy Visiting Professor. I thank the president of Amherst, Peter Pouncey, for his invitation to lecture, for the kindness he extended to me during my visit, and for his response to what I said. For their questions and criticisms in the discussion period, I am grateful to the generous audience, and in particular to Roberto Alejandro, Alan Babb, Jack Cameron, Shin Chiba, James Der Derian, Thomas Dumm, Alexander George, Dale Peterson, William Pritchard, Austin Sarat, Kim Townsend, Dana Villa, and Helen von Schmidt.

For their help in thinking about Emerson I also wish to thank David Bromwich, Eduardo Cadava, Stanley Cavell, Peter Euben, Amy Gutmann,

John Hollander, Mark Johnston, Leo Marx, Barry O'Connell, Richard Poirier, Jason Scorza, Tracy Strong, and Richard Teichgraeber.

To the late Judith Shklar I owe much, including the stimulation of her conversation about Emerson, whose work she loved and suspected.

I thank Stephanie Jinks for word-processing the manuscript in several drafts and helping me prepare it for publication.

Key to Citations

All page references, except where otherwise noted, are to *Ralph Waldo Emerson: Essays and Lectures* (The Library of America, 1983). In some cases where a text from some other volume is cited only by title and page number, the volume's title appears close by. For texts not in the Library of America and found in *The Complete Works of Ralph Waldo Emerson*, edited by Edward Waldo Emerson (12 vols., Boston and New York: Houghton Mifflin, 1903-1904), I have used the following abbreviations:

Society and Solitude: *Society and Solitude* (vol. 7).
Letters: *Letters and Social Aims* (vol. 8).
Lectures and Sketches: *Lectures and Biographical Sketches* (vol. 10).
Miscellanies: *Miscellanies* (vol. 11).
Natural History: *Natural History of Intellect* (vol. 12).

Occasional references to other volumes in this edition are indicated by the volume number and page.

Other abbreviations are:

Early Lectures: *The Early Lectures of Ralph Waldo Emerson* (Vols. 1-3). Quotations reprinted by permission of the publishers from *The Early Lectures of Ralph Waldo Emerson*, edited by Stephen E. Whicher, Robert E. Spiller, and Wallace E. Williams, Cambridge, MA: The Belknap Press of Harvard University Press, Copyright © 1959, 1964, 1972 by the President and Fellows of Harvard College.

Journals: *The Journals and Miscellaneous Notebooks of Ralph Waldo Emerson* (Vols. 1-16). Quotations reprinted by permission of the publishers from *The Journals and Miscellaneous Notebooks of Ralph Waldo Emerson*, Vols. 1-16, edited by William H. Gilman et al., Cambridge, MA: The Belknap Press of Harvard University Press, Copyright © 1960-1982 by the President and Fellows of Harvard College.

Carlyle-Emerson: *The Correspondence of Thomas Carlyle and Ralph Waldo Emerson* (Vols. 1-2). Boston: Osgood, 1883.

Full citations of various works not by Emerson are given in the Bibliography.

Preface

For all his eventual respectability, Ralph Waldo Emerson (1803-1882) was during much of his life a disturbing thinker. His "Address" to the Senior Class at the Harvard Divinity School in 1838 scandalized established religious opinion, and indeed all his writings from *Nature* (1836) to *Essays: Second Series* (1844) aroused unease. His later lectures against slavery were also found threatening, especially close to home, in a supposedly free society. It is right that his world judged him a radical: that reaction meant people had chosen to give greater importance to those passages in which Emerson speaks his mind than to those reassurances—often at the end of the essay or lecture—suggesting that his truth is compatible with the prevailing views.

I believe that Emerson retains the power to disturb, that he remains radical. He can no longer affront orthodox religions: they perceive threats from other quarters. The slavery crisis has long since passed. But the underlying commitment setting him in opposition to the religions of his day and to the system of evil that was slavery fits him to stay radical in all situations. That commitment is to individualism, which he expounds as an ideal suitable for modern democracy. Indeed, he expounds it in a manner that has never been equalled. Though he wrote programmatic lectures and essays that specifically uphold the individual against the group mind or institutional constrictions, his articulation of individualism is constant, no matter what the subject is before him. He not only advocates individualism, he exemplifies it. He responds to life and the world with an individualistic sensibility, as if to show that to be an individual means not eccentricity but centrality. To be an individual means, above all, to see life and the world with one's own eyes, with eyes cleansed of the effects of the group mind and institutional constrictions. His aim is not to get us to agree with his judgments but to persuade us to take a chance and think for ourselves. Finally, we may agree with Emerson, but the agreement would concern the worthiness of life and the world, not the quality of the things that are in it.

Emerson's word for individualism is chiefly *self-reliance*. In this book, I have tried to understand what self-reliance means. It is not an easy or obvious concept. I will distinguish between mental self-reliance and active self-reliance in order to suggest that Emerson tends to elevate intellectual independence above independence of character and practical achievements. I will explore the reasons for this comparative evaluation, while knowing that if I am right in thinking that Emerson makes it, he does so only after trying hard to resist it. Or at least he tries hard to convince us that he wants to resist it. It may be self-serving for a thinker to esteem thinking above doing: Emerson must guard against his natural inclinations. He must also avoid the appearance of confining his aspirations for self-reliance to a small number of full-time thinkers. His mission, after all, is to encourage all human beings to think for themselves, to transfer their religious preoccupations to a determined reception of life and the world. Emerson assumes that most people lead spiritual lives some of the time. He tries to reorient the spirit in the direction of self-reliance and hence of openness to everything around the self. To be truly self-reliant is to be self-concerned, but mostly so one can prepare to receive life and perceive and interpret the world. On the other hand, to be self-concerned in order to assert or develop or realize oneself in the world is better than the usual conformity, but is perhaps fated to failure or merely to a higher conformity.

Given that I believe that Emersonian self-reliance is an ideal for the life of the mind more than it is a guide for how to live in the world, it may seem odd that I have written about Emerson with Nietzsche in mind. Isn't Nietzsche a theorist of the active life? Doesn't he say, in any case, that most people are inadequate for the ardors of real thinking? Yes, these sentiments have a place in Nietzsche's work. But the Nietzsche of greatest value is like the Emerson of greatest value. They both set down precepts for how to think and then devote their lives to thinking in accordance with those precepts. They both seek out what is valuable in whatever they observe. They also challenge the validity of their observations and make powerful arguments for precepts and causes they oppose. I do not deny that there are substantial differences in the method of intellect each advocates and exemplifies. There are, however, also significant similarities.

We know that Nietzsche read a fair amount of Emerson. Nietzsche had strong feelings of admiration tending to reverence towards Emerson, despite occasional exasperation. It is simple enough to find traces, and more than traces, of Emerson in Nietzsche. What is striking is that if you read Emerson after Nietzsche you see a good amount of Nietzsche in Emerson. But, of course, Emerson did not read Nietzsche. Rather, in important respects, Nietzsche was Emerson's best reader. It may be wise to approach Emerson after one has been immersed in Nietzsche. This is a way to disregard Emerson's reputation for softness, or to dispel the ignorant familiarity that surrounds him.

I offer not exactly a Nietzschean rereading of Emerson—such an attempt would be presumptuous and misguided. Instead, my hope is to give a reading of Emerson that is friendly to Nietzsche's interests. For such a reading to be possible, we must not underestimate the influence of Plato over both Emerson and Nietzsche, for good and for bad. Plato is their bond, their common source and allegiance. As will be apparent, I have also kept in mind some interests of later Nietzscheans like Weber, Heidegger, Arendt, Leo Strauss, and Foucault.

Emerson is not, however, exhaustible by the Nietzschean connection. Nor is he exhaustible by even the fullest account of self-reliance. He is a great moral philosopher. He can be enlisted in many causes or none at all. His powers exceed any person's or any age's use. He stays permanently fresh if read without condescension. At the same time, I have concentrated on Emerson as a theorist of self-reliance, as a theorist of democratic individuality. He was the first to say what individualism means in a modern democratic society, and no one has done it better since. The only others in his class are Thoreau and Whitman, who both came under Emerson's influence and owed him the initiating inspiration. To say, as I have, that I have written with Nietzsche's interests in mind is neither to place Nietzsche in the camp of democratic individuality nor to submit democratic individuality to the need to square accounts with Nietzsche. To the contrary, I only wish to say that friends of democratic individuality have much to learn from Nietzsche—as much as he learned from Emerson.

1

Self-Reliance and the Life of the Mind

In Emerson's thought about individualism, the idea of self-reliance occupies the central place. The essay "Self-Reliance" (*Essays: First Series,* 1841) is perhaps his most famous statement of it. Many sentences and passages in this essay are commonly quoted. Indeed, some have lent themselves to ideological exploitation and have even been used in advertisements and commercials. The essay has fame and notoriety, both. Thanks to the essay, the very phrase "self-reliance" has become a common synonym for individualism. Yet the idea of self-reliance is everywhere present in Emerson's thought, not only in the essay named "Self-Reliance." For all its familiarity, the idea is certainly difficult and elusive, just as Emerson's thought usually is. Though much has been written on Emersonian self-reliance, and though Stanley Cavell has recently written about it in three powerful books, perhaps something is left to say about it. By trying to work through some of the meanings and suggestions of self-reliance we can add, I believe, to our own thought about individualism—especially the sort of individualism that I have been calling democratic individuality.

It is well to emphasize at the start Emerson's difficulty and elusiveness. He is full of assertive sentences that may seem unconditional. Every sentence seems a declaration of faith. He seems to stand behind every utterance with his whole being, and risks his being by the completeness of his candor. His variety of declarations tempts us to say that he contradicts himself, but even if we resist the temptation, we are still not sure where he finally stands. We can admit the force of his impeachment of consistency in "Self-Reliance" (p. 265), but may still wish that his assertions did not so frequently collide and perhaps qualify one another to the point of damaging all of them, leaving us suspended and uncertain.

Let us say, however, that he intends to qualify his assertions. In fact, many of the assertions are not assertions at all. He does not stand behind most of his utterances, even though he expends his full virtue in them. In his experiments, he is more like Plato than even Nietzsche is. Emerson is not Thoreau. As he says in one of his numerous programmatic formulations, an intellectual person must have "no engagement in any thought or feeling which can hinder him from looking at it as somewhat foreign." (Emerson usually means "something" when he says "somewhat.") He adds that "the true scholar is one who has the power to stand beside his thoughts or to hold off his thoughts at arm's length and give them perspective" ("Natural History of Intellect," *Natural History,* pp. 39-40).

An almost exasperated Walt Whitman can therefore say of Emerson:

> He does not see or take one side, one presentation only or mainly, (as all the poets, or most of the fine writers anyhow,)—he sees all sides. His final influence is to make his students cease to worship anything—almost cease to believe in anything, outside of themselves. ("Emerson's Books, (The Shadows of Them)," *Whitman, Complete Poetry and Collected Prose,* p. 1052)

A genuinely exasperated Henry James says that Emerson "was never the man anyone took him for" (*Literary Criticism,* p. 266). I assume that James's formulation applies to Emerson's thought, and if it does, it is most apt. The key is found when we see that Emerson makes Plato—whom he regarded as the world's greater thinker and as indispensable to all creative thought—sit for the portrait of Emerson. In *Representative Men,* he says of Plato:

> He has not a system. The dearest defenders and disciples are at fault. He attempted a theory of the universe, and his theory is not complete or

self-evident. One man thinks he means this, and another that; he has said
one thing in one place, and the reverse of it in another place. (p. 652)

Emerson means these words as praise; in turn, we praise Emerson for
transferring them to him. His purpose is to have no system, but a theory
instead—a theory of the need not to have a system in any usual sense. "At
bottom he had no doctrine at all," said Santayana ("Emerson," *Interpretations of Poetry and Religion,* p. 131).

Emerson *aims* at making his philosophy difficult and elusive. He means
to disappoint the expectation that he will supply doctrinal conclusions.
His belief in the possibility of truth requires him, he thinks, to commit
himself only for a time to a particular value, principle or idea (or to any
practice or institution derivative from them), and then to a contrasting one
for a time, trying at the same time to withhold a final judgment, a definite
assent, whenever possible. We may finally observe in him an unreserved
commitment, but it is a commitment to a method of intellect. A commitment to method enables him to withhold lesser, substantive commitments.
(I use the ascetic or Cartesian word "method" because Emerson favors it.)
Hence we must be as careful as possible in assigning beliefs to Emerson.
It is not skepticism but his understanding of truth that makes him so
sparing in acquiring commitments. The matter does not stop here: the core
of self-reliance is a proper engagement with truth, requiring as much
substantive withholding as possible.

Truth is our element of life, yet if a man fasten his attention on a single
aspect of truth, and apply himself to that alone for a long time, the truth
becomes distorted and not itself, but falsehood. ("Intellect," p. 424).

It should always be difficult to attribute commitments to a self-reliant
person—whether it is Emerson himself or anyone who conceives of
self-reliance as he does. Why? What are the connections between self-
reliance, truth-seeking, and substantive withholding?

Emerson thinks that every important value, principle, idea, (or derivative practice or institution) is permanently indispensable for life, even
though any may be at odds with any other. Taken together, they are forces
"by whose antagonism we exist" ("Fugitive Slave Law," 1854, *Miscellanies,*
p. 231). Man himself, Emerson says, is a "stupendous antagonism," the cause

and effect of the world's constitutive antagonisms ("Fate," *The Conduct of Life,* p. 953). Life is a "gale of warring elements" ("Works and Days," *Society and Solitude,* p. 172). When there are two "metaphysical antagonists," he says, "each is a good half, but an impossible whole" ("The Conservative," p. 175). If "the world stands by balanced antagonisms" the thinker must temporarily stand by each antagonistic element in turn ("Natural History of Intellect," *Natural History,* p. 53). Emerson is a sustained practitioner of a multiple perspectivism. He tries to make each element believable, giving it its own essay or passage, or he dwells on its different facets in several essays, while his whole work sets an example of abundant but also sympathetic withholding. But he withholds nothing, it would seem, from the principle of self-reliance, which is the method of sympathetic withholding. It earns Emerson's true loyalty. The principle is Emerson. In the main respects, therefore, self-reliance is not one particular substantive or doctrinal principle like other ones. At its best, self-reliance is nothing but an intellectual method, a method of truth. Emerson's whole work illustrates it, and it may very well define any person's self-reliance as such. This will be my main emphasis, but other meanings of self-reliance will also be examined.

Mental or philosophical self-reliance means, precisely, the readiness to treat with sympathetic understanding ideas and values that have no sympathy for one another. In order to develop such understanding, one must try to remain not free of substantive commitments, but sparing of them. This is the highest aspiration of self-reliance. Emerson acknowledges the temptation to selectivity when he says in "Spiritual Laws" that:

A man is a method, a progressive arrangement; a selecting principle, gathering his like to him wherever he goes. He takes only his own out of the multiplicity that sweeps and circles round him. (pp. 311-312)

Despite these words, Emerson's work shows the effort of achieving a method that refuses any "selecting principle" which derives from something as narrow as one's "own" personality, and which has so limited an aim as to gather one's like wherever one goes. Emerson's method aims to embrace as much as he finds possible. That is the example he would set. His practice is faithful to most of the formulated precepts of his method that recurrently appear in his writings, but not the one just quoted. Self-reliance as a method of thinking with its own intrinsic value means more than any substantive commitment to a particular value, principle or idea, or to any practice or institution that embodies or derives from them. (But I do not deny that self-reliance has institutional preconditions and effects, as we shall see.)

One relies on oneself rather than seeking support in external commitments. One stays within oneself in order to enter imaginatively into all the commitments that social life displays, and must display. One increases the amount of value in the world by keeping oneself from embracing favorite ideas and works exclusively.

Emerson is persuaded of two things: every position is held for at least plausible reasons and perhaps for necessary ones; and every position is inevitably accompanied by or engenders an opposition that is also (though not always equally) plausible or necessary and also narrow. Opposition appears,

> because something has been overstated or omitted by the antecedent sect and the human mind feels itself wronged and overstates on the other side as in this. Each of our sects is an extreme statement and therefore obnoxious to contradiction and reproof. But each rests on this strong but obscure instinct of an outraged truth. Each is, as it were, a cry of pain from the violated soul. ("Society," *Early Lectures, 2,* p. 108)

That antagonists need each other for the sake of their own sanity is shown, Emerson thinks, in the political sphere where parties goad, check, and define each other. But antagonism—not just in politics—is the health of the whole world: its value is perpetual and to be preferred over synthesis or diluted compromise. No position is arbitrary or accidental. The self-reliant thinker will try to disclose, in every case, why a partisan must say what he says and what "insurmountable fact binds him to that side" ("The Conservative," p. 176). As one example, Emerson thinks that "No Burke, no Metternich has yet done full justice to the side of conservatism" ("Lecture on the Times," p. 158). The steady message from Emerson is that no side—no principle or value or practice—has yet been done full justice. But he will try to make amends. He says, "The finer the sense of justice, the better poet" ("Sovereignty of Ethics," *Lectures and Sketches,* p. 185).

In the work he does, he displays and inspires what we may call the democracy of intellect; he gives an example of the spirit of democracy at its best. That is self-reliance. It is sometimes overt in Emerson's work, more often unspoken, that he is presenting and defending the aspirations of the mind of democratic culture, nothing less. It is a mind needed to understand the culture in which it grows, but that can also extend its receptivity to other cultures and also to nature. Henry James said in a review (1883) of the Carlyle-Emerson correspondence:

> In a genuine democracy all things are democratic; and this spirit of general deference, on the part of a beautiful poet who might have availed himself of the poetic license to be fastidious, was the natural product of a society in which it was held that every one was equal to every one else. (*Literary Criticism*, p. 245)

I am not sure that Emerson's spirit is "a natural product" of anything. He is more like one who reveals a secret obscured by its obviousness and kept obscure because it is too radical in its perfect appropriateness. He is revealing democracy. But James is right to insist on Emerson's democracy: his receptivity, his power of uncommitted sympathy, is democracy. Receptivity is the highest form of self-reliance.

Emerson's method of apprehending general ideas and practices—the kinds whose names provide titles for many of his essays—is the heart of his self-reliant intellectuality. But he sometimes devotes his attentive powers to human and natural particulars, on the one hand, and he aspires to a transcendent vision of the totality of things, on the other hand. For a while, however, I will concentrate on his methodical treatment of general ideas and practices. Later, I will say something about Emerson's reception of particulars and his sense of totality.

One of the most compressed statements of his self-reliant method is found at the beginning of "Fate," the first of nine essays in *The Conduct of Life* (1860). He says:

> If we must accept Fate, we are not less compelled to affirm liberty, the significance of the individual, the grandeur of duty, the power of character. This is true, and that other is true. But our geometry cannot span these extreme points, and reconcile them. What to do? By obeying each thought frankly, by harping, or, if you will, pounding on each string, we learn at last its power. By the same obedience to other thoughts, we learn theirs, and then comes some reasonable hope of harmonizing them. We are sure, that, though we know not how, necessity does comport with liberty, the

individual with the world, my polarity with the spirit of the times. The riddle of the age has for each a private solution. If one would study his own time, it must be by this method of taking up in turn each of the leading topics which belong to our scheme of human life, and, by firmly stating all that is agreeable to experience on one, and doing the same justice to the opposing facts in the others, the true limitations will appear. Any excess of emphasis, on one part, would be corrected, and a just balance would be made. (pp. 943-944)

"Excess of emphasis" characterizes all of Emerson's writing.

The excess is meant to compensate for the reserve that Emerson feels in the face of the way people esteem the things they do. Their estimation tends to be blindly or insanely excessive—it is too partial and unduly favors a few worthy things to the exclusion of others that have equal or comparable claims. Commonly, exaggeration makes every thought a prison and hence is "incipient insanity" ("Intellect," p. 424). However, Emerson can say a good word even about one-sidedness:

Exaggeration is in the course of things . . . to every creature nature added a little violence of direction in its proper path, a shove to put it on its way; in every instance, a slight generosity, a drop too much . . . without a spice of bigot and fanatic, no excitement, no efficiency. ("Nature," p. 549)

A person "can't make any paint stick but his own." Nevertheless, insofar as one is a self-reliant thinker, one cannot be a partisan either for oneself or one's cause. A person of one idea is a monotone and must be treated as if a little deranged ("Natural History of Intellect, *Natural History,* p. 50). Only the mediocre, he says, take sides (Notes to "Self-Reliance," *Works, 2,* p. 391).

For Emerson to give everything its due requires that he overcome his characteristic revulsion to unconscious idolatry. In contrast, his own idolatry is deliberate: he will write about something as if it were the best or only thing, but then go on to another. He as it were impersonates ideas and principles, practices and institutions. His impersonations explore actualities and their latencies, and are thus sources of endlessly fertile suggestion. Emerson shows a different power from that of writers who create fictional characters, which are explorations of invented possibilities, or pictures of unrealizable personal roundedness. These interest him less. Following Nietzsche, however, I must not make absolute the difference between the power of conceptual impersonation and the power to create characters. The basic link between the two powers, Nietzsche says, is found in a common "self-possession": "a way of viewing himself as a mirror of the world" (*Philosophy in the Tragic Age of the Greeks* [M. Cowan, Trans.], p. 44). I do still think the difference is substantial.

"I should think water the best invention if I were not acquainted with fire and earth and air" ("Religion," *Early Lectures, 3,* p. 284). He also has to say, "I should think fire the best thing in the world if I were not acquainted with air, and water, and earth" ("Art," p. 433). He approvingly allows that it is the

> habit of certain minds to give an all-excluding fullness to the object, the thought, the word they alight upon, and to make that for a time the deputy of the world . . . The power to detach and to magnify by detaching is the essence of rhetoric. ("Art," p. 433)

This rhetoric is a power "to fix the momentary eminency of an object" ("Art," p. 433). The true benefit of rhetoric, however, comes only when we see it bestowed on contrasting or antagonistic ideas and objects, one after another.

Therefore when the self-reliant individual receives instruction, as he or she must, from the "rhetoric" of others as it is contained in great or good writings, variety must be the rule. Great writers, Emerson says, "are antidotes to each other's influence." After one great writer has been studied,

> then comes by another luminary . . . and with equal claims on our wonder, and affords us at once the power of self-recovery, and that of comparing system with system, influence with influence, and, at last, man with man. ("Lord Bacon," *Early Lectures, 1,* p. 321)

Yet because Emerson is so little partisan, it is hard to know which writers could serve as antidotes to him. He is an antidote to many others.

Emerson means to persuade us to a *happy* responsiveness to contrasting or antagonistic thoughts and phenomena, and he makes it the salient quality of his method. He does not necessarily want us to agree with his insights or judgments, or even to go on discussing all his subjects. He only wants us to feel delight with him in the spectacle of contrariety that the world offers and that he tries to capture in his work. His great lesson is that some large part of the interest or fascination in the world comes from the fact that meaning or beauty or truth can be found in conflicting or incompatible ideas, principles, forces, and practices. The common tendency is to escape such clamor and seek clarification, or to come to the world fully armed with dogma and preconceptions. Rather than feeling dismay from opposition to oneself or from the very abundance of seemingly irreconcilable antagonisms, one can strive for a self-mastery that rides above one's likes and dislikes, and one's cravings for simple clarity.

One can profess what Emerson calls "the joyous science" ("The Scholar," *Lectures and Sketches,* p. 262), and do so by looking at one's mutable opinions "as a bird that flieth" and thus "put himself out of the reach of skepticism" ("Prospects," *Early Lectures, 3,* p. 379). Only the self-reliant person can aspire to the joyous science. Each of the things in contention can be seen separately as worthy or beautiful, but so can the contending things when juxtaposed and held together. What is involved in Emerson's joyous science is something less like seeing all sides of a disputed issue, and more like admiring all sides in an unstoppable struggle. Emerson is eager to present the struggle. I do not think that Emerson typically seeks to create, say, a third thing better than the two seen in contention or held in contrast; nor does he want to "harmonize" them, despite what he says in "Fate." He does not aspire, as John Stuart Mill does, to combine the best elements from contrasting ideas into a new idea better than those from which it selects. Nor is he very eager to compare, because comparison necessarily deprives anything of its "munificence" and makes it "look less" (Notes to "Character," *Lectures and Sketches,* p. 532). He may theorize harmonization, but fortunately, he does not practice it. Rather he seeks to keep each thing alive by giving it good words, considering it "as if it existed for itself alone" and not as if it were to be judged by its conformity to one's wishes ("The Head," *Early Lectures, 2,* p. 17). Each idea or value, practice or movement, has an equal right to exist, even if it does not have a right to an equal influence. The world is full of gods, joined in enmity and kinship. Self-reliance embraces this condition. It seeks to guard the world's complexity and search out the necessity of its turmoil.

In the following pages I will often quote Emerson in support of one idea (or practice) or another. But I know that his statements often stand in a relation of mutual qualification, or are offered exaggeratedly because they are tentative. I do not deny that he favors some outlooks, conceptions or attitudes as well as some institutions and tendencies more than others. He had views, after all: loyalties and inclinations, apart from or in spite of his philosophy. But he deems it essential to struggle against his own mere preferences in order to make almost everything valuable. "A man should be a guest in his own house, and a guest in his own thought" ("The Sovereignty of Ethics," *Lectures and Sketches*, p. 194). Feeling too much at home in one's inclinations, one refuses accommodation to what is different. In reading Emerson, one runs the risk of arbitrarily deciding which statements more nearly represent Emerson's views, and which statements he is only trying out. I am sure that I have not avoided that danger while I persistently go about attributing views to him. Alternatively, one can say that he means everything he says, but that must mean that he moves beyond belief into undiscriminating acceptance. In either case, when we quote him we must believe him, but we should do so with (Emersonian) reservation.

I am sure, however, that whenever self-reliance (in any of its several forms) is at stake, Emerson is always finally on the side of any idea or practice that creates or sustains or favors it. In the form of intellectual method, self-reliance does itself necessitate that Emerson be attentive to and appreciative of the opposition to self-reliance and also be aware of its inherent difficulties and uncertainties. But despite all the indeterminacy that Emerson's work fosters, he is unwaveringly committed to self-reliance. The result is that I have tended to treat his words as expressing his unreserved beliefs when they contribute to the elaboration and defense of the idea of self-reliance and of its institutional preconditions and effects. Of course, not everything in the world is causally or directly related to self-reliance; not everything favors or threatens it. There were almost no democratic societies in the past and therefore self-reliance in its democratic manifestation was not a possibility. Yet the self-reliant mind must absorb the past hospitably. On the other hand, the safety of the ideal of self-reliance is not always at stake amid the disagreements and struggles of democratic life. All the parties, factions, and sects cry for sympathy. These facts leave him a large field for the play of his sympathetically disengaged intellect. That is to say, these facts leave him a large field for the display of mental self-reliance, understood as a method of intellect. Where does Emerson's greater power show itself? In formulating the meanings and implications of self-reliance or in practic-ing mental self-reliance by engaging with the vastness of life and the world in the manner of sympathetic disengagement? It is not necessary to decide.

Emerson does not lie. He makes sure that he will not have to lie by not dwelling on what repels him. In fact, he engages only with what attracts or tempts him. He thus limits the scope of his method. He can say of the hospitable soul that it "entertains in its spirit all travellers, tongues, kindreds, all employments, all eccentricities, all crimes even, in its vast charity and overcoming hope" ("The Poet," *Early Lectures, 3,* p. 356). But Emerson is no friend of crimes. Some readers may think his digestive powers too narrow or selective or driven by a metaphysical bias. His range is not, in any case, as synoptically or historically wide as Hegel's in *The Phenomenology of Spirit* or *The Philosophy of History,* to mention a remotely analogous enterprise. In compensation, he has only a subdued disposition to believe in teleological historical (as distinct from bio-evolutionary) advance, and hence in the chance that obsolescence can overtake most ideas or many practices. He tends to see, I think, permanence, not eventual supersession, in the phenomena he interprets. He says:

> Without hurry, without rest, the human spirit goes forth from the begin-ning to embody every faculty, every thought, every emotion which be-longs to it, in appropriate events. But always the thought is prior to the fact. All the facts of history preexist in the mind as laws. Each law in turn is made by circumstances predominant, and the limits of nature give power to but one at a time. Therefore there is no progress to the race. Progress belongs to individuals and consists in becoming universal. ("Introduc-tory," *The Philosophy of History, Early Lectures, 2,* pp. 13-14)

He therefore does really lend himself to many and diverse phenomena, while nevertheless *giving* himself only to his self-reliant method of encompassing these phenomena.

His exaggerated defense of some phenomena is better than arguments that exclusive partisans could mount, and at the same time, it is a defense that is qualified (explicitly or implicitly) by exaggeration in support of competing objects of idolatry. The qualification may come immediately or be deferred; it may be stark or sly. He sees worth everywhere. Yet it is also true that he sees more worth than he instinctively feels. "I love everything by turns, and nothing long" ("Nominalist and Realist," p. 587). His mind is always desirous because it is only briefly and incompletely appeasable. The self-reliant mind must grow voyeurist and promiscuous, to use opprobrious terms favorably—terms that he of course does not use. Indeed he sometimes criticizes his own tendency. In the first edition of "History" (1841) he can praise "intellectual nomadism" without qualification: "eyes which everywhere feed themselves" (Notes to "Self-Reliance," *Works,* 2, p. 384). But in the second edition (1847) he says that in its excess, intellectual nomadism "bankrupts the mind, through the dissipation of power on a miscellany of objects" (p. 247). The first edition is truer to Emerson than the second.

Henry James said of Emerson that "He liked to taste but not to drink— least of all to become intoxicated" (*Literary Criticism,* p. 265). That is a good description of Emerson's aspiration. To condemn it is to condemn Emerson. This aspiration does not make him playful or merely ironic. His inexhaustible impersonations are not exhibitions. No, his writings as a whole are a battleground; often, any single essay is, too. That is why he tastes, not drinks. He is a battleground and therefore ends up appearing above the battle.

Exactness cannot be reached directly, undialectically. Impersonation requires close attention to the impersonated, but it is more than close attention. In the face of complex and contending phenomena, honesty compels extravagance. Present exaggeration may turn into future accuracy because it discloses unsuspected but latent virtues. Present exaggeration may also be good because it can delineate and detect "occult symmetries and unpublished beauties" ("The Scholar," *Lectures and Sketches,* p. 262).

One other purpose is served by present exaggeration in Emerson. It contributes to recovering the original "inspiration" of any long-standing precept or permanent human tendency. Emerson sometimes practices a benign genealogy. In a lecture, "Religion" (1837), he says:

> As I have said, the invariable badge of virtue is usefulness. It serves the temporal need of the human race. The law which it gives to the listening enthusiast, "Be just," comes to serve for the protection of all the society in the form of "Thou shalt not steal." The law which he heard in his heart, "Serve no furious passion," comes to serve for the police of society in the form of "Thou shalt not kill," "Thou shalt not commit adultery." Mean-

time when, at intervals, to each heart the Supreme Reason reveals itself it perceives the deep truth of these prior commandments and adds to them new titles and rules of veneration to secure the precious palladium to mankind. (*Early Lectures, 2,* p. 93)

Exaggeration can therefore reinflate something to its real size and show how large or great it really is, more so than is commonly thought. Exaggeration wars against the shrinkage that time indefatigably inflicts. An idea or practice can be better than its own faithful adherents know, better than its own most favored perspective on itself suggests that it is.

Is exaggeration permanently necessary to any mind seeking to communicate its self-reliance? Probably. There may have been greater pressures in Emerson's time to refuse receptivity than we currently feel, and his fight may have been a good deal harder than ours today. But the fight has to be fought always. He exaggerates in order to get his audience to attend to what it unjustly feared, despised, ignored or depreciated. A self-reliant mind today will also feel the need to rescue many things and encourage receptivity to them, despite supposedly greater openness. Exaggeration or extravagance can awaken generosity, which always tends to be in short supply.

The truth is got, then, not when one adheres to the precept of moderation, but when one pursues conflicting excesses that qualify each other. The qualifications are meant to deepen our responses, not to impoverish them. In "Circles," he says, "Our moods do not believe in each other" (p. 406). But his steady suggestion is that *we* must believe in them, provided that we believe in all of them, excluding none and letting none exclude any other or all the others. Knowing that the full power of a mood is discernible only after the mood passes, we must be wary of thinking that we can ever rest in a present certainty. Mobility is the check on mood. "I am always insincere, as always knowing there are other moods" ("Nominalist and Realist," p. 587). But though "insincere," Emerson surrenders to every mood and utters its message without letting his awareness that he will later speak in and for a different mood inhibit his utterance or make it less one-sided. He carries out the program he urges for all of us:

The commonest remark, if the man could only extend it a little, would make him a genius; but the thought is prematurely checked, and grows no more. All great masters are chiefly distinguished by the power of adding a second, a third, and perhaps a fourth step in a continuous line. Many a man had taken the first step. With every additional step you enhance immensely the value of your first. ("Natural History of Intellect," *Natural History,* p. 25)

To be sure, each of Emerson's essays is more than the statement of a mood, but its core is a mood—if not a present mood, then a remembered or expected or imagined one.

A mood may attune itself to the matter under consideration and therefore provide greater receptivity; or, contrastingly, it may qualify what one said earlier on the same matter, in a different mood. Thus different moods are many eyes for looking at the diversity of the same thing or looking sympathetically at many contending things.

What claim is Emerson making for his impersonations? To speak truthfully. But is that to grasp essences? I think not: his tone is not that of one who presumes to say the last word. A profound idea or a durable practice can inexhaustibly engender interpretations. Analysis of it is interminable; it is richer than any one mind can know, no matter how many perspectives on it that the same mind, in various moods, is able to take, and no matter how hard that mind tries to befriend it and make the best case for it. But it is also true that Emerson is not a pure perspectivist. Although he lets his moods speak, and although he goes to the limit of the perspective that a mood opens up, he appeals to others, if not for their agreement, then for their provisional assent. He is not speaking only on his own behalf, or simply adding just one more perspective. He takes a broad view. What he sees we can see, and not just because he has instructed us, but mostly because our own resources permit us to understand him and perhaps confirm him, even as they should sustain us in the effort to amend or abandon him. But on the most important matter anyone's self-reliant mind will not amend or abandon Emerson, but be like him: receptive to contrast and antagonism as such and to each element that takes a part in the play of life and the world.

As I will try to show later at some length, Emerson's principal tactic of receptivity and response is to see beauty where others do not. "Beauty," he says, "is the form under which the intellect prefers to study the world." He is faithful to the office of the poet as he defines it in "The Poet": it is "announcement and affirming" (p. 452). His whole work teaches that

"Thought makes every thing fit for use . . . What would be base, or even obscene, to the obscene, becomes illustrious, spoken in a new connection of thought" (p. 454).

What is it that can dispose a person to receptivity and response? I believe that the most sustained answer Emerson gives is found in "History," the first essay of *Essays: First Series*. In this piece, Emerson asks us, as Whitman does later on, to see the human world's historical mutability and diversity as either a projection of elements in every soul or an enactment, on a large scale, of private events in any person's life. History could not be understood if all people were not similarly manifold and equally experienced. "This human mind wrote history, and this must read it. The Sphinx must solve her own riddle" (p. 237). The aim of the study of history is to demonstrate that all history is the work of the generic human being and that it is nothing more than the display of powers lodged in any human soul. The study of history

> will pierce into the subtile streams of influence that pass from man to man, from society to society and uncover the outer and inner bands by which neighborhoods, societies, nations, and the whole race are knit up into a common hope and fear, a common aim and nature, into one man. ("Introductory," *The Philosophy of History, Early Lectures, 2*, p. 10)

(This thought is distinct from Emerson's contention that the processes of nature are projections of a divine mind that is not totally separated from the human mind, and hence are rational and ultimately moral.) The benefit of a greater self-acquaintance is a greater sympathetic understanding of the world's past and present cultures, and of their deeds and achievements. Emerson speaks of "the knowledge of all men which belongs to self-knowledge" (Notes to "Works and Days," *Society and Solitude*, p. 394). Knowledge of the world leads in turn to deeper self-knowledge.

"Man is explicable by nothing less than all his history" ("History," p. 237). One will find in oneself the raw material of every configuration or position or tendency; or one will find in one's life "quite parallel miniature experiences of his own" (p. 249). Nothing human should count as inhuman:

> There is nothing but is related to me; no mode of life so alien and grotesque but by careful comparison I can soon find my place in it; find a strict

analogy between my experiences and whatever is real in those of any man. ("Introductory," *The Philosophy of History, Early Lectures, 2,* p. 19)

Let us notice that Emerson is willing to include the "alien and grotesque" in the scope of his sympathetic understanding.

To be sure, Emerson allows for distorted and therefore unrecognized resemblances:

> As in dreams, so in the scarcely less fluid events of the world, every man sees himself in colossal, without knowing that is himself . . . Every quality of his mind is magnified in some one acquaintance, and every emotion of his heart in some one. ("Spiritual Laws," p. 314)

But howsoever remote and seemingly unlike, any given part of history is potentially stored in every soul.

> Every thing the individual sees without him corresponds to his states of mind, and every thing is in turn intelligible to him, as his onward thinking leads him into the truth to which that fact or series belongs. ("History," p. 247)

It is worth noticing that in this essay Emerson refuses to absorb animal and vegetable nature because they are not made by human beings, as history is:

> What is the use of pretending to know what we know not? . . . I hold our actual knowledge very cheap. Hear the rats in the wall, see the lizard on the fence, the fungus under foot, the lichen on the log. What do I know sympathetically, morally, of either of these worlds of life? (pp. 255-256)

Nevertheless, within the human realm, every fact is available to the self-reliant mind, the mind willing to search itself and face what it finds without orthodox or conformist narrowness or fear.

*   *   *

To repeat: we must not expect anything simple when we take up Emerson on self-reliance. The point put in academic language is that democratic individuality is nothing simple. What, then, more explicitly, is self-reliance? What is reliance on oneself, what does it come to? Though I believe that self-reliance in its highest Emersonian form is a method of intellect, it presents itself memorably as a principle for the conduct of a whole life. In the essay, "Self-Reliance," Emerson mingles reflections on mental self-reliance and active self-reliance. In passing, he does distinguishes between "actual" and "intellectual" life, but appears to suggest that they are inextricably copresent, or indeed, that if a distinction can be made, mental self-reliance is merely preliminary and instrumental to active self-reliance (p. 263). Let us therefore stay awhile with the idea of self-reliance as a way for the self to be and to act in the world. Eventually I will try to force a sharp distinction between mental self-reliance and active self-reliance, a distinction that not only ranks mental higher than active self-reliance, but actually severs them and places them in nearly untouching spheres of life. I think Emerson himself intends such a distinction. Let us for a time, however, work with an unsorted idea of self-reliance.

I have said that Emerson develops the idea in numerous places besides "Self-Reliance." An invaluable concentration is found in this essay; it is, all in all, one of his greatest performances of impersonation. But other writings, before and after, contribute to our understanding of the idea. A way into the idea is to suggest what Emerson thinks is opposed to self-reliance. The most general negative conception is that self-reliance is a refusal to rely on church religions. To be self-reliant is to be free of attachment to church doctrine, church worship, church ritual, and church prayer. Implicit in Emerson's work is the assumption that when church religions are weakened in (and, in part, because of) democratic society, self-reliance will appear, not the nihilism of despair or of frivolity. I do not say that self-reliance is independence from religiousness. To the contrary, Emerson's ultimate meaning of self-reliance is to be properly religious; "self-reliance, the height and perfection of man is reliance on God" ("The Fugitive Slave Law," 1854, *Miscellanies,* p. 236). We will come to Emerson's religiousness later. For now, let us see that Emerson's war, especially vivid in his writings throughout *Essays: Second Series,* is against the effects of church religions on their adherents and communicants. That he resigned his ministry in the Unitarian church in 1832 is a great emblematic fact. Emerson thinks that not only in his time, but also throughout time, church religions take, for the most part, the side of the social given and thus strengthen its hold. Acceptance of society is the normal posture of church religions, what they eventually come to, no matter how disruptive their beginnings may be. Church-faithful minds are dependent minds, and dependent minds produce expected and conformist behavior, even when such behavior seems at odds with church doctrine.

Another rough way of indicating what is opposed to self-reliance is to emphasize the continuous antipathy that Emerson shows toward the social given. Not only does he find the prevailing aims of action and some of the arrangements of life questionable and probably unsatisfactory to those who uphold them, he also, I think, is temperamentally given to shuddering at the thought of clustered humanity, lost together because each is lost to himself or herself. This shudder is part of what it means to be a principled individualist. He exceeds Nietzsche in queasiness. But his reproaches of the herd-spirit, in the name of self-reliance, usually proceed without malice or vanity. One vivid exception to his generosity occurs when, apparently speaking in his own voice, he says that "enormous populations, if they be beggars, are disgusting, like moving cheese, like hills of ants, or of fleas—the more, the worse" ("Uses of Great Men," *Representative Men,* p. 615).

He preaches self-reliance because he thinks that all people already have self-reliant moments and could more successfully become self-reliant if they tried. Self-reliance is thus not a doctrine of superiority to average humanity. Rather it is a doctrine urging the elevation of democracy to its full height, free of the aristocratic, but also free of the demotic.

I wish also to indicate summarily other attitudes opposed to Emersonian self-reliance. As Emerson works out his ideas, we are able to see that the defense of self-reliance is an attack on the common tendency to act on the idea that the core of individualism is economic self-centeredness and that the true individual is acquisitive or possessive or consumerist. For Emerson, the exclusively materialistic life is not life, but a misdiagnosed dying. Relatedly, Emerson's self-reliance does not amount to a celebration of intimacy or of privacy. His elaborations in "Love" and "Friendship" are unhomelike. Finally, self-reliance is not thinking and acting on the belief that one is alone in the world, but that only oneself is real, that the world is what I say or think it is. Emerson is a qualified critic of subjectivity, as in chapter 7 ("Spirit") of *Nature* (1836). He denounces everyday egotism; he is skeptical of philosophical egoism. Indeed, so far is Emerson from praise of the ego that he sounds a remarkable note of existential indebtedness. He says:

> Indeed what is our own being but a reproduction, a representation of all the past? I remember the manifold cord—the thousand or the million stranded cord which my being and every man's being is,—that I am an aggregate of infinitesimal parts and that every minutest streamlet that has flowed to me is represented in that man which I am so that if every one should claim his part in me I should be instantaneously diffused through the creation and individually decease, then I say I am an alms of all and live but by the charity of others. What is a man but a congress of nations? (Notes to "Private Life," *Early Lectures, 3,* p. 251)

In sum, Emerson as a theorist of self-reliance is a theorist of democratic individuality, and he is therefore averse to all the sorts of individualism that I have just mentioned.

Positively, self-reliance is self-trust. "In self-trust all the virtues are comprehended" ("The American Scholar," p. 65). Napoleon commands our respect, says Emerson, "by his enormous self-trust" ("Greatness," *Letters,* p. 314). He goes on to define Napoleon's self-trust as "the habit of seeing with his own eyes." From such self-reliance or self-trust would flow a further daring: to experience honestly and act adventurously. The power which resides in every person is "new in nature" ("Self-Reliance," p. 259). Every individual is a new individual and can, with self-trust, do in the world something not yet done but worth doing. Creativity is always possible; creativity is actual when people trust themselves:

> There are creative manners, there are creative actions, and creative words; manners, actions, words, that is, indicative of no custom or authority, but springing spontaneous from the mind's own sense of good and fair. ("The American Scholar," p. 58)

Such creativity is released only when conformity gives way: "imitation is suicide" ("Self-Reliance," p. 259). "Whoso would be a man must be a nonconformist" (p. 261). With a rare vehemence, Emerson says in his essay, "Persian Poetry":

> We accept the religions and politics into which we fall; and it is only a
> few delicate spirits who are sufficient to see that the whole web of
> convention is the imbecility of those whom it entangles. (*Letters*, p. 248)

A nice uncertainty is in this sentence. It seems to suggest either that
conventions are imbecile in substance; or that they are not imbecile, but
the devout way in which they are accepted is imbecile. Emerson elsewhere defends both sentiments. In sum, "Custom is the defacer of beauty,
and the concealer of truth" ("English Literature: Introductory," *Early
Lectures, 1*, p. 226). "Decorum is the undress of virtue" ("The Present
Age," *Early Lectures, 2*, 162).

Conformity rests on being ashamed. Shame converts virtues into pen-
ances and life into one long expiation. Conformity is the postponement
of life, not life; it scatters one's force, blocks the work that one can do
well, or especially or uniquely well; but "with the exercise of self-trust,
new powers shall appear" ("Self-Reliance," p. 275). The only absolution
is self-forgiveness. Only self-trust can induce self-forgiveness. Without
self-forgiveness, people are "timid and apologetic" (p. 270). Indeed, so
timid and apologetic, that they are no longer upright; they are "ashamed
before the blade of grass or the blowing rose" (p. 270).

It is no revelation to say that Emerson's mission is to preach courage,
inspire hope. He aims to carry out his mission radically. The amazing
passion that drives Emerson's "Address" to the Harvard Divinity School
(1838) is to proclaim the divinity of each person, as if to ground an
absolute self-trust. In this address, he says:

> That which shows God out of me, makes me a wart and a wen. There is
> no longer a necessary reason for my being. (p. 81)

Each of us must be convinced that he or she has an indispensable
existence: the world would be unthinkable without any one of us. To feel
this way is to have the right kind of self-trust. But Emerson does not find
it in the society he knows.

He looks around him and sees a people with immense energy, but the
energy is misdirected, usually deriving from the desire to prove oneself;
"raging riders, who drive their steeds so hard, in the violence of living to
forget its illusion" ("New England Reformers," p. 603). Despair and

self-doubt frantically impel. The animation is in the service of conformity, but adequacy to conformity seems an endless task. From all this waste Emerson tries to reclaim his hearers and readers. Like his greatest European heir, Nietzsche, he tries to seduce us to life. But Emerson makes the job sound less burdensome than Nietzsche does; he has much more trust in the people around him. He even may be said to love them.

From this poetical or Socratic love, Emerson produces images and examples in order to encourage more self-reliant being and acting. What Nietzsche playfully but meanly calls the will to power, Emerson considers common creativity or a common need for self-expression. Emerson's premise is stated on many occasions, but one statement is all the more compelling for being made in the essay "Experience," which is mostly devoted to presenting the best case for the *unlikelihood* of genuine expression. He says:

> I had fancied that the value of life lay in its inscrutable possibilities; in the fact that I never know, in addressing myself to a new individual, what may befall me. (p. 475)

The fact of human unpredictability must be insisted on. There is fearful resistance to it. In fact, people can act as if they did not believe it and thus provide mechanistic determinism a temporary vindication. People sleepwalk: that is how conformist obedience can strike the disappointed observer, and Emerson uses the trope. But Emerson is not resigned to disappointment. He hopes to coax self-reliance.

Self-reliance is a process, not a state in which one can rest. Self-reliance is too difficult to be possessed securely; on the other hand, life's unexpectedness (its "inscrutable possibilities") can and will unsettle even the most self-reliant individual. In the essay "The Transcendentalist" (1842), Emerson attributes to the young and disaffected idealists or transcendentalists (and eventually claims for himself) the occurrence of "a certain brief experience, which surprised me in the highway or in the market, in some place, at some time—whether in the body or out of the body." He continues:

> God knoweth—and made me aware that I had played the fool with fools all this time, but that law existed for me and for all; that to me belonged

trust, a child's trust and obedience, and the worship of ideas, and I should never be fool more. Well, in the space of an hour probably, I was let down from this height; I was at my old tricks, the selfish member of a selfish society. My life is superficial, takes no root in the deep world; I ask, When shall I die and be relieved of the responsibility of seeing a Universe I do not use? I wish to exchange this flash-of-lightning faith for continuous daylight, this fever-glow for a benign climate. (p. 205)

Emerson refers to this condition of occasional illumination and habitual self-loss as "double consciousness." The "two lives" are disconnected or "parallel" for the most part ("Duty," *Early Lectures, 3*, p. 143). Yet he clings to the hope that "the moments will characterize the days" ("The Transcendentalist," pp. 205-206). "How slowly the highest raptures of the intellect break through the trivial forms of habit" ("Duty," p. 144). Perhaps not only slowly but forever incompletely: "all men do value the few hours of real life," as if even the purest vision left the self untransformed, and confined its effects to only a short time ("Address" [Harvard Divinity School], p. 89).

I read the passage from "The Transcendentalist" as an indication of the sense that, for Emerson, self-reliance as an intermittent process is more than a mood, but only with persistent struggle, something appreciably more than a mood. The point is to make self-reliance attractive. He knows how unattractive it can be. In an early lecture he speaks of how it feels to reach the age of one's majority: "The burdensome possession of himself he cannot dispose of" ("The Present Age," *Early Lectures, 2*, p. 170). The temptation is to live on terms prescribed anonymously or by nameable others. American democracy, the opportunity of the New World, exists, however, for the sake of self-reliance, for the sake of weakening the grip of routine and subservience. Democracy may make it possible for people in society to stop being "puppets of routine" ("Reforms," *Early Lectures, 3*, p. 265). If poetical thinking is "departure from routine," then so is living in the spirit of independence ("The Poet," p. 462). To be free and equal is to be self-reliant: that is one short way of putting it. Yet ordinary persons hold back. They are often content to "slide into the vacant places of the last generation" ("Address on Education," *Early Lectures, 2*, p. 197). Emerson will, then, appeal to them. He imputes to all people, as I have said, a fundamental need (and capacity) for self-expression. He is insistent:

> all men live by truth and stand in need of expression. In love, in art, in avarice, in politics, in labor, in games, we study to utter our painful secret. The man is only half himself, the other half is his expression. ("The Poet," p. 448)

(Notice that he includes avarice.)

In an earlier version of "The Poet," he gives another articulation of the half-buried urge to express oneself. He says:

> Does happiness depend on "uninterrupted prosperity," as it is called? Oh no, but on Expression. Expression is prosperity. I must say what is burning here: I must do what I shall perish if I cannot do, I must appear again in my house, in my fortune, in my marriage, in my speech, or else I must disappear, and the brute form must crowd the soul out of nature. (*Early Lectures, 3,* p. 349)

Emerson proposes that as observers we should try to see almost all activity as expression, as self-expression, as exertion motivated as much by the urge to disclose oneself as by the wish to get a job done. The attempt to expose or discover one's secret, one's real talent, is often displaced or off-center, and thus a person's secret may remain a secret even to that person. It is very hard to find one's own way; one falls back on conventionally-defined opportunities. The greater the element of conformity, the greater the chance of avoiding one's deepest truth. Only independent conduct can be perceived as the truth of a person.

In "Self-Reliance," Emerson likens any attentive activity to prayer, the only genuine prayer:

> As soon as the man is at one with God, he will not beg. He will then see prayer in all action. The prayer of the farmer kneeling in his field to weed it, the prayer of the rower kneeling with the stroke of his oar, are true prayers heard throughout nature, though for cheap ends. (p. 276)

The complication is that activity may very well seem like prayer only to the contemplative observer. The inwardness of the worker may not be prayerful. To take inspiration from a kneeling farmer may be to play a trick on oneself. But Emerson's point is probably more generous to the worker.

Especially in his writings before *Essays: First Series,* but not only there, Emerson makes much of finding one's vocation as the key to being oneself. This frequent sense is that each person exists to do what only that person can do well or can do at all. Singularity or individuation is tied to one's active vocation. Self-reliance means yielding to one's real work, if one is released enough to insist on discovering it. One's active vocation is the expression and completion of one's being, but it is also the reason for being. Later on, I will discuss Emerson's idea of vocation at some length. I simply want to indicate its salience here.

Just as steady as Emerson's praise of vocation is his dismay at most occupations. We thus come up against a major obstacle in our efforts to see the essence of self-reliance as a principle of action or as an existential choice rather than as a method of intellect. He can go only so far in investing daily work, even when undertaken as prayer, with a dignity commensurate with the proper expectations for human individuals. The abrupt phrase "though for cheap ends" in a lyrically adorative passage on activity as prayer is indicative of Emerson's attitude. He does not instinctively love the expression he sees. In "The Poet," he can speak of how "hunters, farmers, grooms and butchers" express their love of nature by their very choice of life, "and not in their choice of words." They worship "nature the symbol . . . body overflowed by life." Yet their active life, which is their worship, is constituted by "coarse, but sincere rites" (pp. 453-454). Emerson sees the coarseness, not only the sincerity. He is desperate to praise in order to encourage, so he says that the "aboriginal Self" in each, the unknowable inner power, "shoots a ray of beauty even into trivial and impure actions, if the least mark of independence appear" ("Self-Reliance," p. 268). He labors to love labor, and succeeds partly. However, he says in "The Poet:"

> Notwithstanding this necessity to be published, adequate expression is rare. I know not how it is that we need an interpreter; but the great majority of men seem to be minors, who have not yet come into possession of their own, or mutes, who cannot report the conversation they have had with nature. (p. 448)

Emerson certainly exemplifies his theory that the poet's vocation is to interpret human beings to themselves. He is a poet because he could not endure the world if it were left uninterpreted: It would be "cheap," "coarse."

It is therefore not surprising that when Emerson gives in *Nature* examples of activities that rise above the usual condition wherein "man applies to nature but half his force," they make up an amazingly unnormalized sampling:

> the traditions of miracles in the earliest antiquity of all nations; the history of Jesus Christ; the achievements of a principle, as in religious and political revolutions, and in the abolition of the slave-trade; the miracles of enthusiasm, as those reported of Swedenborg, Hohelohe, and the Shakers; many obscure and yet uncontested facts, now arranged under the name of Animal Magnetism; prayer; eloquence; self-healing; and the wisdom of children. (pp. 46-47)

For the most part, he reaches for the extraordinary or the unadult, as if only these are worth expressing. Though *Representative Men* is a kind of rebuttal to Carlyle's worship of heroes, still the very fact that five of the six representative men are thinkers (and the other is Napoleon) makes it hard for us to believe that Emerson appreciates the typical activities of ordinary persons in the world. As for the realm of the extraordinary, he says in a lecture:

> I like artists better than generals. Goethe and Swedenborg are far more formidable agitators than Napoleon or O'Connell . . . These persons can never compete with the artist. . . . He takes his counters from heaven and plays his game by a skill not taught or quickened by his appetites. ("Literature" [Second lecture], *Early Lectures, 3,* p. 225)

I believe that Emerson gives us indications throughout his work that self-reliant existence or action and endeavor can only be marginal or eruptive; it is dependent on the chances the world gives to make a difference. If the idea of self-reliance is to be realized more self-sufficiently, less contingently —difficult as its realization must always be—it must find its location elsewhere than in worldly appearance or activity. Self-reliance must then refer primarily to the work of the inner life, to the life of the mind. But let me hold off this insistence of mine a bit longer.

Is there a completed picture of a truly self-reliant ordinary individual in Emerson's writing, of one who, leading an everyday life, projects the powers within and independently makes his or her life expressive? Perhaps we find one in the sometimes harrowing essay on his aunt, Mary Moody Emerson—an essay that also looks like a self-portrait. Perhaps his eulogy of Thoreau is a picture of self-reliance; but the reservations he inserts add up to a deep ambivalence, which Emerson voiced on other occasions. Indeed it is the very self-reliance of being and acting, common to his aunt and Thoreau, that elicits Emerson's ambivalence. It is as if the project of existential or active self-reliance verges on the inhuman. Its success may not be success. In any case, it is perhaps right that Emerson leaves all forms of self-reliance except mental self-reliance undefined or ill-defined. Persons have to find their own way. Whatever the reasons, the conceptualization is incomplete. What we have instead of a full portrait is an image of an ideal, an image of being oneself by realizing oneself, of being self-reliant rather than imitative (or conventional and hence unnatural). This image, however, signifies Emerson's inevitable failure to redeem the idea that the principal realization of self-reliance lies in independent being, doing, or acting.

After lamenting everyone's timidity and apology ("he dares not say 'I think,' 'I am,' but quotes some saint or sage"), Emerson says:

> These roses under my window make no reference to former roses or to better ones; they are for what they are; they exist with God today. There is no time to them. There is simply the rose; it is perfect in every moment of its existence.

He goes on:

> But man postpones or remembers; he does not live in the present. . . . He cannot be happy and strong until he too lives with nature in the present, above time. ("Self-Reliance," p. 270)

But the lovely image is not lovely. Human beings characteristically *postpone* too much; but we do not think unless we *remember*. Trying to live in the present is hopeless; so is assimilating living to being, living one's life to being oneself. In what I say I only repeat what Emerson usually says, rose or no rose. The fact is that Emerson insists with a characteristic insistence that we can assimilate our active experience only retrospectively and that this condition is not lamentable but productive of intense intellectuality. It may be easier to observe immediately than to experience immediately, but memory is needed even to make the best of one's immediate observations. To exist or live in the present is to live the past intellectually, not to live actively now, or be fully there. Though Emerson did not write a piece on memory until rather late in life (1857), memory in the form of active recollection is fundamental to his notion of mental life. This thought is crystallized in words from the earlier version of "Love" (1838), which tell of the impact of falling in love: "when we became all eye when one was present, and all memory when one was gone" (*Early Lectures, 3,* p. 57). The best of life, including love, is all eye and all memory.

I grant that there is a sense of living in the present which avoids some of the objections that can be made to the image of the rose. In a lecture given in 1836, Emerson advocates "The present moment against all time" ("Modern Aspects of Letters," *Early Lectures, 1,* p. 384). I read this formulation as an incitement to seize the day and to live or act in defiance of the knowledge that time without beginning precedes one's existence, and time without end will roll on after one's death. One strains to overcome the futility inherent in the comparison of eternity with the brief flash of one's existence. "Works and Days" in *Society and Solitude* develops this thought. There can be, in Emerson's striking phrase, "consent to be nothing for eternity" ("Natural History of Intellect," *Natural History,* p. 56). "The day is great and final. The night is for the day, but the day is not for the night" ("Success," *Society and Solitude,* p. 307). If, then, living in the present means not wasting one's life, though it is absurdly brief, then the thought is salutary. But the image of the rose does not best represent this thought. Human beings cannot be, as roses are. We may look like roses, now and then, to the friend or lover, or to the poet. But only now and then. And if we try to exist as roses exist, we will be foolish or insensitive or cruel or mad, or merely vulgar. The complaint of "double consciousness," to which I referred above, is impossible to assuage, except falsely. The most we can have are moments of activity in which we feel as if all our powers were under our control, in which we feel that the present moment is worthy of lasting forever, that we achieved or restored our identity. Emerson complains that:

> A man acts not from one motive, but from many shifting fears and short motives; it is as if he were ten or twenty less men than himself, acting at discord with one another, so that the result of most lives is zero. ("The Preacher," *Lectures and Sketches,* p. 224)

He outdoes Plato in rendering the wasteland of self-division. But is there reality in his prophecy? He says:

> When he shall act from one motive, and all his faculties play true, it is clear mathematically, is it not, that this will tell in the result, as if twenty men had cooperated. (pp. 224-225)

The distancing phrase "is it not" and the insertion of "mathematically" are meant to reveal, I think, Emerson's strain, his doubt that self-unity can ever be anything but hit and miss.

If, too, we are unpredictable, if our deeds often surprise ourselves as well as others, that can mean, in a good or bad sense, that we are beside ourselves, but not that, at last, we are all that we can be. Roses in any case are predictable. A rose is only a rose. It does not have the "infinitude" that Emerson is intent on attributing to human beings. Infinitude is a concept that precludes living in the present because the all-sufficient present precludes endless potentiality. Emerson says all that is needed to subvert the aspiration to a composed essence:

> Other creatures are generic but have no individuals. Every lion is like every other lion: all horses of the same breed will act alike in given situations: but every man is a new and incalculable power. (Introductory, *The Philosophy of History, Early Lectures, 2,* p. 9)

In several ways, then, Emerson undercuts the idea that the supreme realization of self-reliance should lie in being and acting. He encounters everywhere reasons to be dissatisfied with attempted expressiveness, despite his profound dislike of the unexpressiveness of conformity. His genius, in its power, and perhaps also in its temperamental limitations, inclines to the view that a contemplative mind can be more truly self-reliant than a person striving for self-reliance in the world. With an independent mind, one can see and know, observe and trace the intricacy and complexity of the world. This mental process more nearly reaches self-reliance than being and acting individualistically do. Evidence seems to compel Emerson's judgment.

There are impediments to active self-reliance that Emerson ponders and that I will explore in the next chapter. But even if these impediments were less strong, active self-reliance would still be, in his theory, inherently less worthy, less dignified, than mental self-reliance. I think there are two reasons for this. First, only mental self-reliance can be impersonal. Second, active self-reliance—even when and to the extent that it can be achieved—seems incomplete or inadequate unless one makes the effort to disclose it and make it signify, and such an effort of contemplation and interpretation is of course a mental one. I will take up the second reason in the context of discussing impediments to active self-reliance, but at this moment I wish to attend to the theme of impersonality.

Emerson frequently suggests that to truly be an individual one must become "public"; it means losing "personality" as well as losing the partiality or distinctiveness flowing from one's identification with a group. The attempt may make one resemble an impervious egoist, or a person without qualities; but the appearance would be deceptive. One tries to overcome obstacles to receptivity, to "impressionability" ("Success," *Society and Solitude,* p. 301). We go out of ourselves so that we may enter the world, rather than remaining imprisoned in ourselves. Emerson renders this going out of oneself as a kind of self-forgetting, where the self to be forgotten is the everyday self, a prisoner of habitual mental associations converting newness into a mere exoticism. He says:

> How tedious is the perpetual self preservation of the traveller. His whole road is a comparison of what he sees and does at home with what he sees and does now. Not a blessed moment does he forget himself and yielding to the new world of facts that environ him, utter without memory that which they say. Could he once abandon himself to the wonder of the landscape he would cease to find it strange. (*Journals, 7,* pp. 235-236)

Regularly going out of our selves prepares for the possibility of occasionally losing oneself—being beside oneself, lost in ecstatic contemplation. We ascend by abandonment—that is, by the deliberate struggle against being calculating, against becoming obsessively self-absorbed, self-furthering, even self-realizing. "We are not strong by our power to penetrate, but by our relatedness. The world is enlarged for us, not by new objects, but by finding more affinities and potencies in those we have" ("Success," *Society and Solitude,* p. 302). We abandon pride of personality. We mitigate what I have called "positive individuality" because it distorts self-reliant receptivity. There is a wonderful passage in a letter by Keats, which he wrote under the influence of Hazlitt's great reflections on Shakespeare in *Lectures on the English Poets* (1818), that makes almost the same point in an unusually spirited way, and thus throws light on Emerson's meaning:

> A poet is the most unpoetical of any thing in existence; because he has no Identity—he is continually in for—and filling some other Body—The Sun, the Moon, the Sea and Men and Women who are creatures of impulse are poetical and have about them an unchangeable attribute—the poet has none; no identity . . . It is a wretched thing to confess; but is a very fact that not one word I utter can be taken for granted as an opinion growing out of my identical nature—how can it, when I have no nature? When I am in a room with People if I ever am free from speculating on creations of my own brain, then not myself goes home to myself: but the identity of every one in the room begins . . . to press upon me that, I am in a very little time an[ni]hilated. (To Richard Woodhouse, 27 October 1818, *Letters of John Keats,* pp. 157-158)

Emerson, unlike Keats, does not separate the poet from all other persons, but rather urges all of us to have moments when we lose our identities for the sake of poetical apprehension. He democratizes Keats's thought by trying to persuade us that impersonality is generally available. And he provides a basis for the capacity to become impersonal. Our impersonality is actually a refusal to shut out any aspect of oneself from the reach of cultivated self-awareness in order to position ourselves to use all our aspects—all our warring impulses and thoughts—as bridges to the kindred phenomena actualized in the world.

Nietzsche's rendering of the Dionysian condition in a passage later than *The Birth of Tragedy* also resembles Emersonian impersonality:

> It is impossible for the Dionysian type not to understand any suggestion; he does not overlook any sign of an affect; he possess the instinct of understanding and guessing in the highest degree, just as he commands the art of communication in the highest degree. He enters into any skin, into any affect: he constantly tranforms himself. ("Skirmishes of an Untimely Man," *Twilight of the Idols* [W. Kaufman, Trans.], Sect. 10, pp. 519-520)

We are impersonal not only when we regard everything with as much sympathetic withholding as possible but also when we have sufficient self-acquaintance to know that all that has happened in the world has a source or echo in ourselves. The power to impersonate depends on impersonality. Impersonality registers an individual's universality or infinitude. Such an impersonal aspiration is a decisive indication that for Emerson, self-reliance is most itself when it is a method of intellect rather than a way of being or acting in the world. Let us, therefore, give a definition of self-reliance at its best: it is the steady effort of thinking one's thoughts and thinking them through. It is intellectual independence, reactive and responsive self-possession. Here, rather than in worldly appearance or enactment, we find the greater possibility of a more sustained independence.

Really, how could determinate being or specific doing and acting follow from the cultivation of a readiness to lend oneself to contrasting or even directly opposed ideas and values, practices and institutions? What Emerson says of Plato can apply to Emerson himself: "his garment, though of purple, and almost sky-woven, is an academic robe, and hinders action with its voluminous robes" ("Swedenborg; or the Mystic," *Representative Men,* p. 677). Some of one's particular commitments and engagements must survive sympathetic understanding of forces antagonistic to oneself or a sense of their beauty or appropriateness or necessity. But in comparison to the universe in one's liberated mind, being merely oneself, as well as doing and acting as oneself, can feel like such a narrowing of possibility and such a forcing of choice as to look capricious or willful. Grace lies in impersonality.

Action has to be hindered if the mind is to be liberated and thus made adequate to the vastness of the world:

> Nature can only be conceived as existing to a universal and not to a particular end, to a universe of ends, and not to one,—a work of ecstasy, to be represented by a circular movement, as intention might be signified by a straight line of definite length. ("The Method of Nature," p. 120)

The work of ecstasy ("ecstasy is the law and cause of nature") deserves an ecstatic response (The Method of Nature, p. 127). One's personal "intention" is little in comparison. Emerson says that all nature, "oppressed by one superincumbent tendency, obeys that redundancy or excess of life which in conscious beings we call ecstasy" (p. 121). The conscious ecstasy comes only when we witness the ecstasy endured unconsciously by all creatures, including ourselves most of the time. In a journal entry, Emerson says, "Live all you think, is a noble ethics which I cannot now forget" (*Journals, 7,* p. 342). But this ethics is not possible. Philosophical thinking in Emerson's sense always exceeds the possibilities of realization, whether public or private. No individual (or group) can sanely enact the whole range of indispensable contrasts and contradictions. Even the whole world at any given time omits and loses.

"Shakespeare taught us," Emerson says, "that the little world of the heart is vaster, deeper and richer than the spaces of astronomy" ("Shakespeare," *Miscellanies,* p. 448). The word, not the deed, makes the individual impersonal or infinite: isn't that Emerson's meaning? Still, it would be absurd for me to divorce self-reliance from being and acting or doing altogether. Emerson does not permit it. Rather, he makes active self-reliance lesser than mental self-reliance. In "Tendencies," a lecture of 1840 which supplied thoughts for some of *Essays: First Series,* Emerson gives a preliminary summary of his comparative estimation:

> Yet a strong will is a feeble force. It is a surrender of a man to the visible facts of his desire, the habit of proceeding directly to them without any reckoning of other wills, of opposition or of favor. It is a low species of self-reliance and inspires among the trustless fear and respect. But it has no power over the good. It is strong beside custom, imitation, and indulgence. It is weakness beside the renunciation of will. Beside love and wisdom, the self-abandonment of goodness and of truth, this which seeks merely low and conventional gratifications, power and fame, self-aggrandizement, is unholy and profane. (*Early Lectures, 3,* p. 312)

Later, he rephrases the idea:

> in the scale of powers, it is not talent, but sensibility, which is best: talent confines, but the central life puts us in relation to all . . . Such a man feels himself in harmony, and conscious by his receptivity of an infinite strength. ("Success," *Society and Solitude,* p. 295)

In "Self-Reliance," the motive that Emerson often (though not exclusively) appeals to is not the self-reliance of "self-aggrandizement," but the wish to be oneself, to live as one thinks best, to take chances deviantly, to pursue one's special vocation, to define oneself as different from others, to follow the line of one's distinctiveness without deflection. By Emerson's reckoning, this composite motive is better than many or even most social or worldly motives, even though it retains a conformist (because comparative) element. It is the project of practical democracy. Of course it can never and should never be completely or continuously abandoned. Much should be said in its defense. (In later chapters I will return to active self-reliance.) The question is whether there is any self-reliant activity (or manner of presence) in the world that follows naturally from, or is in perfect consonance with, mental self-reliance, indefinite receptivity. Or does an aroused and energetic contemplation leave one immobile, while relegating *all* one's activity and presence, even self-reliant kinds, to a secondary status and a separate realm of realization? I have already indicated my sense that mental self-reliance is discontinuous with active self-reliance. But let us say a little more.

With effort, can the "biographical Ego," as he calls it, be reduced, and another kind of self-reliant practical activity show itself ("Natural History of Intellect," *Natural History,* p. 62)? It is not motivated by the wish to be oneself and act as oneself, but rather by the determination to act, if at all possible, at the behest of "the grand spiritual Ego," at the behest, that is, of one's impersonal reception of the world. The positive individuality of the biographical Ego will result from independent practical thinking, but thinking that is not yet philosophical or poetical. What, on the other hand, may result from the grand spiritual Ego? It is very difficult, if at all possible, to specify the nature of activity that may flow from a philosophical or political reception of the world.

It may be tempting to think that Emerson has solved the difficulty in the following words:

> But in the face of our libraries it must still be affirmed that every subject of human thought down to most trivial crafts and chores ought to be located poetically,—religion, war, law, politics, money, housekeeping. It would be easy to show that they must all be handled poetically in action in order to any success. A judge and a banker must drive their craft poetically as well as a dancer or a scribe. That is, they must not suffer the facts to stand superior to them . . . Then they are inventive; they detect the capabilities of their affair. ("Politics," *Early Lectures, 3,* p. 239)

But "poetical" in Emerson usually means something other than mastering or constraining facts for the sake of a practical advance. Poetry in action is better than caution or routine; it shows imagination. But the practical imagination serves the biographical Ego; it may enable that Ego to act rapaciously or sordidly; it is self-concerned, not open to the world. Why not just say that thinking, speaking, and writing are the activities that comprise the highest self-reliance, that verbal expression is the only philosophical or poetical activity, and that it is therefore the greatest activity, especially when words affirm life and liberate wonder? This view certainly finds abundant support in Emerson.

Is there more to say? Can one say that if one is filled with a sense of the world's beauty, one wants the world to go on and hence will feel an irresistible desire to do what one can to preserve the world? Consequently, practical activity resulting directly from self-reliant thinking that has achieved, if only some of the time, a philosophical or poetical relation to life's splendid contraries and antagonisms, would consist in doing what lay in one's power to keep the world going and spreading to others the feeling of attachment to it. The project would be the avoidance of human and natural extinction or reversion to a scarcely describable simplicity. Not only self-reliant words but innovative action amid unprecedented circumstances would comprise the activity. But Emerson does not formulate the idea of preservative politics; I elicit it. In any case, to act even out of the most philosophical or poetical purpose would require submission to the discipline of partisanship. The means seem inconsistent with the purpose.

Let us take another tack. Is conscientious action, especially conscientious political action, an expression of self-reliance in the highest sense? It certainly shows independent thinking. But is the thinking philosophical or poetical, or only moral and practical? That question is not easy to answer. Did Socrates's conscientious courage in the face of wicked commands come from his possible belief that there was no afterlife? Was it assisted by a receptive love of individuals and their thwarted potentiality? In regard to Emerson, nonviolent objection to war seems mandated by Emerson's statement that,

If we believed in the existence of strict *individuals,* natures, that is, not radically identical but unknown, unmeasurable we should never dare to fight. ("The Heart," *Early Lectures,* 2, p. 285)

(He says in an earlier version of "Politics," "Let us treat all men as gods. Let us drop violence" [*Early Lectures, 3,* p. 245].) Because he is not satisfied to base his opposition to the waste of war on the preciousness of individual distinctiveness, Emerson returns in the same essay to the "radical identity" he had for the moment forsaken:

⌈Courage is grounded always on a belief in the identity of the nature of my enemy with my own; that he with whom you contend, is no more than you . . . It will be found the mind is too much One to be any longer English or French, Indian or White; that for the same reason why a soldier can muster spirit now to attack a soldier he will then feel that the blow aimed at his brother's heart strikes his own. ("The Heart," pp. 285-286)⌋

The insistence on the radical identity rather than the radical incommensurability of individuals is thus the deeper ground for nonviolence as both a tactic and a condition of life, because it recognizes the equal vastness of every heart. It sees each person as a universe of splendid antagonisms and contradictions. Just as the self-reliant mind may feel impelled to act so as to try to preserve the world for the sake of its scarcely conceivable variety, so such a mind may feel impelled not to take a single life, because every person's equal internal richness makes him or her sacred.

It is therefore possible that no-saying action, not only forbearance from action, comes from the inner voice; that nonviolent resistance well suits or is indeed necessitated by self-reliance in the highest sense; that it is philosophical politics. Though Emerson disapproved of Thoreau's civil disobedience in 1846, he concurred, after 1850, in the refusal to obey the Fugitive Slave Law, and spoke warmly of principled disobedience. (But he also idolized John Brown for his very violence.) It may be more sensible, however, to say that the no-saying deed is the best kind of action that is independent, but that its source is not clearly philosophical or poetical. It falls short of the latter qualities because it takes sides, even though the side it takes is the side that helps people gain or keep the preconditions of self-reliance. It judges harshly and dualistically, praiseworthy though it is. It is, however, the best kind of practical action because there is greater reality in resistance than initiative, in refusal than in the effort to shape the ungraspable and impenetrable world. (In the next chapter I will discuss Emerson's reasons for thinking the world so unamenable to an individual's constructive effort.) But I offer these views knowing them to be inconclusive.

In any event, no matter where we turn in Emerson's world we find the intellect elevated above the manual, the physical, the practical, the non-verbal or the mental that serves any of these. All these latter modes of expression can suit self-reliance, but it must be of a lower sort because these modes are not impersonal and hence not intrinsically poetical or philosophical. They can be made so only in the observation and contemplation of someone who does not engage in them. Is, then, self-reliant comprehension of the world the end itself? I think that Emerson's answer is yes, after all is said; but he says a lot to make that conclusion uneasy. It turns out, as I hope to suggest later, that though no worldly activity, in Emerson's account, manifests the highest self-reliance, two personal relationships—love and friendship—are intimately bound with it. These are not, of course, activities in the usual sense, but they are engagements with the world.

2

Redeeming the Frustrations of Experience

Before looking more closely at a few implications of self-reliance as an intellectual method, I would like to explore some passages in which Emerson explicitly calls into doubt the very possibility of directly self-reliant activity or expression, or even a self-reliant relational engagement with the world. The point is not merely that self-reliant perception and understanding are, because of their impersonality, more inherently worthy than self-reliant being and doing, but also that self-reliant being and doing, whatever their worth, come up against tremendous obstacles in oneself and in the world, and approach impossibility. On whatever terms, active engagement with the world or aspiring to present oneself as oneself in the world partakes of unreality too much, and incurably. It is also likely that the feeling of unreality—the dislocation or alienation—increases with the effort of worldly, active self-reliance. In contrast, great intellectual advantage exists in the feeling of unreality.

Characteristically, Emerson praises the life of the mind not as one who looks for consolation amid the sorrows and failures of action and being, but as one who is enraptured by the life of the mind, immersed in a condition of what he calls "entranced waiting" ("Natural History of

Intellect," *Natural History,* p. 56). This waiting and watching is world enough. But, to be sure, he can also sound regretful that the active life fails to satisfy, fails in reality. In some Emersonian moods, the self-reliant life of the mind can therefore appear as a refuge, a condition to fall back on when the world proves obdurate, impenetrable to the exertions of being and doing. Mental self-reliance, self-reliance in the highest sense, can occasionally seem the highest, can seem good, only by default. Regret may tinge allegiance to it. Such regret, and its causes, are concentrated in "Experience" (*Essays: Second Series*).

Much has been written on this essay. It is hard to grasp, because it seems unstructured, almost random. It also seems philosophically despondent, lacking Emerson's usual luster, the luster that his unequaled generosity bestows on whatever it receives most of the time. The essay's tendency may be as dispiriting or life-denying as Emerson believes church religions to be. I agree with the common judgment that "Experience" is meant to represent caution, to give poetical words to caution's sobriety. For that reason, passages in it are especially suitable for qualifying the exuberant invitations to expressiveness of being and courage in action that are the heart of "Self-Reliance." It is, however, as great an impersonation as "Self-Reliance." Contending impersonations are equally matched. And far more than "Self-Reliance," "Experience" is about the inward relation of the self to itself and thus opens the question of the reality of the self.

Just from the essay's title, one could expect that Emerson will present the best case for experience. Presenting the best case is his usual mode. But what would a case for experience be a case for? Would we be urged to have experience—to have experiences, to grow by accumulation, to unfold by acquainting ourselves with as much life as possible, to submit as much as possible of ourselves and our aspirations to the test of attempted realization? But "Self-Reliance," "Circles" and other writings already make that case. Or, instead, would it be a case for heeding the voice of experience, for not daring too much lest one suffer defeat at the hands of easily identifiable adversaries? One soon discovers that "Experience" is not a case for having experiences or for trying to live as much as we can. It does turn out to be an essay in caution. On the other hand, the source of caution is not the voice of experience, the disappointed voice of chagrin or exhaustion, or the enraged voice of self-spite. I believe that something else is going on in this strange essay; something that is quite relevant to the strategy of deliberately perplexing Emerson's own appeals for active self-reliance.

I read the essay as proposing (with the exaggeration induced and allowed by Emerson's method of tentativeness) two main things. First, to experience, to do and act, to have experiences in the world, to be marked by them, to be touched or affected by them, to feel in touch with them, Emerson says is inordinately difficult. One can scarcely experience oneself. An almost constant condition is feeling haunted, feeling unreal, feeling alienated (in a sense that is both like and unlike that found in Marx's *Economic and Philosophic Manuscripts* of 1844, written in the same year as the publication of "Experience"). Second, to leave one's mark on experience, to make a difference, to be thought to exist, to be experienced, is also inordinately difficult. The two difficulties reinforce each other; indeed, they imply each other. I cannot register on others for the same reasons that others cannot register on me. Thus, there are barriers between anyone and the worldly ability to experience and be experienced. "Experience" is not, of course, a case *against* experience; that would be absurd. The essay, however, does surprise by the force of its doubt that we do live by experience and that we should try to live more intensely.

In a rare personal reference in public, Emerson mentions the death of his 5-year-old son (whose name, Waldo, he does not give). The point of the reference is to say how hard it is to experience (perhaps the preponderant difficulty the essay takes up). The sentences planted in the paragraph are tremendous:

> There are moods in which we court suffering, in the hope that here at least we shall find reality, sharp peaks and edges of truth. But it turns out to be scene-painting and counterfeit. The only thing grief has taught me is to know how shallow it is. . . . An innavigable sea washes with silent waves between us and the things we aim at and converse with. . . . In the death of my son, now more than two years ago, I seem to have lost a beautiful estate—no more. I cannot get it nearer to me. . . . I grieve that grief can teach me nothing. . . . Nothing is left us now but death. We look to that with a grim satisfaction, saying, There at least is reality that will not dodge us. (pp. 472-473)

These are grief-stricken sentences. In Stephen Whicher's beautiful words: "The grief that he cannot grieve is for Emerson a form grief takes"

(*Selections From Ralph Waldo Emerson,* p. 491). Emerson's unstated question is, If grief is deep, why didn't I die of it when the being I loved most, more than myself, who I felt was myself, died? If I survived, grief is shallow. I cannot feel even that I have lost my own life; I cannot grieve even for my own lost life. How, then, can one speak of being able to experience? Emerson is presuming to rebut the wisdom about wisdom spoken by the chorus in Aeschylus:

> Zeus, who guided men to think,
> who has laid it down that wisdom
> comes alone through suffering.
> (*Agamemnon* [R. Lattimore, Trans.], lines 176-178)

To the contrary: "The only thing grief has taught me is to know how shallow it is." This is not the wisdom the chorus promised. The lines from Aeschylus, not mentioned, must lie behind Emerson's account.

What is it that thins out experience, that makes it so difficult to experience and be experienced? In the prefatory poem, Emerson names "the lords of life," the facts of life that create "the innavigable sea" that cuts us off from ourselves and each other. They are Use (mute custom, ordinariness, or habituation), Surprise, Surface, Dream, Succession swift, spectral Wrong, and Temperament (p. 469). Later in the essay, Emerson names the lords of life as "Illusion, Temperament, Succession, Surface, Surprise, Reality, Subjectiveness" (p. 490). (Use and spectral wrong, from the first list, are dropped; dream is changed to illusion; and reality and subjectiveness are added.) Practically every paragraph in the essay is devoted to presenting the case for the force of one or another of these lords. Every lord on both lists makes an appearance; some more than one. Each stands in the way of feeling and being felt, of feeling real and feeling the reality of the world. We can say that they all conspire to deprive us of the feeling that we are or can ever be at home in the world. Emerson acknowledges that "I dare not give their order, but I name them as I find them in my way" (p. 491). The essay has the abruptness or the "lubricity" or seeming unconnectedness that Emerson says stamps the experience of living. "I know better than to claim any completeness for my picture. I am a fragment, and this is a fragment of me" (p. 491). That is, I am at any moment only one or another fragment of myself, and my words at this moment are only a fragment of my whole thought. I cannot bring my whole mind to bear on the question of why I and my thought always remain a fragment. But the fragments in "Experience" do add up, if not to a complete picture, then to a powerful net impression. The disposed reader experiences "Experience" as vividly as any essay Emerson wrote. Or, at least, one can be haunted by it more than by any other.

In "Self-Reliance" an image of being altogether oneself is the rose. In "Experience" the essence of being able to experience and be experienced is to do both directly, without mediation. A common element in both essays is praise for the absence of self-consciousness and thus for the ability to be one and to be at one with what is external. In "Natural History of Intellect," he produces noteworthy sentences that concentrate what he wants to say about the effects of self-consciousness (and, derivatively, detachment). He grants that intellectual distance is a privilege, but says:

> It is not to be concealed that the gods have guarded this privilege with costly penalty. This slight discontinuity which perception effects between the mind and the object paralyzes the will. . . . That indescribably small interval is as good as a thousand miles, and has forever severed the practical unity. Such is the immense deduction from power by discontinuity.
>
> The intellect that sees the interval partakes of it, and the fact of intellectual perception severs once for all the man from the things with which he converses. Affection blends, intellect disjoins subject and object. For weal or woe we clear ourselves from the thing we contemplate. We grieve but are not the grief; we love but are not love. (*Natural History,* p. 44)

This passage fills out a thought from "The Method of Nature" (1841), that "all knowledge is assimilation to the object of knowledge" (p. 126).

Let us emphasize that he says that "the intellect that sees the interval partakes of it." The words suggest that there is always distance between oneself and one's experience, but only those who carry self-consciousness far have the honesty to notice the distance and feel it. But before we say that feeling it should turn us away from the impossible project of perfect unity with one's experience and induce us to try to exploit self-consciousness precisely for the sake of a sensation of greater reality, we must stay a while longer with Emerson's impersonation.

Just as one may take issue with the aspiration to become a rose (no matter how fleeting the aspiration), so we may worry over the basis

Emerson gives for saying that it is almost impossible to experience and be experienced. If self-consciousness prevents us from being like a rose, rooted in oneself while self-sufficiently unconnected to external reality, it also prevents us from entering into an immediate relation to reality. But there is no honest remedy for self-consciousness. Emerson, as much as anyone, says so. In the essay "Experience," however, whose title may suggest that it will present the best case for the value of experiencing, he must allow himself the utterance of disappointment. He says,

> It is very unhappy, but too late to be helped, the discovery we have made that we exist. That discovery is called the Fall of Man. Ever afterwards we suspect our instruments. We have learned that we do not see directly, but mediately, and that we have no means of correcting these colored and distorting lenses which we are, or of computing the amount of their errors. (p. 487)

Language (a half-god, as he calls it in the earlier version of "The Poet," *Early Lectures, 3,* p. 358) creates the possibility of knowing that we exist, of being able to say "I think, therefore I know I am" (my words, not Emerson's); just by doing that, language guarantees that there will be distance between one and oneself, and hence between one and everything else. A fall occurred before the fall, and that prior fall was fated; it was, however, only the grant of speech. It made inevitable the second fall, the act of disobedience, the establishment of distance. In the words of Wallace Stevens, "Adam in Eden was the father of Descartes" ("Notes Toward a Supreme Fiction," Sect. 4, p. 383).

I believe that Emerson also includes among language's gifts the ability to say, "I think, therefore I know that I will die." Let us recall the opening of "Experience":

> Where do we find ourselves? In a series of which we do not know the extremes, and believe that it has none. We wake and find ourselves on a stair; there are stairs below us, which we seem to have ascended; there are stairs above us, many a one, which go upward and out of sight. (p. 471)

When we really wake, we know what "out of sight" means: nothingness. The condition of being in a condition, of having language, is, however, "too late to be helped"—as long as we stay honest. A true sense of mortality will color all perception.

Emerson means something special when he calls language a half-god or a demi-god. If, instead, speech were wholly a god, then perhaps we could cancel all distance between the object and ourselves. Each would speak only his or her own words; words would hit their mark and pass into that supersession by which one selflessly apprehends essences. Language would be the instrument by which self-consciousness is lost, not gained. But even if such a wish were intelligible, it is not for us to have. Language, "being applied primarily to the common necessities of man, it is not new-created by the poet for his own ends" ("Art," *Society and Solitude,* p. 43). Only words will do, but they can do only so much.

There is, furthermore, no doubt that Emerson sees in individualism an intensification of self-consciousness. In a remarkable passage from "Historic Notes of Life and Letters in New England," a piece written in 1867, he goes back to the 1820s and 1830s, the period of what he calls "the Movement" (in distinction from "the Establishment"), a time when the reformist tendency was strong. The Movement's message was that "the nation existed for the individual" and that "the individual is the world." But this idea creates an age of "severance, of dissociation, of freedom, of analysis, of detachment" (*Lectures and Sketches,* p. 326). The result is that the "social sentiments are weak—People grow philosophical about native land and parents and relations." His description reaches its most dramatic moment when he says that the "young men were born with knives in their brain, a tendency to introversion, self-dissection, anatomizing of motives." Emerson is aware that a cultivated individualism, especially at its best when it is mental, when it becomes philosophical self-reliance, can intensify the feeling of unreality. But he does not seek an abatement of individualism. The danger contains the saving remedy. But he is desirous, characteristically, of first impersonating the idea that he must eventually confine to a subordinate role.

Even when not yearning for the direct experience of a complete merger with oneself and everything else, the difficulty of experiencing and being experienced remains considerable. Emerson exaggerates the difficulty of experience, but not by much—only as much as he has to in order to alert us. He brilliantly formulates the frequent sensations of unreality that we all have: the fog or cave or confusion or hallucination or dream or sleep that we recurrently feel that we are lost in, or have just been lost in. As a balance, Emerson adds what seems to go against the feeling of unreality:

the force of temperament, as if to say that if experience does not register on us, then at least by self-persistence we could register on the world:

> Thus inevitably does the universe wear our color, and every object fall successively into the subject itself. The subject exists, the subject enlarges; all things sooner or later fall into place. As I am, so I see; use what language we will, we can never say anything but what we are. ("Experience," p. 489)

Temperament imposes itself. Or, at least, the strong ones impose their temperament on the others around them. But Emerson likens temperament to a "prison of glass" (p. 474). We only think that we are successfully making things become like us. The actuality is that we cannot help thinking that we do so, but the world remains untouched, almost completely. There is no breaking out on our own terms:

> The individual is always mistaken. He designed many things, and drew in other persons as coadjutors, quarrelled with some or all, blundered much, and something is done; all are a little advanced, but the individual is always mistaken. It turns out somewhat new, and very unlike what he promised himself. (p. 484)

Scattered throughout "Experience" are encouragements to disregard the tenor of the essay. There is, however, too much truth in the case that Emerson makes to disregard it. Such truth does not depend on an impossible ideal of unmediated oneness with oneself and with what is around one. By a very much less demanding standard, the difficulty of connection, of experiencing and being experienced, is pronounced.

The larger tendency in Emerson's work, as I have already mentioned, is to capitalize on self-consciousness, to make it the instrument of self-reliance rather than allowing it to be the source of doubt and inhibition, or of permanent estrangement. It alone can lead to a deepened sense of being real and finding the world real. The corrective to "Experience" is actually found earlier, in "The American Scholar" (1837):

> Our age is bewailed as the age of Introversion. Must that needs be evil? We, it seems, are critical; we are embarrassed with second thoughts; we cannot enjoy anything for hankering to know whereof the pleasure consists; we are lined with eyes; we see with our feet; the time is infected

with Hamlet's unhappiness—"Sicklied o'er with the pale cast of thought." Is it so bad then? Sight is the last thing to be pitied. Would we be blind? (pp. 67-68)

I mean to suggest that Emerson's tendency is to hold that the most real experiences come when we are separated by time from the events we usually call experiences. Only then are we able to be detached, and in such detachment the intellect can capture the truth or meaning or reality of experiences. The detachment that time may bring can be supplemented by another detachment that Emerson always urges, which comes from purging egoism and self-interest, the engines of action. As he says in "Natural History of Intellect":

> An intellectual man has the power to go out of himself and see himself as an object; therefore his defects and delusions interest him as much as his successes. He not only wishes to succeed in life, but he wishes in thought to know the history and destiny of a man; whilst the cloud of egotists drifting about are only interested in a success to their egotism. (*Natural History,* p. 39)

Immediate experiencing can be blind or numb, too self-engrossed or too passive; it is suffered. The mind of the detached ego is more successfully or genuinely active than the acting self. Only intellectual mediation can produce what Geoffrey Hartman (1984) has called, in an Emersonian phrase, "unmediated vision." Unmediated vision is not possible through unmediated (that is, immediate) experiencing, even if it is possible at all. This is not to deny that immediate perceptions (as distinct from worldly experiences) can be intense and accurate, but retrospection assists the revelation of their meaning as well. Retrospection ministers to shock.

But how, it may be asked, can we arrive at reality through intellectual and personal detachment when, to begin with, the "lords of life" impede our capacity for having experiences and being experienced, for acting successfully in the world and feeling the reality of the world impinge on us? What is primarily at issue is not the human relation to nature but one's relation to others. If our feelings are unable to reach their objects, reach human social reality, how can thinking about our feelings and objects do so? How can the retrospective or contemplative mind cross "the innavigable sea . . . between us and the things we aim at and converse with"?

How, more generally, can the mind penetrate the human world when the whole person cannot?

The short answer is that Emerson thinks that the mind's powers far exceed any other human capacity. The sixth part ("Idealism") of *Nature* is his most concentrated tribute to these powers. The mind can do what the feelings or the energies of action cannot do: touch. But, we may ask, is it reality that is touched? Or is it only a picture of it, put in its place, whether deliberately or not? Perhaps the mind inevitably constructs what it claims to perceive? Perhaps the self-reliant mind proceeds actively to "consider the passage of things and events purely as a spectacle and not as action in which we partake," and thereby consummates its divorce from reality? ("English Literature," *Introductory, Early Lectures, 1,* p. 226). Is it in touch only with itself? And what reality to itself could it have, so cut off? Do one's thoughts have more reality than what occasions them? Does Emerson commit himself to Idealism? I do not think that he finally does. Yet he does come close.

Notice the powers of mind surveyed in the section "Idealism" in *Nature*. They include these: the capacity of alien detachment which makes things become "unrealized" and thus gives "the whole world a pictorial air" (p. 34); the poetical capacity of imagination: "The Imagination may be defined to be, the use which the Reason makes of the material world . . . the power of subordinating nature for the purposes of expression" (p. 34); the philosophical capacity to generalize, to find laws or regularities that defy the senses or startle common sense; and the capacity to "put nature under foot" and thus, by "degrading nature," perform "the introduction of ideas into life" and establish ethics and religion (p. 38). By invoking these capacities, especially in regard to human social reality, is Emerson describing mental self-reliance as arbitrary power, and therefore putting the mind as far from touching reality as "Experience" puts the feelings? Even further? Or is he altogether substituting mind—subjectivity—for reality? Is mind the only reality for human beings, and is our reality therefore only a fiction? A formulation of Lacan's nicely captures the tendency Emerson flirts with or by which he may even be enraptured:

> And the Greek *nous* is the myth of thought accommodating itself in conformity with the world, the world (*Umwelt*) for which the soul is responsible: whereas the world is merely the fantasy through which

thought sustains itself—reality, no doubt, but to be understood as a grimace
of the real. (Lacan, *Television,* 1974, in Rajchman, *Truth and Eros,* p. 48)

I do not know that Emerson offers a theoretical conclusion. The philosophical questions involved are enormous and will not be discussed here.
Let us leave the matter by simply saying that Emerson seems to commit
himself, if not to Idealism, then to the view that feeling and doing and
acting—experiencing and being experienced—fail to achieve that close-
ness to human social reality that only the powers of the mind can achieve.
Reality is not my mind imposing itself as it pleases; if my mind is
self-reliant, its task is to open up reality by being open to reality. If there
is no reality independent of what my mind thinks about it, there could be
no need for those other powers, those interpretative powers by which one
seeks to know one's own experience and the world at large, and to know
by observation, retrospection, and contemplation. There would be no need
for—no possibility of—mental self-reliance. Instead, there would be only
"the fantasy through which thought sustains itself." I believe that Emerson
does not adopt Idealism despite strong temptations to do so. The world
(human and natural) is there, and the aim of self-reliance is to interpret it
as unarbitrarily as possible. The true powers of mind, the powers that
Emerson continually demonstrates and encourages, are not faithfully
defined in the inventory present in the Idealism section of *Nature.* Some
of them are almost parodied. The exaggeration is deliberate, as is usually
the case with Emerson. *Nature* attempts to domesticate oneself or all humanity in Nature, the social and natural world, which often looks or feels
oppressively foreign. But attributing sovereign powers to mind, which turn
out to be arbitrary, in order to make us feel at home, threatens to dissolve
the world and thus surrender us to the wrong kind of homelessness.

The net effect of "Experience" is that Emersonian self-reliance at its
best must finally be grasped as something mental, not active, and if
mental, then not arbitrary but interpretative. Whether in disappointment
with experience's remoteness, or with pride in the unarbitrary powers of
the mind, especially when it is impersonally self-reliant, Emerson is
committed to saying that self-reliance cannot best show itself in worldly
presence or activity.

I mention here that Emerson, rather late in his publications, expresses
some hesitations about the adequacy of speech to deliver what the powers

of the self-reliantly receptive mind may accumulate. This fact should be noticed, but it does not draw acting closer to self-reliance than thinking. He says:

> Our perception far outruns our talent. We bring a welcome to the highest lessons of religion and of poetry out of all proportion beyond our skill to teach. And, further, the great hearing and sympathy of men is more true and wise than their speaking is wont to be. ("Success," *Society and Solitude,* p. 301)

Emerson does not theorize other inadequacies of speech than the major one he refers to in this passage. There are many sensations, for example, that are not describable or only poorly so. Also, there are kinds of deep emotion that resist adequate expression, even retrospectively. One has experiences that cannot be put into words but nevertheless strike one as real; they can make one speechless. His grief, which Emerson calls shallow, left him with only deflected words, perhaps. They disguised the presence of an impossibly deep grave—an abyss. Speechlessness is not the same as shallowness. As a scarcely equaled master of the word, Emerson expects unlimited success, but not even he can achieve it. But the word remains, in any case, the way to reality.

*   *   *

Mental self-reliance, thinking one's thoughts and thinking them through, does not issue necessarily in some determinate mode of being in the world, or in becoming like a rose or a work of art, or in living one's life as a self-authored story. Of course, one's independence must show itself, but at its highest level it does not enact itself:

> All I know is reception; I am and I have: but I do not get, and when I have fancied I had gotten anything, I found I did not. ("Experience," p. 491)

One tries to possess one's mind and hence one's reception of the world. Life is thought. "What is life," asks Emerson in "Natural History of Intellect," "but what a man is thinking of all day?" (*Natural History,* p. 10). Self-reliance will show itself in the quality of consciousness, in self-reliant words. I would like to think, therefore, that Emerson does stand behind these words from "Experience":

> I know that the world I converse with in the city and in the farms, is not the world I *think*. I observe the difference, and shall observe it. One day I shall know the value and law of this discrepancy. But I have not found that much was gained by manipular attempts to realize the world of thought. . . . Worse, I observe that in the history of mankind there is never a solitary example of success—taking their own tests of success. I say this polemically, or in reply to the inquiry, Why not realize your world? (pp. 491-492)

Up to this point, I have tried to show that Emerson's idea of self-reliance is not a simple one. What seems to be only a charter for an independent and energetic involvement with the world or for a deliberate project of self-expression and self-assertion is something more, something higher. Involvement and expression are, of course, never forsaken by Emerson. Rather they are made secondary to a conception of the workings of the independent mind. In this conception, ridding oneself of traditional religion, with its derivative or sanctioned or conformist dispositions, is the indispensable beginning of receiving the world in a new way, a way that perfectly suits and exploits the spiritual possibilities of democratic culture.

The question, then, is, What is the point of self-reliant thinking? Emerson wants to help us see. To see is to be receptive, to take things in as truly or honestly or accurately as one can. What is to be seen? Having tried to absorb "Experience," we may now distinguish between seeing (making sense of) one's own social experiences or activities through retrospection, and seeing (taking in and making sense of) the world at large through honest perception completed or enhanced by retrospection. Seeing is thus either reliving one's experiences or suspending one's rush of living in order to watch life, human and natural. These two kinds of seeing are easily conflated because retrospection can make one's activity, to some extent, less one's own and more like the rest of observed life, which cannot be one's own. So far in this discussion, I have been conflating the two kinds, and will continue to do so, except when the subject needs the distinction to be made. In this double sense, seeing is the heart of mental self-reliance. At the same time, Emerson teaches that

searching for the meaning of one's experience for one's own sake matters
much less than using one's experience retrospectively as a bridge to
interpret the world for the sake of the world. The best moments are those
when one loses sight of oneself and looks at life and the world apart from
oneself. The pinnacle is impersonal. To be sure, it is possible to validate
one's perceptions by studiously consulting one's inner life, but the world
realizes what one could never foresee or imagine.

Emerson's premise is roughly Plato's: to see right is at once (and
interconnectedly) a source of intense pleasure, the highest manifestation
of doing justice and the most intimate embrace of reality. When Emerson
is secular, he produces a Platonism of the visible world. The trouble for
him is that church religions enable only a distorted seeing. "What is called
religion effeminates and demoralises" ("Worship," *The Conduct of Life,*
p. 1075). Church religions prejudice vision. They discourage appreciation
of the self and the world, and thus incapacitate seeing and reduce visibility. Of adherents and communicants, Emerson says, "They cannot see in
secret; they love to be blind in public" ("Address" [Harvard Divinity School],
p. 88). Church religions refuse to countenance appreciation of contrasts,
gradations, and antagonisms. By encouraging the will to believe, the will
to certainty, the will to one-sided commitment, they discourage the sort
of exaggerated, tentative, constantly qualified and antithetical thinking
that is the heart of self-reliance. They retard the effort to make everything
possible a cause for affirmation. But sight and love can and should
mutually strengthen each other. In a work published late in life, *Society
and Solitude* (1870), he says:

> The affirmative of affirmatives is love. As much love, so much perception.
> As caloric to matter, so is love to mind; so it enlarges, and so it empowers
> it. Good will makes insight, as one finds his way to the sea by embarking
> on a river. ("Success," p. 309)

Secession from church religions can open up the world. Without explicitly preaching secession, Emerson urges its necessity in every essay,
not only in the Divinity School "Address." It is right—up to a point, at
least—that a number of early reviewers found Emerson to be an atheist
or radical heretic. (See Richard Teichgraeber's *"Sublime Thoughts" and
"Penny Wisdom": Emerson, Thoreau, and the Market.*)

In "Self-Reliance," Emerson says that creeds are "a disease of the intellect" (p. 276). His position is that church doctrines are false for two reasons: They are held as doctrines, as creeds; and they inhibit or deny life. They are an indoctrinated and ruinous asceticism. He says:

> Everywhere I am hindered of meeting God in my brother, because he has shut his own temple doors and recites fables merely of his brother's God. Every new mind is a new classification. If it prove a mind of uncommon activity and power . . . it imposes its classification on other men, and lo! a new system. In proportion to the depth of the thought, and so to the number of the objects it touches and brings within reach of the pupil, is his complacency. But chiefly is this apparent in creeds and churches, which are also classifications of some powerful mind acting on the elemental thought of duty and man's relation to the Highest . . . The pupil takes the same delight in subordinating every thing to the new terminology as a girl who has just learned botany in seeing a new earth and new seasons thereby. It will happen for a time that, the pupil will find his intellectual power has grown by the study of his master's mind. But in all unbalanced minds, the classification is idolized, passes for the end and not for a speedily exhaustible means, so that the walls of the system blend to their eye in the remote horizon with the walls of the universe. . . . They cannot imagine how you aliens have any right to see,—how you can see. (pp. 276-277)

Emerson's deadliest attack on the conventionally religious mentality is concentrated in these words. Emerson is persuaded that the truth, if any part of it can be captured at all, cannot be captured whole in any one system; that the "completeness of system which metaphysicians are apt to affect" is not a goal to be sought ("Natural History of Intellect," *Natural History,* p. 12); that there can be only provisionally useful efforts to make sense of the world's inexhaustible, generative beauty, which Emerson renders as "the flowing or metamorphosis" ("The Poet," p. 456); but that such beauty cannot be seen properly by the conventionally religious mind, which is made disposed to interpret the world so as to see sin, guilt, hostility, and opportunities for timidity, compensatory desperate exertions, or melancholy withdrawal. "I think men never loved life less," he says publicly in 1841 ("Lecture on the Times," p. 66), but he had been saying it in his journals for quite some time.

We must also observe that Emerson thinks that religions often misdirect the moral sense and conform it to wrongdoing under the cover of piety.

The link between religions and sanctified immorality is especially vexatious in the decade before the Civil War:

> The fatal trait is the divorce between religion and morality. Here are know-nothing religions, or churches that proscribe intellect; scortatory religions; slave-holding and slave-trading religions; and, even in the decent populations, idolatries wherein the whiteness of the ritual covers scarlet indulgence. ("Worship," *The Conduct of Life,* p. 1058)

The larger constant point, however, is that emancipated thinking, that is, honest thinking, is never creedal and always life-affirming. In being such, honest thinking—honest retrospection as well as honest initial perception submitted to vigorous meditation—is intensely pleasurable because it touches reality and, in touching reality therefore does justice to all things. This is a new Platonism, a democratized one. To say that Emerson is a philosopher who wants to encourage his readers to be more philosophical, and hence more mentally independent and active is to say, I suppose, something. But to say as much does not capture the excitement and urgency of his mission. He believes in his genius, which is the power to see and say freshly. But he also believes in the genius of all other persons. He therefore does not want to tell them what to see and say. The only faithful student of Emerson is one who finds his or her own way, finds subjects, finds words. By looking freshly, one will say new words, not quote Emerson's new words.

Emerson sincerely thinks that everyone can become self-reliant in the sense of having, to an extent, "an original relation to the universe," rather than a relation borrowed from a creed (*Nature,* p. 7). He laments the snobbish claim that ordinary persons are not capable of philosophical illumination or ecstatic thinking. Emerson's role—his vocation—is to stimulate his readers into some attempted originality, which is their vocation. What is the right use of books? he asks in "The American Scholar," and answers that they "are for nothing but inspiration" (p. 57). "Truly speaking, it is not instruction, but provocation, that I can receive from another soul" ("Address" [Harvard Divinity School], p. 79). He expects his books to do no more than inspire and provoke. He cannot give detailed instructions for mental self-reliance; he can only offer an example. To do otherwise would be self-defeating for him and for his audience.

Even if his readers think his powers greater than their own, he hopes that he will be used as he uses those better than himself:

> I perceive that we have heard the same truth, but they have heard it better ... But it is only as fast as this hearing from another is authorized by its consent with his own, that it is pure and safe to each; and all receiving from abroad must be controlled by this immense reservation. ("Character," *Lectures and Sketches,* p. 100)

Yet if he will not give a set of instructions, if he will not devise a new creed, he will try, undeniably, to move our minds in a certain direction. In what I have so far said, I have tried to indicate that direction. I now turn again to two matters in order to draw out some further implications and thus fill out an answer to the question of what the point of mental self-reliance is. First, there is the superior rank of mental over active self-reliance; indeed, acting and being are only means to the end of thinking. Second, there is insistence on thinking as reception, as the effort to entertain the claims of contending philosophical ideas and worldly practices. The result of these two emphases is, to say it again, to touch reality and hence to feel the highest pleasure and do the greatest justice.

On the first matter, we have already noticed that self-expressive activity—a determination to be real and engage actively with human social reality—encounters or induces a haunting sense of one's unreality and the unreality of so-called reality. The consequence is that if for no other reason than to gain the sentiment of being, one must exploit the possibilities of thinking, even though, to begin with, self-reliant thinking in its self-consciousness and detachment threatens to dishearten us because it is candid about our distance from reality. The only surety comes, however, from thinking, from knowing and accepting one's identity as a thinking being, and then thinking one's own thoughts. To say it again, the way to reality is the word. Emerson tends to agree with the Idealists that "retirement from the senses" is needed to discern facts. Until transformed by the word, reality is inert ("The Transcendentalist," p. 193). Emerson thus proposes that activity does not really give whatever satisfaction it can give until it is interpreted or contemplated or mulled over and put into one's best and ripest words. Activity is squeezed or confused until thinking about it saves it:

Self-accusation, remorse, and the didactic morals of self-denial and strife with sin, is a view we are constrained by our constitution to take of the fact seen from the platform of action; but seen from the platform of intellection, there is nothing for us but praise and wonder. ("The Method of Nature," p. 122)

In "Love" he says, "Every thing is beautiful seen from the point of the intellect, or as truth. But all is sour if seen as experience" (p. 328). "The sea is lovely, but when we bathe in it, the beauty forsakes all the near water" ("Beauty," *The Conduct of Life,* p. 1110). Activity, one's own or that of others, seems to lack inherent value; its value is derivative from unencumbered perception and retrospective meditation:

The actions and events of our childhood and youth, are now matters of calmest observation. They lie like fair pictures in the air. Not so with our recent actions,—with the business which we now have in hand. On this we are quite unable to speculate. . . . We no more feel or know it than we feel the feet, or the hand, or the brain of our body. The new deed is yet a part of life—remains for a time immersed in our unconscious life. In some contemplative hour it detaches itself from the life like a ripe fruit, to become a thought of the mind. Instantly it is raised, transfigured; the corruptible has put on incorruption. ("The American Scholar," pp. 60-61)

Emerson goes further in the comparative evaluation of thinking and acting. Acting not only does not have real existence without retrospection, it exists for the sake of retrospection and most generally for the processes of mind.

He says, "The true scholar grudges every opportunity of action past by, as a loss of power." But what actually is the loss? It is the loss of an opportunity for thought. The very next sentences make action instrumental to thought:

It is the raw material out of which the intellect molds her splendid products. A strange process too, this by which experience is converted into satin. The manufacture goes forward at all hours. ("The American Scholar," p. 60)

To be sure, in the same essay Emerson goes the other way:

> Character is higher than intellect . . . A great soul will be strong to live, as well as strong to think. Does he lack organ or medium to impart his truths? He can still fall back on the elemental force of living them. This is a total act. Thinking is a partial act. (p. 62)

This statement represents the minority view, so to speak, in Emerson's work. He will never silence it but he does not let it rule. Even so, living one's truths is a falling back in comparison to imparting them. This judgment is an almost sly reversal of the conventional valuation.

In an essay called "The Superlative," Emerson says words of profound modesty:

> And fit expression is so rare that mankind have a superstitious value for it . . . and to the most expressive man that has existed, namely, Shakespeare, they have awarded the highest place. The expressors are the gods of the world, but the men whom these expressors revere are the solid, balanced, undemonstrative citizens, who make the reserved guard, the central sense of the world. (*Lectures and Sketches,* p. 173)

Despite these gracious gestures toward enactment (and there are quite a few others) and toward those who appear less disposed to make words about their lives, I still would say that the preponderant force of Emerson's work is to find in self-reliant thinking the only reliable self-reliance. "The poorest experience is rich enough for all the purposes of expressing thought" ("The Poet," p. 455). I think that Emerson's world revolves around that sentence.

His essay on the science of dreams, called "Demonology," contains the formulation that "The Ego partial makes the dream; the Ego total the interpretation. Life is also a dream on the same terms" (*Lectures and Sketches,* p. 20). Sleep awakens helpless egotism. Only wakeful intellect can retrospectively decide the meaning of the dream. But, more important, the reason for saying that waking life is itself a dream seems to be that self-expressive acting and doing are confusion and distortion and hence vague and unreal. The Ego partial when awake is metaphorically the sleeping self; in being partial, it is only part of itself, and not the best part. The other meaning of "partial" is partisan or self-preferring. Thus we live and act with only part of ourselves, but we interpret (meditate, retrospect) with our whole being (or our best being). In "Spiritual Laws," he says that the events of the world are "scarcely less fluid" than dreams (p. 314). Self-reliant interpretation alone lends reality to acting and doing (one's own or others') by investing it with coherence. Self-reliant thinking makes things fit. (I do not wish to obscure the fact that in his major essay, "Poetry and Imagination," Emerson pays exquisite homage to dreams as the one aspect of life demonstrating that even a dunce is a poet of invention when he dreams and thus composes an "unwritten play in fifty acts" (*Letters, 8,* p. 45).

Emerson attributes to the Idealist—the one who shakes or dissolves a simple or naive faith in the solidity of things and their complete independence from the human mind—the striking view that

> it [the soul] accepts from God the phenomenon, as it finds it, as the pure and awful form of religion in the world. . . . No man is its enemy. It accepts whatsoever befalls as part of its lesson. It is a watcher more than a doer, and it is a doer, only that it may the better watch. (*Nature,* p. 39)

Presumably, for some, watching is only watching; it is not full receptivity, it is too removed or cold; it is not wholehearted attention. Yet reception can be initiated by watching. Watching is the first stage of seeing, as seeing is the reason for knowing. Emerson criticizes Idealism, but he accepts it as his basis before qualifying it:

> Let it stand then, in the present state of our knowledge, merely as a useful introductory hypothesis, serving to apprize us of the eternal distinction between the soul and the world. (*Nature,* p. 41)

Such words are enough to associate Emerson with the Idealist elevation of thinking over doing and acting.

In the remarkable essay, "Love," he can insert the thought that "We are by nature observers, and thereby learners. That is our permanent state" (p. 337). In a number of passages, he affirms the supremacy of thinking. And toward the end of "Experience," he gives the palm to thinking:

> Life wears to me a visionary face. Hardest roughest action is visionary also. It is but a choice between soft and turbulent dreams. People disparage

knowing and the intellectual life, and urge doing. I am content with knowing, if only I could know. (p. 491)

If one could not know, if one could not interpret, nothing would be left. Or, only troubled sleep would be left. In *On The Genealogy of Morals,* (Preface, sect. 1), Nietzsche says that one cannot both experience and think about experience: One has to choose. Emerson is saying that one cannot experience (or one has not experienced) unless one thinks about it afterwards.

In sum, when Emerson says in "Self-Reliance" that "life only avails, not the having lived. Power ceases in the instant of repose" (p. 217), his work as a whole says that only the having lived avails; confusion and meaninglessness cease only in the instant of repose. Of course, unless there were acting and doing and engaging with the world there would be nothing to think about, no sense to impute; there would be little to see or perceive. One must live as the world understands living; one must attempt and engage; one must try to experience and be experienced. One must gather the raw material of self-reliant thinking. It is not enough that one merely observe. Although living vicariously by sympathetic under-standing of other persons and by the attempted impersonation of various and contradictory ideas and practices, and also as it were suspending living in order to look, may all contribute enormously to one's self-reliant reception of the world, one must live a life, and then one will have the riches of retrospection. "Action," he says in "The American Scholar," "is with the scholar subordinate, but it is essential" (p. 60). The interpretation of life makes life, but without one's experience and the flux of life, there would be nothing to interpret. But the retrospective or interpretative thinking that gives value to activity by giving it meaning is of a higher order than the thinking that animates and guides activity. The latter is partial, the former inclusive.

Let us turn now to the second matter: Emerson's emphasis on thinking as reception. I have already said that the essence of Emersonian reception is to see beauty where others do not. (Seeing means to take pains either to notice or grasp conceptually or both.) All his work means to awaken the sense of beauty—beauty not only in nature but also in human social life. He says in *Nature*:

> The world thus exists to the soul to satisfy the desire of beauty. This element I call an ultimate end. No reason can be asked or given why the soul seeks beauty. (p. 19)

It is in the sense of beauty that he finds release from life-denying creeds. Many things beside creeds obscure beauty: all the anxieties and terrors of life. (From the other side, he admits that the very search for beauty can be motivated by a wish to escape the terrors of life, of "finite nature.") But church religions comprise an obstacle that may be dealt with. Emerson thought his way free of them; he hopes to inspire his audience to do the same. I suppose that it must be said that for Emerson every self-reliant person will eventually come to see beauty where formerly he or she had seen nothing or something dismaying, disheartening, or trivial. In the lecture, "Genius," he is succinct: "What self-reliance is shown in every poetic description!" (*Early Lectures, 3,* p. 77) The world (human and natural) must be looked at again. The poet and philosopher exist to connect individuals to the world in a new way, a way that the spirit of conformity derides or misunderstands and that church religions betray. He says in "Poetry and Imagination," "Poetry must be affirmative. It is the piety of the intellect" (*Letters,* p. 64).

Everyone needs awakening. "Sleep lingers all our lifetime about our eyes, as night hovers all day in the boughs of the fir-tree" ("Experience," p. 471). The beauty of some piece of writing may lead out of itself to the beauty in the world that has inspired it but that also transcends it. Emerson says in "The Poet":

> With what joy I begin to read a poem which I confide in as an inspiration! And now my chains are to be broken; I shall mount above these clouds and opaque airs in which I live—opaque though they seem transparent. (p. 451)

Great writing saves us from false transparency and points us to a genuine one; at least, it saves us from fantasizing transparency where there is only opacity: the habitual responses, the conformist certainties, the mist of unexamined purposes. The great writer "turns the world to glass" (p. 456). The "true nectar" is not the excitements of the world (for example, "war, mobs, fires, gaming, politics, or love, or science,") but "the ravishment of the intellect by coming nearer to the fact" (p. 460). To see rightly is to be ravished. If you want to perceive truly, you can want nothing else; and if you can perceive truly, you will want nothing else. Only the self-reliant want to and are able to see.

The question may be asked, Why is the world worth affirming? If, to begin with, reality seems to be constantly falling short, if it is so thoroughly dependent on philosophical or poetical words for its meaning and hence its value, why define the point of self-reliance as touching reality? Why make thinking, supposedly superior to acting and doing, the servant of what is inferior to itself? I am not sure that I am asking the right questions. But, if I am, or nearly doing so, then I propose the following but temporary answer; I will soon call aspects of it into question. Self-reliant thinking, in Emerson's case, is not expected to affirm the world because the world participates shadowly or symbolically in a metaphysical realm better than itself, but nevertheless resemblant to itself, and dependent on it to lead the mind upward. Nor does self-reliant thinking affirm the world because it is a designed, intentional Whole, greater than any of its parts and more than the sum of them (though the beauty of the world may derive to a degree from the interconnectedness of things). Instead, the world is to be affirmed because all things (people, creatures, relations, objects; values, principles, ideas; tendencies, forces, patterns) are better than they know they are or than people casually or habitually think. As given, all things are imperfectly themselves because they are imperfectly received. The mind must get to work. In regard to human beings (including oneself) their outward enactment, their expressiveness, are inadequately judged by the usual standards of success, but redeemed when seen (and seen truly) as driven by aspirations that are admirable. (Action can be regarded as prayer, for example; further, not all admirable worldly aspirations are those of active self-reliance.) In regard to the human and the nonhuman alike, they all provide a tremendous scene of delight; no other delight can compare to looking at them. The self-reliant mind explores the depths of human inwardness, beginning and ending with one's own, and, in contrast, looks on the world as a sight to behold, as lending itself to affirmation because it can be transformed into surface. The result is that the mind gladly serves what is inferior to itself, grateful for the supply of the material it works on, but also humble before the spectacle. As Nietzsche says in *The Birth of Tragedy* ([W. Kaufmann, Trans.], sect. 7, p. 57), "The spectator without the spectacle is an absurd notion." The partiality of the actors provides the spectacle that invites the impartiality and hence the comprehensive joy of the spectator.

This answer may not be stable; it must be tested. My hope is that it can survive the test. Unless it does, one then proceeds not to convict Emerson of incoherence but to find that he subscribes to a religiousness—unorthodox as it may be—that threatens to ruin the idea of self-reliance.

*   *   *

As I said at the start, I find that Emerson's power of seeing operates in several ways. The most obvious way is the one with which I began this essay: the method of attention to and advocacy of contending philosophical ideas that try to make sense of human life and of diverse phenomena that embody or reflect these ideas. This method moves on the level of the general or permanent or recurrent or salient: the realm of antagonistic forces that Emerson impersonates with tentativeness and exaggeration. But he directs his seeing also at particulars in their profusion: human and natural particulars, the "infinite variety of things" ("Genius," *Early Lectures, 3,* p. 72). On them he bestows his poetical attention. Thirdly, he tries to see—to comprehend imaginatively—the totality of all particulars, what he sometimes names, in Platonic fashion, the "All."

In any given piece of writing, Emerson gives reception in all three ways. What unites these ways is the steady disposition to perceive and pronounce beauty and hence to see and say what is truly there. The net effect is justice: to see the beauty that is present but often obscured, ignored, betrayed, or self-unclaimed. Beauty is to be looked for especially in particulars and in the totality. On the level of the general—Emerson's usual level, the level of his great profundity—he finds cause for celebration and for delight in contrast and antagonism, which have their own beauty. But the beauty of radiance is what Emerson sees in particulars and in the totality the particulars appear to compose. I will now pay some attention to Emerson's treatment of these latter two categories.

3

The Question of Religiousness

I turn now to Emerson's handling of particulars. The seeing of self-reliant individuals is rendered by Emerson as a kind of ecstasy or experience of "the emotion of the sublime" ("The Over-Soul," p. 392). One source of this emotion is the realization, assisted by the greatest writers, that there is "double meaning, or shall I say the quadruple or centuple or much more manifold meaning of every sensuous fact" ("The Poet," p. 447). The human and natural world of particulars swarms with meaning waiting to be seen or inferred or barely made out—it need not be willfully imputed or constructed. Emerson's writings are full of attention to particulars and of the effort to redeem them from disdain or obliviousness. He often implies that the best way to observe familiar things, especially, is to imagine that one is seeing them for the first or last time. It is as if, for anything, mere being is a cause for congratulation. Each thing is one of a kind. Emerson's sense of a particular moves back and forth between the particular's wondrous unexpectedness and its deserving to be regarded as existing because it is needed by everything else. Both modes of reception in Emerson's work grant visibility to the particular. One aspect, then, of being mentally self-reliant is to take particular things in on one's own terms rather than conventionally. But that is equivalent to accepting things on their own terms, self-reliantly making the best case for each of them in turn; perceiving them as they present themselves while trying to remain free (to a decisive extent) of habit, predisposition, prejudice, and worn-down socialized categories. (I suppose that on a more general level one makes the best case possible even for the phenomena of habit, predisposition, prejudice, and socialized categories.) As he says early in his career:

> The wise man and much more the true Poet quits himself and throws his spirit into whatever he contemplates and enjoys the making it speak that it would say. ("Chaucer," *Early Lectures, 1,* pp. 272-273)

We try to be free of any normal attachment that threatens to block receptivity, so that we may find beauty unexpectedly.

Many of the qualities needed to observe and appreciate the contrasts and antagonisms of general and durable ideas and practices are also needed to do justice to particulars.

One can accurately see particulars for oneself only if one makes the extraordinary attempt to shake off the socialized sleep. But even more arduous is the effort to shove aside one's own temperament or special bias and learn to have "a power to see with a free and disengaged look every object" ("Culture," *The Conduct of Life,* p. 1017). On every contemplative level—from the minutest particular to the most fated general idea or tendency, and beyond to the All—mental self-reliance is the flight from egotism to impersonality. Emerson makes paradigmatic the perceptual aim of artists. The best looking is done with "the eye of the Artist" ("The Naturalist," *Early Lectures, 1,* p. 73) or "with the poet's eye but with a saint's affections" ("Ben Jonson, Herrick, Herbert, Wotton," *Early Lectures, 1,* p. 353). We imitate artists and poets when we "disindividualize" ourselves, when "we aim to hinder our individuality from acting" ("Art," *Society and Solitude,* pp. 48, 49). Why do so? Because only in this way can the observer individualize the world: change it in thought from masses to individuals. One mitigates one's own identity to make room for the identity of other particular persons, creatures, and things. Impersonality is a kind of selflessness, which allows what is outside oneself to fill one's inner space, and which prepares the way for perceiv-

ing and expressing the identity of the otherwise indistinct or unappreci-
ated. Emerson says:

> The wonders of Shakespeare are things which he saw whilst he stood
> aside, and then returned to record them. The poet aims at getting obser-
> vations without aim; to subject to thought things seen without (voluntary)
> thought. ("Art," *Society and Solitude,* p. 49)

All through his work, published and unpublished, Emerson turns his
attention to particular people, writers, scenes, moments, objects, events.
A passage in the essay "Nature," for example, renders with close attention
a series of natural occurrences, including "the blowing of sleet over a wide
sheet of water" (p. 542). (In fact, the first three paragraphs of this essay
exceed in persuasive rapture the moment in the book *Nature* when Emerson
crosses the bare common.) Yet I suppose it is right to say that he does not
have Thoreau's interest in particulars. In speaking of the purple grass, for
example, Thoreau can make an overlooked plant extraordinarily vivid and
then intensify its beauty by means of a shocking observation. He chides
the farmer for not cutting the purple grass even for hay:

> The greedy mower does not deign to swing his scythe; for this is a thin
> and poor grass, beneath his notice. Or, it may be, because it is so beautiful
> he does not know that it exists; for the same eye does not see this and
> Timothy. ("Autumnal Tints," *Thoreau: The Major Essays,* p. 230)

The ecstasy of the gratuitous particular is much more in Thoreau than in
Emerson. (I admit that Thoreau's judgment of the farmer may be more
ecstatic than his description of purple grass.) A lovely passage in Emerson
praises color as such, but no particular color. He beautifully says:

> The world is not made up to the eye of figures—that is only half; it is also
> made of color . . . The sculptor has ended his work, and behold a new
> world of dream-like glory. 'Tis the last stroke of Nature; beyond color she
> cannot go. In like manner, life is made up, not of knowledge only, but of
> love also. ("Success," *Society and Solitude,* p. 300)

There is a noteworthy moment of inverse Platonism when Emerson
finds a particular setting, ordinarily thought lovely, so wanting that its

watery reflection is better than it is. He says that "when a common landscape is reflected in still water . . . every leaf and stake and stone loses its vulgarity and becomes an object of delight" ("Modern Aspects of Letters," *Early Lectures, 1,* p. 384). Sometimes particulars must be transported to an inferior medium—to mere reflection—if they are to reveal or take on their beauty. Reflections are more rare than the things reflected and cannot be used as the reflected objects can be.

The bent of Emerson's mind is to generalize or to detect recurrence, tendency, or pattern. Much of the time, therefore, particulars are incidental and hence lesser. His conception of individuality is friendly to the particular when it is opposed to uniformities of mass or group, but less friendly when claims are made for the particular that sever it from a larger connection. He would not be content to be even Shakespeare, the one he calls the greatest expressor, because Shakespeare is happy to rest in the beauty of particulars and does not ascend to general ideas or tendencies. Even more—and this is what is now crucial for our discussion—Shakespeare does not ascend to the totality, the All. He says that Shakespeare:

> rested in their [visible things'] beauty; and never took the step which seemed inevitable to such genius, namely to explore the virtue which resides in these symbols and imparts this power:—what is that which they themselves say? ("Shakespeare; or the Poet," *Representative Men,* p. 725)

Emerson wants to compel things to speak in a certain way: to owe allegiance to their divine source and to acknowledge that they are only details in a story that is greatly more than just a story about themselves. "There is at the surface infinite variety of things. At the centre, there is simplicity and unity of cause" ("Genius," *Early Lectures, 3,* p. 72). The "material world" is "strictly emblematic" (Discarded lines from "English Literature, Introductory," *Early Lectures, 1,* p. 473).

Emerson is therefore not content to bless particulars as such. I propose that this is or may be his fall. He can admit that "Statements of the infinite are usually felt to be unjust to the finite" ("The Method of Nature," p. 119). Nevertheless, he wants to be thought ready to enclose particulars, compose them into a totality, a metaphysical whole, unbounded as that whole may be. Particulars emanate from a common source and they perhaps add up to a single meaning. The sense of the whole is thus another source of ecstasy or the emotion of the sublime. It appears to be Emerson's deepest source. Particulars as particulars do not suffice, whether they are human or natural. It also seems that, for Emerson, not only particulars are inadequate—so too are the conceptions and the forces on which he preponderantly expends his method of self-reliance. These latter must first be seen as mutually antagonistic, but ultimately as harmonious, because all contribute to one result.

We thus enlarge the point to say that Emerson is ravenously religious. Anything in the world—whether a particular thing or a general idea or a durable phenomenon—matters and is beautiful or sublime only if seen and thought of as part of a designed, intentionally coherent totality; indeed as an emanation of divinity. At least it *seems* to be the case that Emerson's religiousness dominates his receptivity.

⎧ He says at one point that "the critic, the philosopher is a failed poet" ("Poetry and Imagination," *Letters*, p. 56).⎫Is he himself a failed poet by being religious; by allowing the idea of totality to disparage the sufficiency of every particular, on the one hand, and multiple antagonistic ideas and forces, on the other; by allowing metaphysics to overcome his poetry? In turn, should his religiousness interfere with our reception of him? It is a horror to say so, but it may be rather wasteful to study Emerson unless one shares his religiousness. I repressed this thought until rather late. I still cannot quite believe it. One is right to resist it at the start, but eventually one finds the thought so persistent that it must be dealt with, even if we lose Emerson in the process.

I would now like to explore the question of his religiousness in order to see how great a danger it poses. To anticipate: I think the danger can be faced down. A delayed dealing with it can be vindicated. Emerson's religiousness is probably reducible to the effort to make the natural and human world look human, only human, which means legible and satisfactory.

It will be the united effect of the progress of science and the progress of virtue to open the primitive sense of the permanent objects of nature that so all which the eye sees may be to the mind that legible book in which every form, alone or in composition, shall be significant (Discarded lines from "English Literature, Introductory," *Early Lectures, 1,* p. 473).

And not to make it with Nature; with beauty, goodness + truth: the human world come alive?

The world can be free of divinity and still be significant, and therefore satisfy the mind, provided the world is looked at with wonder. And Emerson gives many hints along the way that this is his great purpose—and it is not religious. I am not certain of what I have just said, but close enough to certain. But let us take for a while Emerson's religiousness at face value.

A place to begin is his essay, "The Comic," published in 1843; it is a revision of an earlier lecture, "Comedy" (1839). He says:

> The whole of Nature is agreeable to the whole of thought, or to the Reason; but separate any part of nature, and attempt to look at it as a whole by itself, and the feeling of the ridiculous begins. The perpetual game of humor is to look with considerate good-nature at every object in existence *aloof*, as a man might look at a mouse, comparing it with the eternal whole; enjoying the figure which each self-satisfied particular creature cuts in the unrespecting All, and dismissing it with a benison. Separate any object, as a particular bodily man, a horse, a turnip, a flour-barrel, an umbrella, from the connection of things, and contemplate it alone, standing there in absolute nature, it becomes at once comic; no useful, no respectable qualities can rescue it from the ludicrous. (*Letters*, pp. 158-159)

(Emerson's comedy is not far from Sartre's nausea.) Thus to think that you are independent, that anything is independent, is to deserve derision. "Men celebrate their perception of halfness and a latent lie by the peculiar explosions of laughter" (*Letters*, p. 162). The particular thing or even the more general idea or phenomenon is a mere part of the All; it has no meaning in itself. A detached or isolated particular is as meaningless as a single word usually is:

> Natural objects, if individually described, and out of connection, are not yet known, since they are really parts of a symmetrical universe, like words of a sentence; and if their true order is found, the poet can read their divine significance orderly as in a Bible. ("Poetry and Imagination," *Letters, 8*, p. 8)

Everything has meaning only by reference to the mind of nature.

Emerson would find life meaningless if nature or the world as a whole were meaningless. His assumption often seems to be that meaning must come from a supreme originating intention. Compensatorily, the external source, the more-than-human source, of that intention is deemed continuous with the mind of human beings. What is more, the reason that the things of the world signify the presence of mind is, finally, that all things can be seen as teaching the lessons of morality. At moments, Emerson narrows his definition of unbelief to a rejection of the universal necessity by which all deeds receive their due:

> Shallow men believe in luck . . . . strong men believe in cause and effect . . . fortunes are not exceptions but fruits; that relation and connection are not somewhere and sometimes, but everywhere and always; no miscellany, no exception, no anomaly—what comes out, that was put in . . . There is no concealment, and, for each offense, a several vengeance; that, reaction, or *nothing for nothing,* or, *things are as broad as they are long,* is not a rule for Littleton or Portland, but for the universe. ("Worship," *The Conduct of Life,* pp. 1065-1066)

[margin note: luck or Magic]

Emerson tends to conflate the divine and the mental, the meaningful and the moral, and finds in these associations the wished-for sense of the world, the lineaments of the All. He says in *Nature,* his foundational book, that "Particular natural facts are symbols of particular spiritual facts," and that "Nature is the symbol of spirit" (p. 20). Then he proceeds to show how easily every natural fact lends itself to a human meaning that is also exemplary of morality, while the human meaning is divine. In the words of William James:

> For Emerson, the individual fact and moment were indeed suffused with absolute radiance, but it was upon a condition that saved the situation— they must be worthy specimens,—sincere, authentic, archetypal; they must have made connection with what he calls the Moral Sentiment, they must in some way act as symbolic mouthpieces of the Universe's meaning. ("Address at the Centenary of Ralph Waldo Emerson, May 25, 1903," *William James: Writings 1902-1910,* p. 1124)

[margin notes: beauty / bridges; with regard to when only of truth...]

In sum, Emerson seems to propose recurrently that the world is intended to be a world of moral lessons, and everything in it truly matters only to the extent that its particular lesson (the symbolic significance that it sends forth) can be interpreted morally. The world is an architecture, a coherent network of moral lessons because the divine mind, which is not utterly removed from the human mind, intended the world to be such a place. Perhaps the deepest and most common moral lesson Emerson wants to find is compensation. I discover in Emerson no affirmation of a Platonist realm of transcendental Forms, despite the Platonist talk about appearance and invisibility—that much must be granted to him by secularists and skeptics. The "All" or the "Whole" is perhaps only a name for the world's overall moral nature, which can be seen only when everything is properly interpreted.

It should also be said that Emerson's emphasis varies. Sometimes he seems to affirm metaphysical meaningfulness as such without mentioning the tie to morality. For example, he says:

> The new virtue which constitutes a thing beautiful, is a certain cosmical quality, or, a power to suggest relation to the whole world, and so lift the object out of a pitiful individuality. Every natural feature,—sea, sky, rainbow, flowers, musical tone,—has in it somewhat which is not private, but universal, speaks of that central benefit which is the soul of Nature, and thereby is beautiful . . . And, in chosen men and women . . . They have a largeness of suggestion, and their face and manners carry a certain grandeur, like time and justice. ("Beauty," *The Conduct of Life,* pp. 1110-1111)

In these words is suggested the idea, partly from Plato's *Phaedrus,* that particular persons, creatures, and things remind us of something better than themselves, which is either a perfection that each sketches but none will ever achieve or a role they play in a larger story of which they are not conscious. On another occasion, Emerson proposes a different aesthetic version of metaphysical meaningfulness. The maker or shaper of nature is the supreme artist:

> The circulation of the waters, the circulation of sap, the circulation of blood, the immortality of an animal species through the death of all the individuals, the balance and periods of planetary motion,—these are works of art quick and eternal . . . In our purest hours nature appears to us one with art—art perfected—the work of genius. (Notes to "Art," *Early Lectures, 2,* 390)

But if nature is art perfected, great human art "draws us into a state of mind which may be called religious: it conspires with all exalted sentiments" (Emerson's notes to "Art," *Early Lectures, 2,* pp. 390-391; see also "Genius," *Early Lectures, 3,* pp. 76, 79). Great art is necessary to perfect the one imperfect thing in nature—humanity: "Man is fallen; nature is erect" ("Nature," p. 546). We can see, as well, that for Emerson meaningfulness as such sometimes is the same as beauty, but a beauty arising not from undamaged perception but from the effort of the imagination:

> and there is a joy in perceiving the representative or symbolic character of a fact, which no bare fact or event can ever give. There are no days in life so memorable as those which vibrated to some strokes of the imagination. ("Beauty," p. 1111)

And relatedly, even when metaphysical meaningfulness is deciphered as moral, the beautiful and the moral are scarcely distinguishable: each must also be the other to be itself.

More often, methaphysical meaningfulness is a general morally benign tendency in the course of the world: "No statement of the universe can have any soundness, which does not admit its ascending effort" ("Fate," *The Conduct of Life,* p. 960). Or, on a lower level, meaningfulness is nothing more than one or another common moral lesson which, of necessity, the nature and movement of things obey and which particular actions and events illustrate or emblematize.

In a fragment, Emerson distills his thought:

> Every man may be (as some men are) raised to a platform whence he sees beyond sense to moral and spiritual truth; when he no longer sees snow as snow, or horses as horses, but only sees or names them representatively, for those interior facts which they signify. (Notes to "The Superlative," *Lectures and Sketches,* p. 548)

Nothing in the world suffices on its own; its contribution to the overall moral economy saves it.

The world itself would not suffice unless it could be understood as existing beyond itself, as having a meaning that Emerson sometimes sees as allegorical and sometimes as "metonymic" (his word in "Poetry and Imagination") or what used to be called anagogical. The meaning, moral or aesthetic (preferably both), must be lodged in things from the outside. But what is outside oneself is already inside oneself because what is inside oneself partakes of the divine, creative intelligence that made the outside. If Emerson in *Nature* (p. 8) calls nature the "NOT ME," he will later call it the soul's shadow, the "other me" ("The American Scholar," p. 60).

The position seems paradoxical. Emerson wants things to be symbols, as if they would have more dignity that way. Yet he makes clear that the symbol is inferior to the symbolized. Thus it is more dignified to symbolize, to be charged with a significance not merely the thing's own, than to be just what a thing is, in its richness and complexity, and not symbolize anything. We look at things in order to see through them. Our "second sight" is metaphysical:

> the world exists for thought: it is to make appear things which hide: mountains, crystals, plants, animals, are seen; that which makes them is not seen . . .

> The world realizes the mind. Better than images is seen through them. . . . The poet discovers that what men value as substances have a higher value as symbols; that Nature is the immense shadow of man. . . . The world is thoroughly anthropomorphized, as if it had passed through the body and mind of man, and taken his mold and form. ("Poetry and Imagination," *Letters,* p. 23)

The world suffers a great reduction by this attempted elevation; so may humanity. The world is not loved or affirmed for its own sake. Humanity may be loved in the wrong way—that is, flattered. Everything in this world is denied intrinsic or self-sufficient value. It is one thing for Emerson to find all vocations and activities and worldly experience unequal to his expectations. It is quite another thing to find the very stuff of the world unsatisfying and hence in need of metaphysical enlargement so as to make rapturous the contemplation of the world. At the same time, what Emerson makes crucial for mental self-reliance, the need to appreciate contrast and antagonism, threatens to demand much less self-overcoming. Emerson's own impersonations of diverse phenomena could be seen as sustained by the reassuring sense that all tensions and contradictions are ultimately reconcilable because they all are ultimately in the service of an invisible yet detectable intention, an intention closest to our heart. Where is the risk to complacency in these following words?

> Each new step we take in thought reconciles twenty seemingly discordant facts, as expressions of one law. Aristotle and Plato are reckoned the respective heads of discordant schools. A wise man will see that Aristotle Platonizes. By going one step farther back in thought, discordant opinions

are reconciled, by being seen to be two extremes of one principle, and we can never go so far back as to preclude a still higher vision. ("Circles," pp. 406-407).

Furthermore, Emerson's effort to claim superiority for thinking over doing can come to mean that thinking is actually the highest kind of doing, rather than the intellectually secular completion of worldly doing:

> The poet is enamoured of thoughts and laws. These know their way, and, guided by them, he is ascending from an interest in visible things to an interest in that which they signify, and from the part of a spectator to the part of a maker. ("Poetry and Imagination," *Letters,* p. 42)

In thinking metaphysically, the human mind repeats the acts of the divine agency and hence re-creates the world—re-creates it in mind and as mind. But should we not say that such acting and doing are spectral?

Emerson's religiousness makes the world safe or safer; mental self-reliance becomes a process of constantly renewed metaphysical faith or trust. Subdued or rejected is an omnivorous receptivity that is its own reward just because the things it tries to take in are good enough being what they are and do not have to be symbols or vehicles of a transcendentally ordained moral truth. They do not need to be more than themselves to be real or even to possess moral significance. They must be interpreted, of course, but not in the light of a higher purpose directing them, but rather through the effort to remove them from their inevitable initial obscurity. Moral judgment would then be neither an arbitrary imputation nor a perception of metaphysical truth. It would be an appeal for agreement.

Emerson is led, starting with *Nature,* even to deny the adequacy of beauty when it is not situated metaphysically:

> (But beauty in nature is not ultimate. It is the herald of inward and eternal beauty, and is not alone a solid and satisfactory good. It must stand as a part, and not as yet the last or highest expression of the final cause of Nature. (p. 19))

Possibly, Emerson is afraid that attributing beauty to anything would be unfounded, a merely personal response, unless beauty were an inherent property and therefore an object of metaphysical knowledge. The unguardedness of aesthetic judgment is just like that of moral judgment. The

constant flux of human judgments and interpretations delights him but
also leaves him yearning for sponsorship. Is this philosophical scrupu-
lousness? Or is it timidity—a major defection from self-reliance? Does
Nietzsche settle the matter when he says, "life itself forces us to posit
values" ("Morality as Anti-Nature," *Twilight of the Idols* [W. Kaufmann,
Trans.], sect. 5, p. 490)? There is no alternative to judgment, but aesthetic
and moral judgment cannot appeal to heaven for authentication.

Emerson says in his most famous ecstatic passage:

> Crossing a bare common, in snow puddles, at twilight, under a clouded
> sky, without having in my thoughts any occurrence of special good
> fortune, I have enjoyed a perfect exhilaration. I am glad to the brink of
> fear . . . Standing on the bare ground—my head bathed by the blithe air
> and uplifted into infinite space—all mean egotism vanishes. I become a
> transparent eyeball; I am nothing; I see all; the currents of the Universal
> Being circulate through me; I am part or parcel of God. (*Nature,* p. 10)

Does he not move in these words from free perception to metaphysical
discipline? (Eight years later he publishes an admission in the essay
"Nature": "If there were good men, there would never be this rapture in
nature," p. 545.)

Let us ask, What is "a transparent eyeball"? I think that the meaning of
this strange phrase is disclosed by a passage in "The Over-Soul." After
saying what the soul is not: it is not an organ, function or faculty; it is not
intellect or will; Emerson says that it is a light. "From within or from
behind, a light shines through us upon things and makes us aware that we
are nothing, but the light is all" (p. 387). Elsewhere, Emerson cites with
approval Blake's words: "I question not my corporeal eye any more than
I would question a window concerning a sight. I look through it, and not
with it" ("Poetry and Imagination," *Letters,* p. 28). He does not cite
Schopenhauer, but the similarity is noticeable:

> For at the moment when, torn from the will, we have given ourselves up
> to pure will-less knowing, we have stepped into another world, so to
> speak, where everything that moves our will, and thus violently agitates
> us, no longer exists . . . Happiness and unhappiness have vanished; we are
> no longer the individual; that is forgotten; we are only pure subject of
> knowledge. We are only that *one* eye of the world which looks out from

all knowing creatures. . . . (*The World as Will and Representation,* vol. 1
[E.F.J. Payne, Trans.], pp. 197-198)

Thus, in our transparent, clear-seeing moments, nothing in us, either
social or personal, obstructs the passage of the inner light (or the light of
our genius or daimon) outward on to things. They are illuminated by it
and they thereby become really visible, at last. The universe "becomes
transparent, and the light of higher laws than its own shines through it"
(*Nature,* p. 25). The brightness of truth replaces the poor colors of fiction.
The only Form of the Good is the inner light. The inner light enables sight
and makes things visible. (The inner light does not quite give things their
being: Emerson does not take the last Idealist step.) But the sight it enables
is of underlying reality, which is the underlying moral purpose intended
by divinity, by the nature of things. Emerson thus makes things vanish
into a higher expressiveness. The look of things, which is life's greatest
blessing, is demoted. The sun is not good enough; the unreligious, democratic eye that uses sunlight to see is not good enough. What Emerson
seems to want is what Nietzsche describes as "an eye turned in no
particular direction, in which the active and interpreting forces, through
which alone seeing becomes seeing something, are supposed to be lacking" (*On the Genealogy of Morals* [W. Kaufmann, Trans.], third essay,
sect. 12, p. 555). In his most enraptured passage, Emerson seems to
abandon a secular Platonism that uncovers the beauty already expec-
tantly present in the visible and various world, and to approach a blinded
moral high-mindedness. Our unobstructed inwardness permits us to see
what is there because we see it as part of a resplendent and intentional
unity. For Emerson, the only alternative to honest ecstasy is for us to see
as conformists made yet more docile by church religions: to see by means
of a distorted and depressed symbolism that bestows the wrong kind of
unity.

But does Emerson in his religiousness substitute for the churches'
disparagement of the world his own more subtle kind? He seems to be saying
that all things are nothing without the religiously inspired self-reliant
mind. Things, perhaps people too, do not unfailingly arouse by their own
power. Emerson does in fact directly express woe at the inadequacy of
things, and it is a woe that seems immune to any but the most desperate
consolation. He says:

It is an odd jealousy: but the poet finds himself not near enough to his object. The pine-tree, the river, the bank of flowers before him, does not seem to be nature. Nature is still elsewhere. This or this is but outskirt and far-off reflection and echo of the triumph that has passed by, and is now at its glancing splendor and heyday, perchance in the neighboring fields, or, if you stand in the field, then in the adjacent woods. The present object shall give you this sense of stillness that follows a pageant which has just gone by. ("Nature," p. 553)

The thing is there, but it has always just vanished; it is there, but missing; it has never arrived to itself. Each person is, as a matter of course, insusceptible or impervious. "Experience" tell us so. The wall that blocks our vision is not only conformity or church religions. Is the main reason actually yet another one: that things—nature, but not only nature; human relations and achievements—are intrinsically deficient? Are they worthless or nearly so, unless they are gathered up into a totality? Actually, a moral totality? "But if, instead of identifying ourselves with the work, we feel that the soul of the workman streams through us . . . " (p. 554). Is it only then that anything is given sufficient reason, "a reason why it should be rather than not be?" (D. W. Hamlyn, *Schopenhauer,* 1966, p. 11). Is Emerson too intent on finding sufficient reason?

Notice how in the passage from *Nature* Emerson ties his ecstasy to the feeling that "currents of the Universal Being circulate through me; I am part or parcel of God." When he says "I see all," one thinks that he is really saying "I see the All."

Idealism sees the world in God. It beholds the whole circle of persons and things, of action and events, of country and religion, not as painfully accumulated, atom after atom, act after act, in an aged creeping Past, but as one vast picture, which God paints on the instant eternity, for the contemplation of the soul. (*Nature,* p. 39)

In "The Poet," Emerson reaffirms this sentiment:

For, as it is dislocation and detachment from the life of God, that makes things ugly, the poet, who re-attaches things to nature and the Whole,— re-attaching even artificial things, and violations of nature, to nature, by a deeper insight,—disposes very easily of the most disagreeable facts. (p. 455)

Elsewhere Emerson says,

> Art, in the artist, is proportion, or a habitual respect to the whole by an
> eye loving beauty in details. And the wonder and charm of it is the sanity
> in insanity which it denotes. ("Nominalist and Realist," p. 579)

It is as if details, no matter how beautiful, if unorganized, were only
specimens of insanity. In sum, the sense of the whole is not only supposed
to add a deeper meaning to what already mistakenly appears sufficiently
and acceptably meaningful, but also to give a positive meaning to the ugly
or the repellent:

> Readers of poetry see the factory-village and the railway, and fancy that
> the poetry of the landscape is broken up by these; for these works of art
> are not yet consecrated in their reading; but the poet sees them fall within
> the great Order not less than the bee-hive, or the spider's geometrical web.
> ("The Poet," p. 455)

Emerson as it were forces these much better lines in "The Poet" to be preceded by the lines on ugliness quoted above.

The ecstatic affirmation of life, as concentrated, for example, in the
passage on crossing the bare common, is meant to be the fruit and
justification of self-reliance. But if Emersonian self-reliance is religious,
even if it is not religious as church religions are, then is it actually
self-reliance? Does Emersonian self-reliance rest on a metaphysical fiction? It may be life-affirming and still be as remote from truth as church
religions are. It may work like a creed.

Emerson wants to believe that the mind which permeates nature (and
by nature he means "both nature and art, all other men and my own
body," *Nature,* p. 8) is at one with the soul in each person. The world
manifests the same divinity that is lodged in each human being. There is
a source to things and hence a coherence; the liberated mind can detect
the coherence, and the human soul can move to an ecstatic appreciation
of it. Humanity thus becomes divine, and only as such can it sanely love
itself and can one sanely love oneself. In *Nature,* in "Self-Reliance," in
"The Over-Soul," and many other writings, Emerson teaches the divinity
of the world, its oneness, and its affinity with the divine human soul. His
best summary is in "Natural History of Intellect":

And as mind, our mind or mind like ours reappears to us in our study of Nature, Nature being everywhere formed after a method which we can well understand, and all the parts, to the most remote, allied or explicable,— therefore our own organization is a perpetual key, and a well-ordered mind brings to the study of every new fact or class of facts a certain divination of that which it shall find. (*Natural History,* p. 20)

The consequence is that self-reliance is reliance on an "aboriginal Self," and its innate nature, which is genius, spontaneity, instinct, or intuition ("Self-Reliance," pp. 268-269). To see the truth of totality one must try to discard all social and personal encrustation and establish a direct connection between the soul and the detectable structure of reality. Social and personalized being are obstacles to genuine religiousness. One must be thrown back on oneself in order to know the real, and hence really live in truth for the first time. The Stoicism is unmistakable.

But in Emerson, religiousness stems not only from adoration of the sublime, but also from a certain kind of fear of the sublime—a dread that clings to the human condition. The fundamental fear is of the "NOT ME," a concept found in Fichte, used by Carlyle, and making its way to Emerson (*Nature,* p. 8). To subdue it, Emerson works to convert the "NOT ME" into the me. (Often it is more like converting the NOT US into the us, or the NOT LIKE ANY OF US into any of us.) We can therefore say that when Emerson makes nature unalien by explaining it as the emanation of an intelligence like our own and thus as the emanation of ourselves, although not in a literal causal sense, he is trying to deal with a fear he thinks many feel. Sometimes, however, Emerson follows the strategy of positing nature as invincibly "NOT ME," yet as something that can be worked over by the resolute mind and made ordered, lawful, regular; or made purposive; or rendered unreal in comparison to the mind. This other strategy, which I explored earlier, verges on the arbitrary. If we were to see it as Emerson's real position, he would certainly count as unreligious. He would be a deliberate and condescending contriver of metaphysical meaning, not its faithful translator. But such a move by us could threaten our reception of him as much as his possibly sincere religiousness. Let us stay with the thought he is religious, because he is more likely to be religious than a cynical lawgiver or a thoroughgoing nihilist. Our hope is that his religiousness, though sincere, is so minor as not to pose an insuperable obstacle to our secular reception of him.

One root of Emerson's religiousness is thus the need to reconcile us to the world by dispelling some of its unlikeness. Even if his starting point in *Nature,* his first book, had not been the me pitted against the "NOT ME" (everything external to my consciousness), he would have striven for reconciliation. It is a matter of temperament. He tries to intensify the felt need to seek reconciliation. Another kind of individualism pushes, instead, in a direction that we now would call existentialist, where bliss is found in our being unsponsored by a higher mind and in being unburdened by some supposed resemblance to it.

He is eloquent on the epistemological desolation of a godless world. Without some religiousness, "every thought loses all its depth and has become mere surface" ("Holiness," *Early Lectures, 2,* p. 342). "I cannot keep the sun in heaven," he says, "if you take away the purpose that animates him" ("The Preacher," *Lectures and Sketches,* p. 222). Less dramatically he insists that:

> it is only our ineradicable belief that the world answers to man, and part to part, that gives any interest in the subject. If we believed that Nature was foreign and unrelated,—some rock on which souls wandering in the Universe were shipwrecked, we should think all exploration of it frivolous waste of time. ("Country Life," *Natural History,* 165)

There is also the personal desolation:

> Unlovely, nay, frightful, is the solitude of the soul which is without God in the world. . . . To see men pursuing in faith their varied action, warm-hearted, providing for their children, loving their friends, performing their promises,—what are they to this chill, houseless, fatherless, aimless Cain, the man who hears only the sound of his own footsteps in God's resplendent creation? To him it is no creation; to him these fair creatures are hapless specters: he knows not what to make of it. ("The Preacher," pp. 221-222)

In a proto-Rilkean passage, he even claims that the birds would reject humanity's sympathy for them if humanity were without belief. Emerson seems remote from the sentiment expressed by one of his masters, Plotinus:

> And indeed if the divine did not exist, the transcendently beautiful, in a beauty beyond all thought, what could be lovelier than the things we see?

> Certainly no reproach can rightly be brought against this world save only that it is not That. (*The Enneads,* [S. MacKenna, Trans.] V, 8, p. 419)

There are also times when Emerson professes a faith in progress, but he could not profess it unless divinity sponsored it. Optimism must be cosmic. It cannot be merely social because Emerson sometimes expresses doubt that society ever progresses. He says:

> Society never advances. It recedes on one side as it gains on the other . . . For every thing that is given something is taken. ("Self-Reliance," p. 279)

But he continues to sound the note of *cosmic* hope. He thinks that there is "a force always at work to make the best better and the worst good" ("Speech" [Free Religious Association], *Miscellanies,* p. 486). His famous essay, "The Tragic," is full of devices for thinking away human suffering. Perhaps his best cosmic estimate is found in "The Young American" (1841):

> That genius has infused itself into nature. It indicates itself by a small excess of good, a small balance in brute facts always favorable to the side of reason. All the facts in any part of nature shall be tabulated, and the results shall indicate the same security and benefit; so slight as to be hardly observable, and yet it is there. (pp. 217-218)

In calculating the net good, then, Emerson settles for something like Robert Frost's "a fraction of one per cent at the very least" (in the poem, "Our Hold on the Planet," p. 349). The optimism is parsimonious. Still, Emerson cannot attribute benefit, however small, to chance. Impersonating fate, he says flatly that "there are no contingencies" ("Fate," *The Conduct of Life,* p. 968).

At this point, it is tempting to recall some words from Nietzsche's *The Anti-Christ.* They all go toward shaking one's confidence in Emerson. Nietzsche says:

> would blessedness—or more technically speaking, *pleasure*—ever be a proof of truth? . . . Faith makes blessed: consequently it lies. . . . "Faith" means not *wanting* to know what is true. . . . The man of faith, the "believer" of every kind, is necessarily a dependent man—one who cannot posit *himself* as an end, one who cannot posit any end at all by himself.

The "believer" does not belong to *himself,* he can only be a means, he must be *used up,* he requires somebody to use him up. . . . Every kind of faith is itself an expression of self-abnegation, of self-alienation. . . . By lie I mean: wishing *not* to see something *as* one sees it. . . . The most common lie is that with which one lies to oneself; lying to others is, relatively, an exception. (W. Kaufmann, Trans., sections 50, 52, 54, pp. 631-632, 635, 638-639)

Though Nietzsche names Carlyle as the one who is guilty of these self-deceptions, Emerson appears to be just as guilty. The irony is that Nietzsche's phrases about the religious believer, which are very much like those Emerson uses about adherents to church religions, may be turned against Emerson.

Emersonian self-reliance is therefore reliance on the nature of things metaphysically—that is, religiously—understood. Why could not Emerson content himself with an unreligious emotion of the sublime, with a secular ecstasy? "My inference," he says, "is that there is a statement of religion possible which makes all skepticism absurd" ("The Preacher," *Lectures and Sketches,* p. 223). This formulation—and Emerson's work is full of comparable ones—leads me to believe that he sincerely thought that a moral divinity permeated nature and the world. Yet even if he did not, I doubt that he thought a complete secularism was livable—much less, that its truth, if it were true, could inspire an affirmation of life. He said in his Divinity School "Address" that people suspected that God is dead; but he believed, I think, that humanity would die (for all practical purposes) in that death, in the erasure of transcendental belief. "Worship is the regard for what is above us. Men are respectable only as they respect" ("The Sovereignty of Ethics," *Lectures and Sketches,* p. 213). Atheism is self-destruction, not the beginning of a new sublimity. Emerson left it to Nietzsche to be Nietzsche, or Emerson.

Of course, he would not have been heard if he preached anything resembling atheism. As it is, he is quite aware of his power to unsettle. In a later chapter of *The Conduct of Life* he reflects on what he has been doing:

Some of my friends have complained, when the preceding papers were read, that we discussed Fate, Power, and Wealth, on too low a platform; gave too much line to the evil spirit of the times; too many cakes to Cerberus; that we ran Cudworth's risk of making, by excess of candor, the argument of atheism so strong, that he could not answer it. ("Worship," p. 1055)

Emerson protests that he has "no infirmity of faith." But he seems to let the cat out of the bag: "excess of candor" makes the argument for atheism too strong. But I suppose he hopes that we will not notice. His much earlier Harvard Divinity School "Address" (1838) shocked respectable opinion. He therefore could not have wanted to frighten away forever the people he thought he could help. "The irresistible maturing of the general mind" has reached its endpoint ("Worship," *The Conduct of Life,* p. 1059). His religiousness is a middle way between church religions and the death of God. It takes advantage of a preexistent readiness on the part of all—ordinary persons and philosophers alike—to think metaphysically: to insist that the world is always or must eventually be a coherent and moral totality, or to succumb to an indeliberate aestheticism.

He goes so far in his concessions to popular religiousness as to say in "Self-Reliance" itself that:

> In your metaphysics you have denied personality to the Deity: yet when the devout motions of the soul come, yield to them heart and life, though they should clothe God with shape and color. Leave your theory, as Joseph his coat in the hand of the harlot, and flee. (p. 265)

We want to ask, Flee from what to what? From sophisticated vagueness to a self-indulgent will to believe? Who then is the harlot? Yet how could the elevation of thinking (at its self-reliant best) over all else, including acting (also at its self-reliant best) be made plausible to ordinary persons unless their preexistent religiousness—distorted as it was—was appealed to? How could self-reliance be propagated unreligiously? The unfamiliar had to grow out of the familiar. The contemplative ideal could only be made accessible to multitudes of ordinary persons, Emerson perhaps thought, in a religious guise. The audacity consists in transforming religiousness. Emerson then makes the enormous effort to produce a joyous religiousness that is not, as in church religions, a joyous anticipation of a next life, but a joyous acceptance of this one. He wants to make come true his sentence that "We are learning not to fear truth" ("The Sovereignty of Ethics," *Lectures and Sketches,* p. 213). The truth of science and philosophy reveals that the dualism of Zarathustra is overcome, and thus the world is made a unity and a cause for joy. The pity is that what Emerson needs to sustain himself causes a good part of the later suspicion of him.

William James, George Santayana, and others were and are offended by his optimistic religiousness. That Emerson did not believe in any scriptural revelation is not enough for them. I doubt that it should be enough for us. Yet, even so, we must acknowledge the completeness of his break with revelation:

> The old psalms and gospels are mighty, as ever showing that what people call religion is literature; that is to say, that here was one who knew how to put his statement, and it stands forever, and people feel its truth, and say, *Thus saith the Lord*; whilst it is only that he had the true literary genius which they fancy they despise. (Draft of "The Preacher" quoted in Notes, *Lectures and Sketches,* p. 554)

If it is maddening to think that Emerson appears to retreat from the possible radicalism of self-reliance and head toward religiousness (howsoever unorthodox), it is even more maddening to think that he may not have been able to approach radicalism except through religious inspiration.

It is obvious that I find the religiousness of Emerson an impediment to my reception. I certainly do not deny that because the theory of democratic individuality commits one to the hope that a secular (that is, an unnervously disenchanted) form of the philosophical conception of self-reliance can gain acceptance among ordinary persons, the fact of pervasive religiousness remains a tremendous problem. But let us leave that aside. My question is whether we can say anything to leave open the possibility that Emerson's religiousness is not integral to his redemptive vision. (Of course, there is an unbelieving redemption.) Does he provide any basis for reading him as a secular thinker, or near enough to secularism? Is it at all possible that he did not, in any straightforward way, believe that the world is a divine and moral emanation and that we participate in that divinity? Or, at least, that this belief can be so attenuated as to be minor, though still real? That he retained a saving uncertainty?

I must not try too hard, yet I cannot help doing so. I will point to a few occasions in Emerson when divinity as the source of some kind of meaningfulness in the world or divinity as the guarantor of a specifically moral meaningfulness of the world makes an appearance, but, I am happy to say, in a perhaps self-undercutting manner. Let us look at some of these moments. First, Emerson abandons biblical space and time. The essay,

"Nature," refers to the refutation of Moses and Ptolemy by scientific geology, and to "boundless space and boundless time" as the two cardinal conditions for all changes in nature (p. 546). The essay, later amplified by "Fate" in *The Conduct of Life,* has a genuine sense of the slow accumulative evolution of things. To be sure, Emerson sometimes posits the progress in evolution as the inevitable emergence of man—that is, as the inevitable appearance of thought:

> It is a long way from granite to the oyster; farther yet to Plato, and the preaching of the immortality of the soul. Yet all must come, as surely as the first atom has two sides. ("Nature," p. 547)

But the essay's idea of the boundless does not give religious comfort, even to the heterodox. Also comfortless to the religious are Emerson's words that contemplate the possible surpassing of humanity. Emerson is actually not sure that the emergence of the human race is the undeniable terminus of nature; the race is just not good enough:

> That no end may be selected, and nature judged thereby, appears from this, that if man himself be considered as the end, and it be assumed that the final cause of the world is to make holy or wise or beautiful men, we see that it has not succeeded . . . But nature seems further to reply, "I have ventured so great a stake as my success, in no single creature. I have not yet arrived at any end . . ." ("The Method of Nature," pp. 120-121)

Emerson comes close to leaving nature so open-ended as to appear unregulated.

Second, there are times when Emerson renders with an unusual flatness the meaningfulness of the world that he craves and claims to find. The meanings become obvious and harmless metaphors and seem to do much less work than Emerson almost promises. In *Nature,* he speaks of "that wonderful congruity which subsists between man and the world" (p. 44) and of a "radical correspondence between visible things and human thoughts" (p. 22), but then he contents himself with such illustrations as these: "An enraged man is a lion, a cunning man is a fox, a firm man is a rock, a learned man is a torch." Nature becomes a repository of analogies that anyone can make but that are easily seen for what they are. "But is there no intent of an analogy between man's life and the seasons? And do the seasons gain no grandeur or pathos from that analogy" (pp. 21-22)? Well, to begin with, the truth of an analogy cannot be proven when it is so loose and picturesque. And maybe the seasons lose grandeur and gain only an inferior pathos from that analogy. Emerson does not seem to press his point energetically. By these analogies, he makes the world more homelike but much less interesting. He commits "pathetic fallacies" when we know that he can see through them. He may let the enterprise of instilling the courage of self-reliance become too relaxed.

Even when his analogies are more abstract, they are not especially helpful to his religiousness. In his Phi Beta Kappa address at Harvard in 1867, he says that "Every law in nature, as gravity, centripetence, repulsion, polarity, undulation, has a counterpart in the intellect" ("Progress of Culture," *Letters,* pp. 222-223). The correspondences are easy and unilluminating. It would be good if all that Emerson wants his analogies and correspondences to achieve is a doubling of secular meaning through a ravished but unmoralized or unmetaphysical interpretation. Notice how the advantages of reducing a thing to a symbol are rendered in a way (in an analogy for analogies) that fastens us to the thing's multiplicity and takes interest away from any symbolism:

> Being used as a type, a second wonderful value appears in the object, far better than its old value, as the carpenter's stretched cord, if you hold your ear close enough, is musical in the breeze. ("The Poet," p. 452)

We stay in a happily contingent world when a carpenter's cord turns out to be a musical instrument and also when utility has an unmeant beauty. We are far from using anything as a type: the first words of the sentence are denounced by the rest. Emerson almost indicates that the double meanings that constitute a second world of higher value are only aesthetic ones radiated by the given world of unreflective use, gratifying the secular mind's expectations while the world of use, if seen as also beautiful, can then be seen in its utility all the more instructively:

> The spurious prudence, making the senses final . . . is the subject of all comedy. . . . The true prudence limits this sensualism by admitting the knowledge of an internal and real world. This recognition once made,— the order of the world and the distribution of affairs and times being studied with the co-perception of their subordinate place, will reward any

degree of attention . . . For our existence . . . reads all its primary lessons out of these books. ("Prudence," pp. 58-59)

It is noteworthy that in his essay on Swedenborg in *Representative Men*, he criticizes this mystic in a way that may turn one against Emerson, but he does so with an authority that is breathtaking. He complains that Swedenborg's doctrine of correspondences between visible and invisible things is badly executed and inadequate. What he finds inadequate, however, is fairly like the view he expresses earlier in *Nature*. He says of Swedenborg:

He fastens each natural object to a theologic notion;—a horse signifies carnal understanding; a tree, perception; the moon, faith; a cat means this; an ostrich, that; an artichoke, this other; and poorly tethers every symbol to a several ecclesiastic sense. . . . His theological bias thus fatally narrowed his interpretation of nature. (p. 676)

Emerson insists that "the dictionary of symbols is yet to be written." But I do not think that the sketch he gives of an adequate symbolic procedure can reassure a reader who is fond of religiousness. He says:

The slippery Proteus is not so easily caught. In nature, each individual symbol plays innumerable parts, as each particle of matter circulates in turn through every system. The central identity enables any one symbol to express successively all the qualities and shades of real being. In the transmission of the heavenly waters, every hose fits every hydrant. (p. 676)

Not only is Proteus slippery, Emerson's metaphors for Proteus are also slippery and threaten to leave the doctrine of correspondences in comic disarray. To be sure, Emerson says elsewhere that it is necessary "to suppose that every hose in Nature fits every hydrant," in order to avoid thinking that nature is "chaos" ("Natural History of Intellect," *Natural History,* p. 20). But he does not improve the idea when he says:

The feat of the imagination is in showing the convertibility of every thing into every other thing. Facts which had never before left their stark common sense, suddenly figure as Eleusinian mysteries. My books and chair and candlestick are fairies in disguise, meteors and constellations. ("Beauty," *The Conduct of Life,* p. 1111)

Imagination here is not powerful—it is too close to whimsy.

Third, Emerson is radical in his doubt about immortality and the after-life. In "The Over-Soul," he says:

> Jesus, living in these moral sentiments, heedless of sensual fortunes, heeding only the manifestations of these, never made the separation of the idea of duration from the essence of these attributes, nor uttered a syllable concerning the duration of the soul. It was left to his disciples to sever duration from the moral elements, and to teach the immortality of the soul as a doctrine, and maintain it by evidences. The moment the doctrine of the immortality is separately taught, man is already fallen. (pp. 393-394)

A thinker who abandons belief in personal immortality verges on discarding what matters most to the spirit of religiousness, at least for many people. Emerson is emphatic when he supplies what he thinks is the right answer to give to an "ardent missionary":

> Other world! there is no other world. God is one and omnipresent; here or nowhere is the whole fact. ("The Sovereignty of Ethics," *Lectures and Sketches,* p. 199)

On this point Emerson is more courageous than Whitman. And perhaps when Emerson cites in *Nature* "a certain poet," and challenges the idea of earthly length of life, he is trying to discredit the wish to last forever:

> "A man is a god in ruins. When men are innocent, life shall be longer, and shall pass into the immortal, as gently as we awake from dreams. Now, the world would be insane and rabid, if these disorganizations should last for hundreds of years. It is kept in check by death and infancy." (pp. 45-46)

I must mention, however, that at one point Emerson looks with a sympathetic eye on the wish to live endlessly:

> The race of mankind have always offered at least this implied thanks for the gift of existence,—namely, the terror of its being taken away; the insatiable curiosity and appetite for its continuation.

But he then quickly compromises his sympathy:

> Of immortality, the soul, when well employed is incurious . . . 'Tis a higher thing to confide, that, if it is best we should live, we shall live,—'tis higher to have this conviction, than to have the lease of indefinite centuries and millenuiums and aeons . . . Immortality will come to such as are fit for it . . . It is a doctrine too great to rest on any legend, that is, on any man's experience but our own. It must be proved, if at all from our own activity and designs which imply an interminable future for their play. ("Worship," *The Conduct of Life,* p. 1075)

Who then is "fit" for immortality? "He only is rightly immortal, to whom all things are immortal" ("Worship," p. 1070). We deserve to live forever only if we accept our mortality, accept the fact that things preceded and will outlast us, and "consent to be nothing for eternity" ("Natural History of Intellect," *Natural History,* p. 56).

Fourth, he sometimes conceptualizes the soul in a manner that lends itself to a profound secular understanding. The soul is light, the inner light: such a conceptualization is still too religious. But mixed with these words is the idea that the soul is "the background of our being . . . an immensity not possessed and that cannot be possessed" ("The Over-Soul," p. 387). If we join this statement with Emerson's frequent references to human depth, inscrutability, unpredictability, indefinite potentiality, unconscious powers, and unexpected achievements, we have, I think, a perfectly truthful account of the human mystery. The best metaphor, however, is not light, but dark depths. Although we need not use the word "soul," we must do justice to the facts that so occupy Emerson, among others, and that should occupy us. Some of these facts comprise human infinitude. Perhaps we can say that what counts in reading Emerson is the attention he devotes to these facts, not the needless religiousness with which he surrounds them and further obscures them.

Emerson speaks of "the impenetrable mystery which hides—and hides through absolute transparency—the mental nature" ("Perpetual Forces," *Lectures and Sketches,* p. 72). Because each person is "an inexhaustible mine," a secularist can therefore agree that "the chief end of man" is to explore oneself rather than stay housed in church worship, but then one must draw back when Emerson adds reassuringly that "external nature is but the candle to illuminate in turn the innumerable and profound obscurities of the soul. Do we not see how cunningly for this end he is fitted to the world, to every object in which he has relation?" ("Address on

Education," *Early Lectures, 2,* pp. 199-200). Despite these last words, Emerson's work most of the time provides a secular reassurance just by showing the rewards for individuality of self-exploration. In his concentration on individual infinitude, he consecrates each person and thus promotes the democratic understanding of individuality. Man, he says in "The Over-Soul," is "always leaving behind what you have said of him" (p. 385). There is always a "residuum" that no philosophy has ever resolved. But also and always present in Emerson is attention to the facts of finitude, including human mortality.

Maybe Emerson thinks that it is better for humanity to cherish itself directly, and that it can do so only if it assimilates itself to divinity. There is an indirect way, too. It is more subtle and it is followed by many church religions. As Nietzsche describes it, the indirect way consists in the effort to shift tremendous burdens of guilt and disgrace onto humanity's shoulders, thus imposing a seriousness or even a stature of perverse greatness on it. Emerson will not follow suit. He wants to rescue humanity from depression and still keep it interesting. His religious or theological vocabulary, therefore, sometimes looks merely strategic in order to keep the sense keen that humanity has inscrutable depths and hence infinite creativity.

Early and late, Emerson worries about the drying up of human energy—or at least, its confinement to feats of industry and trade. For example, in his "Introductory" to lectures on *The Present Age,* he speaks feelingly (even if with studied exaggeration) about the threat to intense passions, including and especially religious ones, when economic life and its corresponding devotion to intellectual "analysis" become regnant:

> A nation governed by the religious sentiment, or by the parental sentiment, by the love of military glory, (which is only an impure love of greatness), or by the love of art, is still capable of extraordinary deeds. But an activity of the lower powers once absolved from the dominion of these sentiments, makes life and man mean. It is aimless bluster. All religion departs. (*Early Lectures, 3,* p. 190)

In "Worship," he says that "All the great ages have been ages of belief." Only belief makes the human soul "earnest;" and only earnestness can provoke "any extraordinary power of performance" (p. 1063). In the absence of religious and patriotic enthusiasm, only the practical arts, not the spiritual arts, flourish ("Art," *Society and Solitude,* pp. 56-57). Emerson claims that "If we meet no gods, it is because we harbor none" ("Worship," p. 1070). But he is also sure that the present tendency of skepticism cannot be "cured or stayed by any modification of theologic creeds, much less by theologic discipline." In fact, "The cure for false theology is mother-wit" (p. 1062). Emerson thinks skepticism will cure itself because some belief will introduce itself. What matters for our discussion is to see that he is quite able to hint at strategic considerations which are at some distance from his own beliefs.

Let us also notice a passage on Jesus, who constantly fascinates Emerson. He says that "The excellence of Jesus, and of every true teacher, is, that he affirms the Divinity in him and in us, not thrusts himself between it and us" ("Character," *Lectures and Sketches,* p. 77). Jesus is great; he has only to be human to be great; his greatness is that of "every true teacher"; he is not the only one, but he may be the best teacher because he is the greatest liberator—provided that we first liberate him from church religions. The saving lesson is that God, "that He, that It, is there, next and within" ("The Sovereignty of Ethics," *Lectures and Sketches,* p. 194). Emerson clearly does not think that he can simply say that humanity is just there and to be revered as a stupendous but contingent occurrence. He would not be understood by his audience. He will give, instead, his own this-worldly meaning to the idea that God had to become man so that man could become God.

Fifth, Emerson's idea of cosmic unity, of the All, of the universe as a designed network of moral lessons, is occasionally reducible to the less pious notion that all things are closely or remotely, obviously or obscurely, directly or indirectly, interconnected. Everything needs or is tied to everything else. We have discussed his espousal of contrasts and antagonisms. But there are other forms of unexpected mutual dependence. He says:

> There is no solitary flower and no solitary thought. It comes single like a foreign traveller,—but find out its name, and it is related to a powerful and numerous family. Wonderful is their working and relation each to each. . . . Every new thought modifies, interprets old problems. The retrospective value of each new thought is immense, like a torch applied to a long train of gunpowder. ("Natural History of Intellect," *Natural History,* p. 21)

Though Emerson cannot abstain from ending this paragraph with a reference to the All, the quoted words can, I think, fight their way free of theology and strengthen a sense, not so much of the intended affinity of things, but of the continuously surprising play of influences in the world over time or at any given time. In "Nominalist and Realist," Emerson can personify Nature and invest it with purpose, but the point he makes need not have a metaphysical relevance:

> She will have all. Nick Bottom cannot play all the parts, work it how he may; there will be somebody else, and the world will be round. Everything must have its flower or effort at the beautiful, coarser or finer according to its stuff. They relieve and recommend each other, and the sanity of society is a balance of a thousand insanities. (p. 581)

Or as Nietzsche puts it:

> Nothing in existence may be substracted, nothing is dispensable. . . . To require this requires courage. ("The Birth of Tragedy," *Ecco Homo* [W. Kaufmann, Trans.], sect. 2, p. 728)

(Or is this thought, too, just more "metaphysical comfort"?)

Sixth, there are times when Emerson retreats from his kind of religious certainty (or hope) to a state of bewilderment or puzzlement. The world resists being known even by Plato:

> He has clapped copyright on the world. This is the ambition of individualism. But the mouthful proves too large. *Boa constrictor* has good will to eat it, but he is foiled. He falls abroad in the attempt; and biting, gets strangled: the bitten world holds the biter fast by his own teeth. There he perishes: unconquered nature lives on, and forgets him. ("Plato; or, the Philosopher," *Representative Men,* p. 653)

Emerson had said earlier that "the sun and moon and the man who walks under them are miracles that puzzle all analysis" ("Religion," *Early Lectures, 3,* p. 278). The extreme statement of Emerson's bewilderment is beautifully formulated in the "Natural History of Intellect":

> In my thought I seem to stand on the bank of a river and watch the endless flow of the stream, floating objects of all shapes, colors, and natures; nor can I much detain them as they pass, except by running beside them a little way along the bank. But whence they come or whither they go is not told me. (*Natural History,* p. 16)

Seventh, Emerson's puzzlement at the nature of the world sometimes changes into a sense of wonder that there is a world, and he seems not to need a divinity to instigate the wonder. (Here, I borrow Hannah Arendt's distinction between puzzlement or perplexity and wonder. [*The Life of the Mind,* vol. 1, p. 114].) In a letter to Carlyle, he says that his friend, Bronson Alcott, "is capable of the truth, and gives one the same glad astonishment that he should exist which the world does" (*Carlyle-Emerson,* vol. 1, p. 223). Such astonishment, here casually expressed, is the secular ecstasy of the self-reliant mind. It would be ideal to see the encouragement of secular ecstasy as Emerson's highest teaching. But is it?

Four splendid passages begin with the feeling of wonder and express it in an unhoarse voice. Each paragraph, however, collapses into piety. In "Natural History of Intellect," he says:

> To Be is the unsolved, unsolvable wonder. To Be, in its two connections of inward and outward, the mind and Nature. The wonder subsists, and age, though of eternity, could not approach a solution. (*Natural History,* p. 16)

But then he must mention the "suggestion" of a hidden source and nearly dissolves the wonder.

In "The Sovereignty of Ethics," he says:

> You are really interested in your thought. You have meditated in silent wonder on your existence in this world. You have perceived in the first fact of your conscious life here a miracle so astounding,—a miracle comprehending all the universe of miracles to which your intelligent life gives you access, as to exhaust wonder, and leave you no need of hunting here or there for any particular exhibitions of power. (*Lectures and Sketches,* pp. 200-201)

Emerson waves away Christian texts that threaten such elementary wonder, wonder that the world is a greater wonder than wonder at how it is, in any of its particulars; but then he must associate wonder with "peaceful trust in the Divine Providence." ("The Over-Soul" contains an earlier version of the idea: "Thus revering the soul, and learning, as the ancient said, that 'its beauty is immense,' man will come to see that the world is the perennial miracle which the soul worketh, and be less astonished at particular wonders" [p. 400]. And then trust in God is invoked to distract from the secular mysticism.)

"New England Reformers" ends with an encouragement to wonder:

> All around us, what powers are wrapped up under the coarse mattings of
> custom, and all wonder prevented. It is so wonderful to our neurologists
> that a man can see without his eyes, that it does not occur to them, that it
> is just as wonderful, that he should see with them; and that is ever the
> difference between the wise and the unwise: the latter wonders at what is
> unusual, the wise man wonders at the usual. (pp. 608-609)

The passage is extraordinary, but we stumble with Emerson as he implores
our trust in the Power by which the soul lives. Then, however, we can
recover, if we choose.

Most splendidly, at the start of Chapter 1 of *Nature,* Emerson writes:

> if a man would be alone, let him look at the stars . . . seen in the streets
> of cities, how great they are! If the stars should appear one night in a
> thousand years, how would men believe and adore. . . . But every night
> come out these envoys of beauty, and light the universe with their
> admonishing smile. (p. 9)

A sublime passage, but religiousness imperils it with a reference immediately made to the city of God. To be sure, a certain hesitancy appears:
"One might think the atmosphere was made transparent with this design,
to give man, in the heavenly bodies, the perpetual presence of the sublime" (p. 9). If only we could see in "one might think" a refusal of
religiousness: how truly sublime would this perception of Emerson's be.
But he chooses to trust us only so far. In a lecture from 1840, "Religion," he says that "The mind of this Age will endure no miracle and this
not because of unbelief but because of belief" (*Early Lectures, 3,* p. 278).
I would like to say that the enlightened mind of our age will not endure
Emerson's religiousness—not because of unbelief but because of passage beyond belief, beyond Emerson's acquiescence in the sentiment
that "We are born believing. A man bears beliefs, as a tree bears apples"
("Worship," p. 1056).

All these passages, before they subside religiously, articulate a sense
of wonder that the secularist can deeply admire. Why not just disregard
the ritualist appeals to divinity and selectively take what Emerson has to
give?

*   *   *

Try as one may to be conclusive, the issue of Emerson's religiousness proves as elusive as Emerson wants his thought in general to be. I would submit the view that whenever Emerson seems to retreat from his bravest thoughts into what I have been calling his religiousness, he appears to be mesmerizing himself and voicing a faith or trust helplessly. He believes in the divinity of Nature, but seems able or willing to do little to promote belief in it. His strength is secular; his gestures religious. But the fact remains that he is sincerely religious—that is, sincerely possessed of the idea that the world is permeated by a divine mind that imparts moral shape and hence a meaning to the world. For Emerson, the less important stake is meaningfulness as such, which is supposedly dependent on a more-than-human but not utterly nonhuman source; the moral meaningfulness of nature and of the long-term tendency of human life is the larger consideration. Emerson cannot shake off religiousness because he cannot disregard an intransigent moral concern, whether it be guilty or earnest.

What is this moral concern? Emerson does not think that modern people need church religions to be moral. To the contrary, the moral kernel has now to be extracted from church religions to be kept safer. He is a critic of church religions because, in part, they sully the motives to morality and its content. In any case, he says in 1866, "I consider theology to be the rhetoric of morals" ("Character," *Lectures and Sketches,* p. 108). The progress of civilization is measured by the ability of morality to stand on its own and dispense with the "quaint grotesques of theology" (p. 109). He also says:

> The next age will behold God in the ethical laws—as mankind begins to see them in this age, self-equal, self-executing, instantaneous and self-affirmed; needing no voucher, no prophet and no miracle besides their own irresistibility. ("The Preacher," *Lectures and Sketches,* pp. 222-223)

The problem—if it is a problem—is that Emerson craves a world that can be honestly understood as morally intended (and the intention is divine, not merely human) and ever more morally actual. This craving is the core of his religiousness. I doubt he thinks that people have to be religious in this sense if they are to be moral—much less that belief in this sort of meaningfulness is needed for human life to go on without despair. I doubt he offers his religiousness as an indispensable replacement for waning church religions to fill the void in the public heart. The craving is genuinely his own. (To be sure, the crisis over slavery in the 1850s drives him to moral despair. He says in his *Journals*: "We must have foundations" [14, p. 399]. But this worry over relativism is untypical.)

In a revealing passage he says:

> There is this eternal advantage to morals, that, in the question between truth and goodness, the moral cause of the world lies behind all else in the mind. It was for good, it is to good, that all works. Surely it is not to prove or show the truth of things,—that sounds a little cold and scholastic,—no, it is for benefit, that all subsists. As we say in our modern politics, catching at last the language of morals, that the object of the State is the greatest good of the greatest number,—so, the reason we must give for the existence of the world is, that it is for the benefit of all being. ("Character," *Lectures and Sketches,* p. 91)

Later, impersonating the passion for wealth, Emerson gives a somewhat different reason for the existence of the world:

> Power is what they want,—not candy; power to execute their design, power to give legs and feet, form and actuality, to their thought, which, to a clear-sighted man, appears the end for which the universe exists, and all its resources might be well applied. ("Wealth," *The Conduct of Life,* p. 993)

But the words in "Character" appear closer to Emerson's view; in speaking for character, Emerson does not impersonate. He wants the world to have a reason for its existence, and he wants that reason to be a moral one.

Emerson's craving for a morally intended and ever more morally actual world is, we surely must grant, complex. After all, he affirms the world and asks us to affirm it because of, not in spite of, its antagonisms and contrasts. This desire to affirm cannot possibly suit any simple moralism. On the other hand, as we shall see later on, in Emerson's conceptualization of active or practical self-reliance, the moral motive is not emphasized, even though moral limits are. This view, too, cannot possibly suit any simple moralism. What shall we say? Emerson's religiousness consists in the will to see the world as a place in which the inherent moral intention is made actual only with great beauty. The beauty is in the difficulty, the complexity in the drama engendered by antagonistic or contrasting elements and forces, embodied in nature and humanity, which slowly, slowly, over countless ages, yield a morally acceptable tendency of benefit that is scarcely recognized or recognizable. Let me cite again Emerson's cosmic estimate from "The Young American": "a small excess of good, a small balance in brute facts always favorable to the side of reason" (p. 217). The evidence can justify no higher estimate, but Emerson believes that it does justify the estimate. The appearance of humanity after long evolutionary periods he must see as necessary and as (so far) the supreme benefit. It is no accident; the nature of things requires it. But the benefit is a benefit not only because humanity reflects the divine mind more than anything else in nature and makes a consciousness of divinity possible along with an understanding of divinity as consciousness, but also because humanity, in its devious and usually indirect way, works to realize moral benefit. To repeat words quoted above: "There is this eternal advantage to morals, that, in the question between truth and goodness, the moral cause of the world lies behind all else in the mind" ("Character," *Lectures and Sketches,* p. 91).

*   *   *

All in all, Emerson's religiousness, though everywhere present in his work, may not be an insuperable obstacle. I would like to think that when we see Emerson's religiousness as essentially moral, when we take into account those serious mitigations of his theological metaphysics which I have surveyed, we can judge the problem of his religiousness as minor. His sense of complexity and of beauty or sublimity can seem much weightier than his moralism. His passion for harmony, for reconciliation, for totality, on the one hand, and for natural moral benefit, on the other, may strike us as less vivid than his passion for antagonism and contrast. And when we read a sentence like "There is nothing so wonderful in any particular landscape as the necessity of being beautiful under which every landscape lies" ("Nature," p. 545), we can forgive (if we have to) the possibly metaphysical excess and admire the words in our own way.

In trying, then, to deal with Emerson's religiousness, we have several proceedings at our disposal. First, we can tolerate his religiousness because we judge it to be comparatively minor. It is more than a blemish—perhaps more than a flaw—but it is a good deal less than an insuperable obstacle. Second, we can elicit a secular meaning from his religious conceptions just as he extracted his own religiousness from church religions. We can translate him, as he translated his tradition. We can push him in a more unreligious direction. In doing that, we would actually be far less coercive than he was: we would have much less to do than he did. And, last, we can simply work with the inexhaustible abundance of detachable utterance his writings contain by easing its way, unencumbered by religiousness, to us. Here, too, we would follow Emerson's precept. He speaks of "a class of passages" in Shakespeare "which bear to be separated from their connexion as single gems do from a crown and choicely kept for their intrinsic worth" ("Shakespear" [second lecture], *Early Lectures, 1,* p. 313). We can, by these and other proceedings, be self-reliant readers of the great teacher of self-reliance.

4

Friendship and Love

If we say that self-reliance is the true principle of Emerson, we then ask, Does the self-reliant individual need others? Obviously no one, no matter how self-reliant, can live without others. Emersonian self-reliance is not perpetual solitariness. When we ask whether the self-reliant individuals need others, we mean to see what human relationships Emerson posits as ideally suited to self-reliant individuals. Our distinction between mental and active self-reliance is relevant here. Of greatest concern to Emerson is the prosperity of mental self-reliance. Our purpose now is to show that the relationships Emerson praises most are those that improve the work of mental self-reliance, the attempt to think one's own receptive thoughts and think them through. It is a weighty fact that human relations most conducive to mental self-reliance are simultaneously valuable as expressions of active self-reliance (in the sense of trying to be or show oneself more adequately, more fully). But the contribution that a relationship makes to mental self-reliance matters most. In the next two chapters, I will discuss human relations that display active self-reliance but do not simultaneously improve the work of mental self-reliance.

The furtherance of mental self-reliance provides a perspective on the whole range of relationships that comprise society. In more than one lecture or essay Emerson actually does survey many relationships from that perspective. The first thing we notice is that Emerson takes no sort of relation for granted; none, no matter how long established or revered, can go unexamined. Each must somehow earn the acceptance of the self-reliant individual, and some relationships are especially resistant to acceptance. Rather than advancing one's mental self-reliance they may retard it. Before turning to what Emerson has to suggest about particular relationships, it would be well to pause and simply say that in Emerson's theorization of self-reliance, no sort of relationship should come easily, even if the self-reliant individual accepts it as valuable. But there must and will be relationships. The ideal is that they be truthful and that they also promote a greater receptivity to truth about what is external to them—truth about the world.

I have already taken up Emerson's idea (in "Experience") of the "innavigable sea" that cuts us off from one another, and hence of the near impossibility of honestly experiencing and being experienced. The honesty increases with self-reliance and hence the difficulty of connection may also increase. Allowing for Emerson's pedagogic extremism, we can still find nourishment in his despair. We can be left with a sobering reminder of the gaps between persons and try to discover whether and how Emerson, in the name of mental self-reliance, tries to narrow them, even if he is unable to close them. When I mentioned Emerson's report on the grief he felt or failed to feel over his son's death, I discussed his view of the difficulties of relation in the most general, existential way. However, he has more to say. We should not take as final Emerson's exasperated (or is it exultant?) remark that "All men, all things, the state, the church, yea the friends of the heart are phantasms and unreal beside the sanctuary of the heart" ("Introductory Lecture," *Lectures on the Times,* p. 163). He may posit a "metaphysical isolation" of each person, but he enters a sizable qualification:

> This solitude of essence is not be mistaken for a view of our position in nature. Our position in nature, nature will severely avenge. We are tenderly alive to love and hatred. ("The Heart," *Early Lectures, 2,* p. 280)

The enterprise is, precisely, to discover that others are real, as real as oneself, and that what is outside oneself consists not of phantasms, but of reality. But, for Emerson, with his strenuous concern for truth, it is an arduous enterprise. One's best relations must be both an instrument of truth and an instance of it. One must not have drowned in the innavigable sea while thinking that one is safely ashore. But can the sea be somewhat navigable?

As we take up Emerson's thought on how one may break out of isolation, we should keep to mind that when he was young, and hence more able to adhere to others, he found in intimacy only the confirmation of feelings of isolation. His early words, from 1835, express a recurrent and important mood:

> 'Tis very strange how much we owe the perception of the absolute solitude of the spirit to the affections. I sit alone, and cannot arouse myself to thoughts. I go and sit with my friend and in the endeavor to explain my thought to him or her, I lay bare the awful mystery to myself as never before, and start at the total loneliness and infinity of one man. (Notes in *Society and Solitude,* p. 347)

*   *   *

The very title of Emerson's book, *Society and Solitude,* announces both an antagonism and a complementary connection. As we have seen, the Emersonian sense is that any human phenomenon, even though indispensable, is inevitably incomplete and must be completed and balanced by what is antithetical or at least contrasting. Emerson's title implies that society is better off if people have a taste for solitude, but also that proper solitude looks to the perpetual interruption of itself by relationships, by social involvement. But we must never make Emerson evenhanded, certainly not with respect to the contending and cooperative claims and benefits of society and solitude. The core of Emersonian individualism, the mental self-reliance that he theorizes, demands a larger place for solitude than many other conceptualizations of how to live, what to do, more than many other conceptualizations of individualism. He does not finally say that solitude is the most natural and favorable condition of any self-reliant individual. But its advantages serve as a standard by which to judge many relationships: not all of them—not, for example, being a parent (about which Emerson speaks rapturously); but self-reliance certainly allows one to judge some of the most important ones. Indeed, solitude provides an initial measure for the evaluation of intimacy.

In his Dartmouth college lecture of 1838, "Literary Ethics," Emerson gives his most succinct expression of the high worth of solitude. He is addressing students and advising them, but his words, as always, have a general application. The self-reliant individual, no matter what his walk in life, is, after all, a lifelong student. Emerson asks why the student must often be solitary and silent, embracing solitude as a bride and having his "glees and glooms" alone (p. 104). Why must one often be one's own bride? In periods of marriage to oneself, he says, one "may become acquainted with his thoughts" (104). One lies passive to one's thoughts and thus becomes self-reliant, because self-reliant thinking is built on self-acquaintance. This is not exactly Socratic self-knowledge, which seems tied to the attempt to find out what one really wants and what is really satisfying. Such self-knowledge is not as close to Emerson's heart as it is to, say, Thoreau's. Rather, Emersonian self-acquaintance is the effort to fix one's attention on the steady but confused and elusive stream or sea or ocean of consciousness or semiconsciousness as well as on one's dreamlife. What is happening inside oneself? What is one really thinking? Emerson's premise is that it is too easy to forget to listen to oneself, and to settle, instead, for the thoughts of others, whether others are close to hand or part of some large, anonymous network. Somehow, anyone's own thoughts, often secret or at least unexpressed, are better—more real, more just, more truthful—than thoughts that are held in common and that circulate, whether in a large group or a small one. And this is the case even though, and especially because, many thoughts come unbidden just as dreams do, and despite the fact, which Emerson gives many indications he knows, that one is frequently helpless in relation to the contents of one's inner life, and not only when dreaming. One must try to become self-acquainted. One must try to retrieve what is valuable from the flow of evanescence. The first paragraph of "Self-Reliance" concentrates this advice. In solitude, we grow self-acquainted. In turn, self-acquaintance prepares us for a self-reliant reception of the world.

On numerous occasions, Emerson says that if an individual pays attention to his or her inner life, one gains access to the mind of the universe. In becoming self-acquainted one discards the untruth, the imperception, the slothful sensuality that invariably characterize the thoughts that are socially held in common and that circulate. One makes room for the universe's intelligence to register itself on one's attention. Every person's intuition—that is, untaught perception—derives from participation in the universal mind. This view is part of the core of Emerson's religiousness. We must not allow his religiousness, however, to spoil our reception of him. I want to separate Emerson from his religiousness for the sake of his truth. Therefore, if I am told that, for Emerson, the only point of self-acquaintance is to put oneself in touch with the universal mind, then I would have to say, I hope not. As I have tried to suggest, Emerson himself is much more cagey. He endows his words with the capacity to be detached from his transcendental ambitions, lending themselves to uses more secular. "Literary Ethics" climaxes in the religious insistence that the student "is great only by being passive to the superincumbent spirit" (p. 109). But counsel to the unreligious also works its way throughout the essay. Quite simply, it is good to grow self-acquainted because it is good to know what is one's own—to know oneself in distinction from others. Literal solitude is indispensable to self-collection and self-recollection.

Though solitude is necessary for self-acquaintance, which, in turn, matters most as the indispensable preparation for self-reliant thinking about the world, the reality that encloses one's solitude. As I have already tried to indicate, Emerson thinks that the most immediate knowledge of experienced reality often comes not during immersion in it but afterwards. The closest encounter is retrospective. There is a radical split in Emerson between doing (or being) and knowing (or seeing). Emerson regularly maintains that we most truly know, we get nearest to reality—whether our own experiences or the life around us—after the fact, and, for the most part, in solitary contemplation. That is the great work of solitude: to know oneself, of course, but also (and perhaps this thought seems ironical) to know everything but oneself. Emerson shows little of the hesitation about solitude that Montaigne expresses in his essay, "Of Solitude": "There are ways to fail in solitude as well as in company" (*The Complete Essays* [D. Frame, Trans.], pp. 182-183).

But solitude is not sufficient for the purposes of solitude. There is society. Emerson says:

> Of course, I would not have any superstition about solitude. Let the youth study the uses of solitude and of society. Let him use both, not serve either.

The reason why an ingenious soul shuns society, is to the end of finding society. ("Literary Ethics," p. 105)

Although a person must depend for various reasons on various sorts of relationships in society, only one sort turns out to be from its very nature intrinsic to both self-acquaintance and self-reliance; only one sort of relationship helps solitude accomplish its major work of receiving the world in truth. That is friendship. Finding society means finding the right company; it does not mean looking for the good society. Emerson explains himself:

You say, I go too much alone. Yes, but Heaven knows it is from no disrelish for love and fellow working. I shun society to the end of finding society. I quit a society which is no longer one. I repudiate the false out of love of the true. I go alone that I meet my brother as I ought. ("The Protest," *Early Lectures, 3,* p. 96)

In the central essay, "Friendship," from *Essays: First Series,* Emerson says:

The soul environs itself with friends that it may enter into a grander self-acquaintance or solitude; and it goes alone for a season that it may exalt its conversation or society. (p. 344)

Only friendship establishes the true reciprocity between society and solitude—a reciprocity that cancels the question as to which of them is a means and which is the end. Society and solitude exist for each other, as friends do. And they both serve the highest purpose, which is truth, as friends do.

The demands made of friendship, then, are tremendous. Though the following words from *Nature* are about the difference between all human beings and the rest of nature, the subsequent paragraph makes clear that the favor shown human beings over nature actually derives from Emerson's high estimation of the possibilities of friendship. He says:

Words and actions are not the attributes of brute nature. They introduce us to the human form, of which all other organizations appear to be degradations. When this appears among so many that surround it, the spirit prefers it to all others. It says, "From such as this, have I drawn joy and knowledge; in such as this, have I found and beheld myself; I will speak

to it; it can speak again; it can yield one thought already formed and alive."
... far different from the deaf and dumb nature around them, these all rest
like fountain-pipes on the unfathomed sea of thought and virtue whereto
they alone, of all organizations, are the entrance. (pp. 30-31)

Even if Emerson claims a year later (1837) that "every being in nature
addresses me," I think he believes that the address of one speaking
creature to another is what makes all other reception possible, and that
the speaking of friends intensifies both the need and the power of reception ("Introductory," *Human Culture, Early Lectures, 2,* p. 226).

Emerson sees two elements, as he calls them, that compose a friendship.
He claims that the elements are of equal worth and that there is "no reason
why either should be first named" ("Friendship," p. 347). But he does
name truth first, and tenderness a bit later. I think that Emerson's tendency
is to give the element of truth the larger place. Perhaps it is better to say
that the mysteries of tenderness make possible the search for truth, even
if tenderness is not itself a vehicle of truth. A friend is, then, an accomplice
in truth. What truth? I read Emerson as suggesting, first, that friends help
each other approach the truth about all the reality that is external to them,
the truth about the world. As I have said, the point of self-reliance is to
see or perceive the world honestly and accurately, free of the depression
and falsehood of church religions. Friends encourage mental self-reliance
in each other. Second, a friend is the most real being outside oneself, and
in getting to know that person, I can think that I have at last truthfully
experienced a reality as genuine as myself (when I attend to myself in a
fully awakened and withdrawn state). What is more, Emerson suggests,
in an Aristotelian vein, that a friend can help me feel my own being as
more real. My friend is myself externalized. "Other men are lenses
through which we read our own minds" ("Uses of Great Men," *Representative Men,* p. 616). (Emerson thus reworks Plato's analogy of the
letters.) I can watch him or her as I cannot watch myself and learn
otherwise unknowable truths about myself by watching this other, provided the two of us are—to borrow Mill's phrase about both friends and
lovers in *The Subjection of Women*—"not too much unlike" (*Collected
Works of John Stuart Mill,* 21, p. 334). Emerson would have found the
phrase congenial. Yet Emerson can also praise the bond of substantial
difference, as when he says:

Each man seeks those of different quality from his own, and such as are good of their kind; that is, he seeks other men, and the *otherest*. ("Uses of Great Men," p. 616)

Quite programmatically Emerson states:

Some perceptions—I think the best—are granted to the single soul; they come from the depth, and are the permanent and controlling ones. ("Inspiration," *Letters,* p. 292)

But then he allows that it takes two to find other perceptions. He goes so far as to say:

In excited conversation, we have glimpses of the universe, hints of power native to the soul, far-darting lights and shadows of an Andes landscape, such as we can hardly attain in lone meditation. Here are oracles sometimes profusely given, to which the memory goes back in barren hours. ("Considerations by the Way," *The Conduct of Life,* p. 1093)

These possibilities lead Emerson to say that "the best of life is conversation" ("Behavior," *The Conduct of Life,* p. 1049). The role of friendship is, however, not usually exaggerated. An almost grudging quality is present when Emerson says:

If men are less when together than they are alone, they are also in some respects enlarged. ("Clubs," *Society and Solitude,* p. 228)

The qualifications and hesitations reflect Emerson's constant sense that it is only with difficulty that either a truthful or a truth-serving sort of human relationship can be had. Friendship is not a conquest, but it is an achievement.

Perhaps all of Emerson's qualifications and hesitations come close to being canceled, however, when he comes out and says:

Our affection towards others creates a sort of vantage or purchase which nothing will supply. I can do that by another which I cannot do alone. I can say to you what I cannot first say to myself. ("Uses of Great Men," p. 616)

The one to whom we can say what we cannot say to ourselves is "inestimable." Being known by another whom one trusts is indispensable to self-acquaintance:

> What else seeks he in the deep instinct of society, from his first fellowship—a child with children at play, up to the heroic cravings of friendship and love—but to find himself in another mind, to confess himself, to make a clean breast, to be searched and known, because such is the law of his being that only can he find out his own secret through the instrumentality of another mind? ("Address on Education," *Early Lectures, 2,* p. 200)

An acknowledgment of the capacity to hide from oneself, from one's own most thorough introspection, is rare in Emerson. It goes well with the magic he attributes to the eloquent public speaker: namely, the ability to state a truth that the listener is "most unwilling to receive," that the listener "did not wish to see." Indeed, the statement of truth which one is unwilling to receive may be "so broad and so pungent that he cannot get away from it, but must either bend to it or die of it" ("Eloquence," *Society and Solitude,* pp. 91-92). I doubt that Emerson wants friendship to be as risky as this, but these formulations about public eloquence also fit, up to a point, the office of private friendship as Emerson pictures it. Friendship can also be a rescue from imperviousness: "I cannot tell what I would know; but I have observed there are persons who, in their character and actions, answer questions which I have not skill to put" ("Uses of Great Men," p. 617).

Let us also be aware that before "Self-Reliance" was published, Emerson appears to value what he regrets in "Self-Reliance." In "Society" (1837), he writes:

> What constitutes the charm of society, of conversation, of friendship, of love? This delight of receiving again from another our own thoughts and feelings, of thus seeing them out of us, and judging of them as of something foreign to us. The very sentiment you uttered yesterday without heed shall sound memorable to you tomorrow if you hear it from another. Your own thought and act you shall behold with new eyes, when a stranger commends it. (*Early Lectures, 2,* p. 100)

In the first paragraph of "Self-Reliance," Emerson memorably rebukes us for dismissing our thought without notice just because it is ours. He says:

In every work of genius we recognize our own rejected thoughts; they come back to us with a certain alienated majesty. (p. 259)

Yet the earlier words are more suitable to the best meanings of self-reliance than the later ones.

The way to approach truth is to practice what Emerson calls sincerity. One can be sincere only with a friend. Emerson says in "Friendship" that ordinarily:

> Every man alone is sincere. At the entrance of a second person, hypocrisy begins. (p. 347)

But, against the odds:

> ⌈A friend is a person with whom I may be sincere. Before him I may think aloud. I am arrived at last in the presence of a man so real and equal that I may drop even those undermost garments of dissimulation, courtesy, and second thought, which men never put off, and may deal with him with the simplicity and wholeness with which one chemical atom meets another. (p. 347)⌋

Friendship is mutual intellectual nakedness. Between friends there are "no terrors, no vulgarities" because "everything can be safely said" ("Social Aims," *Letters,* p. 90). Sincerity is thus one of the main solvents of conformist perception and utterance. It helps me to understand what the world means and to mean what I say. Therefore a self-reliant person relies on a friend as he relies on himself ("Behavior," p. 1049).

The medium of friendship is conversation, and the best company is made up of just one other person: one friend at a time. Sincerity permits the proper influence of one on another, which is a kind of contagion that is utterly dissimilar from the unconscious contagion of conformity to convention or public opinion or episodic public moods. Emerson says:

> We are emulous. If the tone of the companion is higher than ours, we delight in rising to it . . . it is because one thought well that the other thinks better: and two men of good mind will excite each other's activity, each attempting still to cap the other's thought. ("Inspiration," *Letters,* p. 293)

As I have said, these formulations on friendship concern the need a self-reliant individual has for others, when they are friends, to the end that he or she can improve a truthful understanding of the world and gather the courage to express it. In this way, friendship enhances one of the principal aims of solitude. In addition, friends assist the self-reliant individual to progress toward a particular and especially personal acquisition of truth: the sense that some other being in the world is as real as oneself. Of course every being is as real to itself as I am to myself. That should go without saying, but it cannot. Rather, a friend is as real to me, perhaps, as I am to myself. Sincerity is once again the key. When two persons are mutually sincere, each can also hope to know the other's reality. Pretense, play-acting, and conformity are gone. The most real is the least social, the most personal. Yet the most personal is also the most universal. We touch human nature by getting near to a true friend. In "Friendship," Emerson says:

> There can never be deep peace between two spirits, never mutual respect, until in their dialogue each stands for the whole world. (p. 352)

Then, in one of the climaxes of the essay, Emerson writes:

> A friend therefore is a sort of paradox in nature. I who alone am, I who see nothing in nature whose existence I can affirm with equal evidence to my own, behold now the semblance of my being, in all its height, variety and curiosity, reiterated in a foreign form; so that a friend may well be reckoned the masterpiece of nature. (p. 348)

A semblance is a likeness. My friend is like me and is, as it were, me. In being with a friend, I am with myself yet outside myself. In seeing my friend, I can see myself in a way that is not otherwise possible. I can therefore add to my self-acquaintance. I add to my knowledge of the truth about myself.

Emerson here approaches agreement with the Aristotelian dictum that a friend is another self—that is, another who is myself, another who is also myself. When in an earlier lecture, "Society," Emerson explicitly likens a friend to "another self," he interprets the phrase in an un-Aristotelian spirit to mean that the friend "occupies another point of view, and sees the same object on another side" (*Early Lectures, 2,* p. 102). In the essay "Friendship," Emerson again departs from Aristotle. He does not base the feeling of having another self on a kind of selfless self-love, as Aristotle does, but on some affinity that does not seem to have anything to do with self-love. He writes:

> The only joy I have in his being mine, is that the *not mine* is mine. (p. 350)

The *not mine* must not become merely mine if it is to be mine in a worthwhile way. It must remain its own simultaneously. I, too, must not be merely mine, and I must also remain my own. (Recall how in *Nature* he tries to show that the "NOT ME" is, with great struggle, me.) We are admonished that "We must be our own before we can be another's," (p. 351) and that "There must be very two, before there can be very one" (p. 350). Genuine separation alone can constitute a genuine union. It is a union of wholes, not parts.

Emerson makes a little effort to theorize the affinity, the initial attraction between friends:

> We are associated in adolescent and adult life with some friends, who, like skies and waters, are co-extensive with our idea; who, answering each to a certain affection of the soul, satisfy our desire on that side; whom we lack power to put at such focal distance from us, that we can mend or even analyze them. We cannot choose but love them. (*Nature*, p. 31)

He also says, "We talk of choosing our friends, but friends are self-elected," and adds:

> Friendship requires that rare mean betwixt likeness and unlikeness that piques each with presence of power and of consent in the other party. (p. 350)

These last are rather strange words—opaque, maybe evasive. Or perhaps they are Emerson's tribute to the arbitrariness or contingency that determines attraction. Emersonian friendship does not calculate advantages; it only derives them. Elsewhere he explains the consent of friendship as "consent of will and temperament" ("Considerations by the Way," *The Conduct of Life*, p. 1093). It may be that what Emerson says about falling in love also applies to coming to have a friend:

> There is the illusion of love, which attributes to the beloved person all which that person shares with his or her family, sex, age, or condition,

nay, with the human mind itself. 'Tis these which the lover loves, and Anna Matilda gets the credit of them. As if one shut up always in a tower, with one window, through which the face of heaven and earth could be seen, should fancy that all the marvels he beheld belonged to that window. ("Illusions," *The Conduct of Life,* p. 1120)

Nevertheless, friendship appears as the one sort of human relationship that manages to take us out of what Emerson calls our "eggshell existence" ("Considerations by the Way," p. 1093) and allows us to find and give reality in the realm of human relationships. And perhaps it also deepens the sense of one's own reality beyond what a practiced introversion gives.

Let me observe in passing that Emerson does not make friendship monogamous, as he says other philosophers may. One friend at a time is best for company, not a gathering, if friendship is to yield its greatness. But the self-reliant individual will have a number of friends:

I please my imagination more with a circle of godlike men and women variously related to each other and between whom subsists a lofty intelligence. ("Friendship," p. 349)

What of tenderness, the second element of friendship? It seems obvious that the emphasis on a friend as an accomplice in truth and in the search for ever more reality need not put much value on warmth—if warmth is what tenderness means. In discussing friendship the word "love" is sparingly or only lightly and teasingly used. I think that Emerson really believes that the transactions of friendship involve feelings that are more important than comradeship and infatuation. To be sure, tenderness is not merely a means to the end of finding truth and reality, or merely a residual form of gratitude for success in attaining that end. Still, it is acceptable in Emerson's theorization of friendship only when it is compatible with that end. The self-reliant individual wants light more than intimacy, which may obscure the light.

Emerson speaks of distance between friends. Let me make some distinctions. He sometimes advocates distance, knowing that the passion of friendship is to overcome distance; he sometimes seems troubled that since the growth of individualism in the 1820s, all sentiments have weakened and an extreme distance or detachment, not intrinsic to the human condition, has developed; and he sometimes resigns himself sadly to the inevitable existence of distance, to the "infinite remoteness" in even the closest sorts of relationships, including friendship ("The Heart," *Early Lectures, 2*, p. 279). Passages in his work sustain all three positions. But his most radical passages, I think, are those in which he speaks as the advocate of more distance—that is, of distance recognized as such, accepted as inevitable, and deliberately turned into a source of benefit. Distance always exists, whether we care to acknowledge the fact or not. People, even friends, are separate beings, in life, in consciousness, in death. The point is to face the fact and make good come out of it. And the good is not the mere advantage of abating one's annoyance at constant proximity, although a journal entry does in fact speak of this practical advantage to distance:

> Our virtues need perspective. All persons do. I chide and rate my wife or my brother on small provocation if they come too near me. If I see the same persons presently after in the road, in the meeting-house, nay, about the house on their own affairs, heedless of me, I feel reverence and tenderness for them. (*Journals, 7*, p. 419)

Tenderness between friends, therefore, must respect distance; it will resemble kindness more than a loss of self in the other. Emerson says that between friends:

> The joy of kindness is here made known, the joy of love which admitteth of no excess. ("Society," *Early Lectures, 2*, p. 104)

And he advises that friends should "Leave this touching and clawing" ("Friendship," p. 351). With friends, "We will meet as though we met not, and part as though we parted not" (p. 354). Friends live in thoughts about each other.

Emerson complains at moments about distance, but the reason for the complaint is that the friend (or at least, the regular companion) unwittingly blocks Emerson's access to the knowledge the friend has but cannot impart. The friend becomes an imperfectly useful resource. Emerson's spoken but unpublished words are not tender at all; they are an impersonation of the institution of social clubs, and they are also a little frightening:

> Barriers of society, barriers of language, inadequacy of the channels of communication, all choked up and disused . . . Each man has facts I am looking for, and, though I talk with him, I cannot get at them, for want of the clew . . . I cannot have society on my own terms (Quoted in Notes to "Clubs," *Society and Solitude,* p. 419).

Emerson knows men of many different kinds of learning:

> I would fain see their picture-books, as they see them.—This was the very promise which mesmerism made to the imagination of mankind. Now, said the adept, if I could cast a spell on this man, and see his pictures, by myself, without his intervention,—I see them, and not he report them . . . lift the cover of another hive, see the cells, and suck the honey . . . draw the most unwilling mass of experience from every extraordinary individual at pleasure . . . Here was diving bell, but it dived into men. (He was the thought vampire.) He became at once ten, twenty, a hundred men, as he stood gorged with knowledge . . . hesitating on which mass of action and adventure to turn his all-commanding introspection. (Quoted in Notes to "Clubs," *Society and Solitude,* pp. 419-421. See also Notes to "History," *Works, 2,* pp. 386-387)

If Emerson had the ring of Gyges, he would steal knowledge somehow, not power and sex.

The most radical passage in the essay, "Friendship," is a plea for a certain kind of distance:

> Worship his superiorities; wish him not less by a thought, but hoard and tell them all. Guard him as thy counterpart. Let him be to thee forever a sort of beautiful enemy, untamable, devoutly revered, and not a trivial conveniency to be soon outgrown and cast aside. (p. 351)

It is hard for me to know what to make of the idea that a friend is a "beautiful enemy." The thought seems to exceed even Nietzsche in its daring, in its espousal of "the pathos of distance," although the passage on "star friendship" in *The Gay Science* (sect. 279, pp. 225-226) has a likeness to Emerson's concept. Is Emerson just playing? Aristotle, Montaigne, and Bacon all influence Emerson's reflections on friendship, but I find this thought in none of them. Emerson is certainly not taking any idea he has found elsewhere and impersonating it, trying to say for it words that are more adequate than those of its committed partisans. The idea had no partisans.

Certainly the idea is not adequately explained in Emerson's early remark (1832) that "every man must learn in a different way. How much is lost by imitation. Our best friends may be our worst enemies" (Quoted in Notes to "Self-Reliance," *Works, 2,* pp. 388-389). The point here is that we may imitate those we love best and thus lose our originality, forfeit "the significance of self-education." But that point is meanly self-regarding. Nor is the grand suggestiveness of the idea of a friend as an enemy suitably framed when Emerson says in "Friendship":

> I hate, where I looked for a manly furtherance or at least a manly resistance, to find a mush of concession. Better be a nettle in the side of your friend than his echo. (p. 350)

In a lecture given before "Friendship" was published, Emerson refers interestingly to enemies in the context of describing friends (and lovers). He says:

> ... sitting with a friend in the stimulated activity of the faculties, we lay bare to ourselves our own mystery, and start at the total loneliness and infinity of one man. We see that man serves man only to acquaint him with himself, but into that sanctuary, no person can enter. Lover and friend are as remote from it as enemies. ("Society," *Early Lectures, 2,* p. 105)

Here, enemies are only enemies: friends are not enemies, although, to be sure, enemies are no further away from one's center than friends are. This passage is not conventional, but it is much less radical than the words in "Friendship," and is not a preparation for them. Furthermore, Emerson is not saying that friendship is a process by which those who are initially hostile are eventually reconciled, as opposites are united. This latter sentiment, the reverse of Emerson's, Nietzsche idealizes as the only genuine love of enemies: "How much reverence has a noble man for his enemies!—and such reverence is a bridge to love.—For he desires his enemy for himself. . . . " (*On the Genealogy of Morals* [W. Kaufmann, Trans.], first essay, sect. 10, p. 475). But Emerson tries not to have enemies in the usual sense; he fights personal enmity, but he will not exclude tension from affection.

Often when Emerson is being radical, he takes a thought from the Gospels or from Plato's *Republic* or *Symposium* and reworks it, making it more fit for the uses of self-reliance. But he does not take the idea of a

friend as a beautiful enemy from these sources; it seems to lack prece-
dents. It is not really the privatization of the agonistic ideal of citizenship.
Nor is it Homeric. William Blake's line, "Opposition is true Friendship"
means that your enemy is, unknown to you, your friend, your benefactor
(*The Marriage of Heaven and Hell,* p. 262). (This sentiment, by the way,
is certainly present in Emerson.) It does not mean that your friend is,
ideally or really, your enemy, but that person is your special enemy
because he or she has a beautiful form to which you cannot help being
attracted. Let us content ourselves by saying that for Emerson, friends
have to remain somewhat strange to each other; actually, the more they
know each other, and the more sincere they are, the more strange to each
other they should, in certain respects, grow. Friends, like lovers, "should
guard their strangeness" ("Manners," p. 522). In this way, tenderness does
not interfere with truth. Friends should continue to surprise one another,
catching each other off guard, refusing to become familiar and hence
wrongly reassuring. Familiarity should dissolve itself by permitting an
opening out into strangeness. What makes friends enemies is not that they
are, in the usual sense, competitive. They are not competitive in Aristotle's
sense, either: they do not try to see which of them can do more good to
the other, and thus turn perhaps into mutually overbearing rivals. They
are *beautiful* enemies; they retain an aura for each other. Perhaps when in
the first Duino Elegy Rilke says (in Leishman-Spender's English) that "Each
single angel is terrible" (p. 21), we have some approximation to Emerson's
meaning. (Rilke's German word *schrecklich* is, however, too strong.)

At the same time I do not wish to deny that even in regard to friendship
Emerson may very well engage in the kind of excess of statement he
thinks that accuracy requires. But his work seems not to offer a contrasting
excess. He seems to be of one mind on the subject of friendship.

A reasonable question, I suppose, is whether he was or tried to be a
friend in the way his theory prescribes. It may be worth mentioning that
Thoreau thought that Emerson spoke the needed truth to him only after
their friendship waned: "When he became my enemy he shot it to me on
a poisoned arrow." If Thoreau is accurate, Emerson did not practice his
precepts—at least with Thoreau in this period. Yet Thoreau could also
complain of candor: "I am more grieved that my friend can so easily give
utterance to his wounded feelings—than by what he says." (See Robert
Sattelmeyer, " 'When He Became My Enemy': Emerson and Thoreau,
1848-49," pp. 190, 201.) A more general characterization of Emerson's

friendship is made by Henry James, Sr., in his remarkably vivid and violently ambivalent memoir of Emerson:

> In his books or public capacity he was constantly electrifying you by sayings full of divine inspiration. In his talk or private capacity he was one of the least remunerative men I ever encountered. . . . He had apparently no private personality. . . . I could find in him no trivial sign of the selfhood which I found in other men . . . he only connected with the race at second-hand . . . he recognized no God outside of himself and his interlocutor, and recognized him there only as the *liaison* between the two. (*The Literary Remains*, pp. 299-302)

But a more measured critique is made by Henry James, the son, who, in his first essay on Emerson, a review of the Carlyle-Emerson correspondence in 1883, said:

> Emerson speaks of his friends too much as if they were disembodied spirits. One doesn't see the color in the cheeks of them and the coats on their back. (Henry James, *Literary Criticism*, p. 247)

James wants to see novelistically; Emerson does not. James knows as much, and in a later essay, which may have no peers in the writing about Emerson, he complains that Emerson kept away from novels. Let us say that Emerson's radicalism includes an anti-novelistic sense of beauty and of truth. He does not want us to be especially interested in his or our friends' cheeks or coats. He defines heaven as the place without melodrama. It is nevertheless good to hear James's reproach.

In the second essay, the 1887 review of James Elliot Cabot's *A Memoir of Ralph Waldo Emerson*, James intensifies the reproach. He says:

> Courteous and humane to the furthest possible point, to the point of an almost profligate surrender of his attention, there was no familiarity in him, no personal avidity. Even his letters to his wife are courtesies, they are not familiarities. He had only one style, one manner, and he had it for everything—even for himself, in his notes, in his journals. (Henry James, *Literary Criticism*, p. 260)

So be it. Emerson tries to be what James does not want him to be. But is James consistent? Emerson, in life and thought, revises human relationships individualistically—a great theme in James himself. He is more equivocal than Emerson, but closer in spirit than he allows.

I cannot help thinking, all in all, that friendship is the only sort of human relationship that Emerson believes is intrinsic to mental self-reliance. It alone helps to do the work of solitude, and that, because friendship alone assists both self-acquaintance and (without paradox, without compromise) self-reliance. Only friendship's tie to the search for truth and for reality is unaccidental. Its tenderness does not directly advance the work of solitude. But there is no friendship without tenderness, which is a need and a passion, relieving us of an otherwise unendurable solitude. Clearly, Emerson reconceptualizes friendship, not merely adapting an old practice.

But what of love—sexual and passionate love? What does Emerson say about it? What does he suggest about the connection between love and mental self-reliance? The brief answer is that to the extent that love includes or turns into friendship, all that can be said in behalf of friendship can be said for love. But that brief answer is not quite adequate, especially when we notice how easily Emerson applies his formulations about friendship to love and how quietly he drifts into discussion of unsexual friendship when his ostensible subject is sexual love.

In two essays on love and in other pieces on domestic life, Emerson tries to look at love—even at personal love—from the perspective of mental self-reliance. It is not always easy to say whether he is being unsettlingly radical or just prudish or cold. Maybe the line between the two is indistinct: radical individualism of Emerson's sort is in principled opposition to possessiveness and exclusiveness in human relations because these qualities are interwoven with the vices of envy, jealousy, and spite. What binds too tightly also blinds: exclusive love presumptuously defines the lover and the loved. None of this suits the effort to know oneself or the world. If exclusive love must be allowed, it cannot be celebrated.

In any case, Emerson as a theorist of self-reliance is not an enthusiast of the sexual passion. He is temperamentally ascetic: "Appetite shows to the finer souls as a disease, and they find beauty in rites and bounds that resist it" ("Prudence," p. 362). That these words of distaste appear when Emerson impersonates the quality of prudence does little to diminish the force of their sincerity. In a rare off-color metaphor he says that "We may all shoot a wild bull that would toss the good and beautiful, by fighting down the unjust and sensual" ("History," p. 253). The sensual male is unjust, if not mean: too vigorous and hence unmindful. He also says:

> The preservation of the species was a point of such necessity, that
> Nature has secured it at all hazards by immensely overloading the passion,
> at the risk of perpetual crime and disorder. ("Culture," *The Conduct of Life,*
> p. 1016)

These words occur when Emerson speaks on behalf of culture, understood
as the restraint on the "goitre of egotism" and hence on all assertive
passions. In the strongest voice, he makes the case of culture, a case which
he will elsewhere correct. But Emerson repeats the sentiment when later,
in *Society and Solitude,* he speaks on behalf of old age. Perhaps we are in
the presence of his true or nearly true feelings when he says the same thing
from two different perspectives.

Emerson would prefer a less sexed world; perhaps that is what self-
reliant individuals may prefer. Then again, maybe not, for he can also say:
"When we speak truly—is not he only unhappy who is not in love? his
fancied freedom and self-rule—is it not so much death?" ("The Method
of Nature," p. 128). Furthermore, he regularly pays tribute to human
physical beauty, male and female. In the section, "Beauty," in *The Conduct of Life,* he says:

> The felicities of design in art, or in works of nature, are shadows or
> forerunners of that beauty which reaches its perfection in the human form.
> All men are its lovers. . . . It reaches its height in woman. (p. 1107)

To be sure, in one of Emerson's reworkings of Plato's doctrine of love's
ascent in the *Symposium,* the lowest rung is not sexual desire but a
sensation more merely physical, but solely human. In the same section,
"Beauty," from which I have just quoted, he says:

> Thus there is a climbing scale of culture, from the first agreeable sensation
> which a sparkling gem or a scarlet stain affords the eye, up through fair
> outlines and details of the landscape, features of the human face and form,
> signs and tokens of thought and character in manners, up to the ineffable
> mysteries of the intellect. (p. 1112)

The love of beauty, although it guides the soul from one thing to something else better, is not at root sexual. It seems to have no root, but is born
in a child's eye. The romance of love itself is partly rooted in such splendid
superficiality. In this passage, therefore, Emerson departs from Plato: he

does not think that sexual arousal and its imaginative sublimations provide the basic adhesive to reality. Thus, in the space of a few pages, Emerson speaks a bit dissonantly. The idea of beauty makes him say that all earthly beauty aspires to the beauty of the human body and is perfected in it; but the idea of culture makes him say that sexual love is love of beauty, but love of beauty is not originally sexual. As we shall see, when he speaks directly on behalf of love, he is less ambiguous. But his reputation for being unsexual or antisexual is partly deserved, I suppose.

Early in the essay, "Love," which was published in *Essays: First Series,* and was a revised version of a lecture given a few years before, Emerson writes:

> I have been told that in some public discourses of mine my reverence for
> the intellect has made me unjustly cold to the personal relations. (p. 329)

The lecture of 1838, also called "Love," already finds Emerson worried that his views on education disparage love of persons (*Early Lectures, 3,* p. 56). I assume that Emerson is haunted by the way in which Socrates, in the *Phaedrus,* turns from impeaching love as hopelessly irrational and begins to defend it so as not to give offense to Eros, who is, after all, a god. To love is to worship and hence to be pious. Emerson, too, will try to compensate for any coldness. The essay "Love" praises human love. "Persons are love's world" (p. 329); love is the "deification" of persons (p. 335). And Emerson will try to defend, at least up to a point, the inclination to single out just one person for the bestowal of a love that excludes everyone and everything else. Friendship too is exclusive, but is so for the sake of opening one's perception of the world. Love seems to have no such purpose and shrinks the world to one person.

Yet Emerson's praise of love reaches its highest point when he describes the effect of love on the ability of the lover to perceive the world with fresh eyes. In a couple of pages he describes this effect in such a way as to bring it close to his constant and overriding ambition, which is to open one's perception of the world. He writes:

> The passion rebuilds the world for the youth. It makes all things alive and
> significant. (p. 331)

These words seem to catch the essence of self-reliant thinking and to indicate that personal love, quite without trying, causes an epistemological miracle. The passage culminates, furthermore, in a formulation that gives to love a power equal to friendship in calling forth knowledge of one's powers and hence increasing self-acquaintance:

> In giving him to another it still more gives him to himself. He is a new man, with new perceptions, new and keener purposes, and a religious solemnity of character and aims. He does not longer appertain to his family and society; *he* is somewhat; *he* is a person; *he* is a soul. ("Love," p. 331)

The trouble is that much of this passage does not seem sincere. Some sentences are willed or fanciful, and one may finish thinking that whatever else sexual love may mean to Emerson, and howsoever grand a place he establishes for it in the structure of life and its necessities, it does not have a lot to do with mental self-reliance understood as the desire to think one's thoughts and think them through. Love seems off to the side. Most people may not care that love appears unconnected to a poetical or philosophical reception of the world. But Emerson does, and so must anyone who takes the aspirations of democratic individuality seriously.

Here are a few of the sentences that illustrate the effect of love:

> The clouds have faces as he looks on them . . . Behold there in the wood the fine madman! He is a palace of sweet sounds and sights; he dilates; he is twice a man; he walks with arms akimbo; he soliloquizes; he accosts the grass and the trees; he feels the blood of the violet, the clover and the lily in his veins; and he talks with the brook that wets his foot. ("Love," p. 331)

I grant that the last phrases have a fine poetic diction and come from Emerson's best skills. Still, if looked at sternly, these words become a parody of self-reliant thinking, which tries to stare the world into beauty and find the world worthy of affirmation. It is as if in such words Emerson illustrates the truth of his remark that the relation of unsexual friendship "is a kind of absolute," and that it is so "select and sacred that it "even leaves the language of love suspicious and common, so much is this (sc. friendship) purer, and nothing is so much divine" ("Friendship," p. 346). Emerson's case for love is not helped when he avers that overwhelming and world-opening love is not a passion that anyone over the age of 30 can feel, even though he hastens to add:

> The remembrance of these visions outlasts all other remembrances, and is a wreath of flowers on the oldest brows. ("Love," p. 329)

These remembrances do not strike me as being those in which the meanings of one's experiences and encounters in the world, or of one's observations of the larger world, are distilled and turned into truthfully poetic perception, either in solitude or with the help of a friend. (I do not deny that other writers may have more successfully portrayed the alliance of sexual passion, self-acquaintance, and mental self-reliance. Who, if not Proust?)

Emerson condescends to love. This becomes clearer when we see how he conceptualizes the relation between the sexes, especially married love. In the lecture, "Society," he says:

> The first Society of Nature is that of marriage, not only prepared in the distinction of Sex, but in the different tastes and genius of Man and Woman. This society has its own end which is an integrity of human nature by the union of its two great parts, Intellect and Affection. For, of Man the predominant power is Intellect; of Woman, the predominant power is Affection. One mainly seeks Truth, whose effect is Power. The other delights in Goodness, whose effect is Love. (*Early Lectures, 2,* p. 102)

The writing is straight; every noun, almost, is capitalized; the abstractions are simple and dualistic. In the preliminary lecture on love, he extends his point by noticing the respective vices of men and women and says that men and women "must balance and redress each other" (*Early Lectures, 3,* p. 63). He also attributes will, daring, and experimentation only to men, while confining women to sympathy, and sympathy to women. I would say that Emerson's commitment to seeing the world as comprised of salutary antagonisms and contrasts and of competing and divergent claims is reduced in these thoughts to a crude dichotomy and hence to a too easy aestheticism, to bad poetry—the kind of all-too-human response to life that Emerson usually deplores and tries to cure so that a superior, democratized aestheticism can take its place. Even at its most conventional, however, Emerson's thought does not exhibit the crassness that denies women any share in the life of the mind. He readily associates the advance of civilization with their ever greater involvement in public and social life. But he makes men or masculinity *represent* the life of the mind.

If we were to leave Emerson's treatment at this point, we would have to conclude that self-reliance neither gains anything from sexual love nor gives anything to it. The relationship of personal love, though fully compatible with democratic individuality, seems immune to its most significant aspect: self-reliance understood as mental self-possession for the sake of affirming the world. Of course, we could say that the sexual love that Emerson theorizes is more than merely compatible with another and lesser aspect of self-reliance—namely, self-expressive activity. Sexual love, when so intensely personalized and made romantic, is, after all, usually thought as the *result* of individualizing tendencies in society that existed well before the establishment of modern democracy. Thus Emerson could be seen as working out in his own way the meaning of those tendencies. I grant validity to this point. But if I am right in holding that the main Emersonian form of self-reliance is shown and must be shown in thinking and perceiving rather than in expressive activity, then this valid point does not reach to the most fundamental issue.

To gain relevance to mental self-reliance, sexual love must surpass itself and become friendship. Emerson further suggests that friendship growing out of sexual love may be even more valuable for perception of truth and the experience of reality than a friendship that does not. This thought is the culmination of the essay, "Love." But the friendship of lovers or former lovers cannot be based on the continuous dualism of masculine and feminine, which is conventionally a dualism of unequals. Friends are equal. A truthful and truth-seeking relationship must be a relationship of equals. This sentiment accounts for a passage in the essay "Character" (*Essays: Second Series*) in which unsexual friendship is definitively elevated above sexual love:

> I know nothing which life has to offer so satisfying as the profound good understanding which can subsist, after much exchange of good offices, between two virtuous men, each of whom is sure of himself and sure of his friend . . . Of such friendship, love in the sexes is the first symbol. Those relations to the best men, which, at one time, we reckoned the romances of youth, become, in the progress of the character, the most solid enjoyment. (p. 506)

In his time, Emerson is reckless in explicitly locating the source of male friendship in romance. But he remains bound by convention to the extent he finds that the love between men and women must be a relationship of unequals and hence philosophically inferior to the friendship of equal men. Sexual love at its best is reduced to a symbol, an imperfect copy of something better, the higher relation of unsexual (or sexually unconsummated) friendship.

If Emerson is to escape convention, he must see through the dualism of masculine and feminine. The dualism must give way, or at least allow its rigidity to be loosened. The most desirable traits of intellect and character must be seen, to a decisive degree, as floating free of biological identity. One must be disposed to regard men and women as equally available for the kind of friendship that is centered in a companionable quest for more truth, more reality. The self-reliant eye, unimprisoned by gendered thinking, will see equal potentiality in men and women to become self-reliant individuals. The project would be to promote the equal education of women so that there may be a marriage of equals. We must go to other writings, some of which are roughly contemporary to "Love," to see evidence that Emerson tries to break free of the conventional dualism that gives men not so much a monopoly of intellect as a monopoly of the highest traits of intellect.

For the most part, Emerson loosens but does not abandon the dualism of masculine and feminine. He follows two loosening strategies. Common to them both is the decision to describe mental activity solely by reference to the categories of masculine and feminine. One strategy is to value masculine mental traits above feminine ones for the purposes of intellectual self-reliance, but also to say that some women show masculinity. (This is not to say that most men are relevantly masculine.) The other strategy is to claim that the most self-reliant person manages to combine in himself or herself both masculine and feminine intellectual traits and that both sets of traits are equally indispensable. What pervades Emerson's views is a readiness to detach intellectual gender from biological sex and point the way to an ideal hermaphroditism. Let me add that even when Emerson's emphasis is on mental life, his words on masculinity and femininity expand to cover the whole character.

I grant that to use the concepts of "masculine" and "feminine," even though distributed apart from the sex of persons, is to fix the possibilities of identity in a manner not consistent with the theory of democratic individuality. The founder of the theory does not think it through to its end. What cannot be denied, I believe, is that much of the time Emerson seems to regard the masculine traits, whether mental or more broadly characterological, as superior to their necessary feminine complement. Still, in loosening the dualism Emerson does unconventional work, the kind of work needed by the theory of democratic individuality, the heart of which is self-reliant perceiving and knowing, but which must also, of course, encompass being and acting.

The first strategy, then, is to suggest that just as many men lack intellectual masculinity, so some women may have it. In *The Conduct of Life,* Emerson says:

> In every company, there is not only the active and passive sex, but in both men and women, a deeper and more important *sex of mind,* namely, the inventive or creative class of both men and women, and the uninventive or accepting class. (p. 973)

It is well to notice that this sentence comes from the chapter titled "Power." As Emerson says at the start of the book, he will speak as favorably for each phenomenon as possible. This sentence thus expresses a sentiment of those who are especially given to the pursuit or admiration of power—namely, all of us much of the time. To repeat: Emerson is impersonating a sensibility. As it stands, his thought at least breaks with the custom of unalterably dividing the world into masculine men and feminine women, even if it reserves for masculinity the better role in mental life. Bad hermaphroditism is common because many men combine a male body with a feminine mind (uncreative, passive); good hermaphroditism means that some women, despite having women's bodies, have masculine minds (creative, active). The natural ideal remains the mentally masculine man.

But this line of thought is not the only one, and I think it is further away from Emerson's true beliefs than other passages where he praises femininity and places it equal to or better than masculinity in mental life, and admires any man or woman who is mentally both masculine and feminine. (This is the second strategy.) After all, it would not be consistent—that is, it would not be honest—for Emerson to celebrate perceptual reception and hospitality and then depreciate passivity when it is as mentally alert and vigorous, indeed as rapacious, as he preaches and practices it. If one is willing to receive, to be impinged upon, to be invaded, to be open to the world, one is not conventionally deemed masculine. For Emerson to call such traits feminine is not ideal, but he nevertheless engages in a radical undertaking. He is dignifying the feminine in a way very few others then did. With a radical simplicity he says, "The stronger the nature, the more it is reactive" ("Uses of Great Men," p. 616).

In a journal entry (1843) he expresses an almost pained tribute to femininity:

> Poets . . . do not appear to advantage abroad, for . . . sympathetic persons, in their instinctive effort to possess themselves of the nature of others, lose their own, and exhibit suppliant manners, whilst men of less susceptibility stand erect around him . . . like castles.
>
> It is true that when a man writes poetry, he appears to assume the high feminine part of his nature. . . . The muse is feminine. But action is male. (*Journals, 8,* p. 356)

At one point he goes the length of citing with approval the words of Henry James, Sr.:

> To give the feminine element in life its hard-earned but eternal supremacy over the masculine has been the secret inspiration of all past history. ("Character," *Lectures and Sketches,* p. 121)

Emerson gives a political slant to this thought in his lecture, "Literature" (1837), where he says that "from their sympathy with the populace arises that humanity even feminine and maternal, which always characterizes the highest class of geniuses" (*Early Lectures, 2,* p. 62).

In a journal entry from 1839, Emerson writes:

> Women see better than men. Men see lazily if they do not expect to act. Women see quite without any wish to act. Men of genius are said to partake of the masculine and feminine traits. They have this feminine eye, a function so rich that it contents itself without asking any aid of the hand. (*Journals, 7,* p. 310)

Emerson's escape from categorical rigidity is effected by praise of the exceptional individual, the genius, although the class of genius seems exclusively made up of men. Yet women as a class are praised for having better perception, the thing that is central to Emerson's depiction of intellectual activity and is a possession Emerson covets for himself.

In a later journal entry (1843), Emerson says:

> Much poor talk concerning woman, which at least had the effect of revealing the true sex of several of the party who usually go disguised in the form of the other sex. Thus Mrs. B is a man. The finest people marry the two sexes in their own person. Hermaphrodite is then the symbol of the finished soul. It was agreed that in every act should appear the married pair: the two elements should mix in every act. (*Journals, 8,* p. 380)

To call Hermaphrodite the symbol of the finished soul is surely noteworthy. Emerson thus extends the idea of hermaphroditic perception to take in the person as such, and now the finest people, not just men, can be ideally hermaphroditic.

Afterward, in *English Traits* (1856), Emerson calls the English national character hermaphroditic for combining kindness and military prowess:

> The two sexes are co-present in the English mind . . . The English delight in the antagonism which combines in one person the extremes of courage and tenderness. ("Race," *English Traits,* p. 802)

These words seem, once again, to confine to men the ability to be hermaphroditic: men alone fight in wars. (The English are "rather manly than warlike.") The feeling is irrepressible that whenever Emerson publishes his work, he reserves the highest privileges of hermaphroditism to men, but grants women the same privileges only in the privacy of his journal. But, as we shall see, he does publish thoughts more radical than any that appear only in his journal. We should also remark that Emerson indicates that only when we *delight* in hermaphroditic antagonism can we achieve the heights. The antagonism is not between ideas or between phenomena, or between us and others, but between one element in ourselves and another element at a distant extreme. The best character and the best mind feel this delight. To feel it to the extent of welcoming or cultivating one's hermaphroditism is the most authentic sign of self-reliance.

Emerson complicates his sense of the hermaphroditic by further loosening the dualism of masculine and feminine. He suggests that as people improve, as they grow more self-reliant, they grow more fluid in character and mind. In his lecture, "Swedenborg; or the Mystic," which was published in *Representative Men* (1850), he entertains the thought that gender, divided between "virility" and "the feminine," (p. 679), is a universal quality that pervades every human phenomenon and stamps the whole human world with its dualism. But he turns on the thought and says:

> God is the bride or bridegroom of the soul. . . . In fact, in the spiritual world we change sexes every moment. You love the worth in me; then I am your husband: but it is not me, but the worth, that fixes the love; and that worth is a drop of the ocean of worth that is beyond me. Meantime, I adore the greater worth in another, and so become his wife. He aspires to a higher worth in another spirit, and is wife or receiver of that influence. (p. 680)

The progress of mental life becomes perpetual worship that is always instigated and accompanied by perpetual self-dissatisfaction. Someone, in some way or on some matter, is wiser than oneself. One opens oneself to him or her. The categories of gender are drastically renovated by being destabilized and made to serve unconformist purposes. This passage may be Emerson's most advanced statement on love.

A related point is made in ungendered language in the essay "Compensation":

> The radical tragedy of nature seems to be the distinction of More and Less. How can Less not feel the pain; how not feel indignation or malevolence towards More? . . . It seems a great injustice. But see the facts nearly and these mountainous inequalities vanish. Love reduces them as the sun melts the iceberg in the sea . . . If I feel over-shadowed and outdone by great neighbors, I can yet love; I can still receive; and he that loveth maketh his own the grandeur he loves. . . . It is the nature of the soul to appropriate all things. (p. 301)

Identification with the superior proceeds from incorporation; the receiver's active love converts the receiver, otherwise passive, into the equal of the superior and thereby abolishes envy. This is not identifying with the aggressor. Rather it is pleasure in thinking that although one does not share privileges, they exist in the world and enhance it. In abandoning resentment, one loses sight of one's lack. To use gendered language, the feminine thus becomes masculine, or overcomes it.

A journal entry (1842) that is a little later than the meditations that found their way into the eventual lecture on Swedenborg fills out the thought in that lecture:

> A highly endowed man with good intellect and good conscience is a Man-woman and does not so much need the complement of woman to his being as another. Hence his relations to the sex are somewhat dislocated and unsatisfactory. He asks in woman, sometimes the Woman, sometimes the Man. (*Journals, 8,* p. 175)

Unfortunately, these words, like the passage from the lecture on Swedenborg, still seem to place the masculine above the feminine and still seem to assume that the good hermaphroditic opportunity is for men, not women. But the appearance is partly deceptive: a true man expects a woman to be able to be a man episodically, just as he becomes a woman. What is more, that as a man in the middle of the 19th century, Emerson can say before a popular audience, as he does in the lecture on Swedenborg, that a developed man becomes the wife of the man from whom he learns is remarkable. Virility is potency to instruct. We may, of course, wish that Emerson could have found an unsexed or ungendered language to express the desirability of being inwardly full of contrasts and antagonisms that are acknowledged, then mastered and made mobile. But I think that Emerson carries self-reliance into new territory. Later radicals can perfect his intuitions. His language conveys in an especially forceful way the idea that the independent mind has no categorial fixity, that receptivity is absent of such fixity. And as the mind is, so should the character endeavor to become. Emerson's reflections suggest that because a true individual is hermaphroditic, a pair of friends, whether or not they are or have been lovers, must each strive to be hermaphroditic so as to grant full play to each other's nature and full scope to each other's thought.

The fact is Emerson believes everyone is hermaphroditic. He says:

> The spiritual power of man is twofold, mind and heart, Intellect and morals; one respecting truth, the other the will. One is the man, the other the woman in spiritual nature. One is power, the other is love. These elements always coexist in every normal individual, but one predominates. ("Natural History of Intellect," *Natural History,* p. 60)

If one element must predominate, the individual will not allow it to injure the claims of the other element. "Each has its vices, its proper dangers, obvious enough when the opposite element is deficient" (p. 61). One must therefore tend both the masculine and the feminine in oneself.

To some appreciable extent, then, Emerson tries to efface the stark distinction between men and women and hence between conventional masculinity and conventional femininity. The point—Emerson's point, not just our own —is to see whether sexual love can, like unsexual friendship, help the intellectual work of self-reliance and not merely be a relationship that is compatible with it or that may have some of the coloration of expressive individuality in a democracy. Lovers must become friends. In "Of Friendship," Montaigne quotes Cicero's *Tusculan Disputations,* 4: "Love is the attempt to form a friendship inspired by beauty" (*The Complete Essays* [D. Frame, Trans.], p. 39). The idea of hermaphroditism is a large step towards theorizing love as friendship, yet a kind of friendship that grows out of sexual love and very nearly replaces it—a kind of friendship that treasures the memory of sexual passion but transmutes the decay of passion into the perfection of friendship. The question in Emerson reduces to whether a husband and a wife can befriend each other.

I believe that a key formulation is found in the lines I quoted from his journal. Let me repeat them:

> A highly endowed man with good intellect and good conscience is a Man-woman and does not so much need the complement of woman to his being as another. Hence his relations to the sex are somewhat dislocated and unsatisfactory. (*Journals, 8,* p. 380)

I read that passage as saying that, contrary to the myth on love that Aristophanes offers in the *Symposium,* a true individual has progressed to the point where one has engendered in oneself the half that most people, still imperfectly individualized, miss in themselves and seek in others. True individuals self-reliantly complete themselves from within. They grow to resemble the original, undivided double self; they have tried to become self-healed. Emerson produces a ferocious statement of the individual's self-sufficiency in "Perpetual Forces," a lecture from 1862, in the time of the Civil War:

> The last revelation of intellect and of sentiment is that in a manner it severs the man from all other men; makes known to him that the spiritual powers are sufficient to him if no other being existed; that he is to deal absolutely in the world, as if he alone were a system and a state, and though all should perish could make all anew. (*Lectures and Sketches,* p. 83)

Emerson's more moderate view is that what the true individual lacks is nothing that another person can steadily supply. Rather, what is required is a company of friends, perhaps one's spouse included, who take turns in supplying what is lacking. The very need to be supplied is diminished: One tends to supply oneself. What is most urgently wanted is not sexual embrace but help toward intellectual fulfillment: the ecstasy of reception of the world. "Hence his relations to the sex are somewhat dislocated and unsatisfactory." The reason is that women, in Emerson's time and place, were not expected to be intellectual.

In a journal entry, Emerson tries to suggest that love is not desire, and that desire diminishes as love increases:

> Remember the great sentiment, "What we love that we have, but by Desire we bereave ourselves of the love," which Schiller said, or said the like.

Schiller's lines, as quoted by Emerson's editors, are:

> One *loves* what he has; one *desires* what he has not; Only the rich soul loves; only the poor one desires. (*Journals, 7,* p. 214)

Emerson finds his thought captured perfectly by another.

Of course, no one is literally self-sufficient. The point is that what one needs from lovers and friends is nothing so tremendous as half a self, as in Aristophanes's story. In relations with the loved one, the source of dislocation is the difficulty in converting love into friendship. Luck is necessary; the project can never be easy. Yet each partner in love, like each unsexual friend, has (or can cultivate) a mixture of masculine and feminine traits, even though they are in different emphases and proportions. In this way they become equals, while remaining diverse. Despite having the same capacities as the other, each necessarily has a different temperament, different experiences, and different tastes, and hence will have a different perspective on life. The couple will never run out of things to say. All this is possible when two persons are "not too much unlike." The mutually attractive unlikenesses, which must also exist between two individuals, can be assured without the cultural system of gender once inner hermaphroditism is encouraged.

To repeat, Emerson does not actually say that lovers or unsexual friends should be or become a pair of hermaphroditic individuals. His thought is hinted, not worked out. But I believe I am taking it in a direction he suggests.

Do I need to add that Emerson's ideal of hermaphroditism is not a doctrine of bisexual activity? The only time Emerson writes about homosexual love is in an undergraduate essay, composed when he was 17, called "The Character of Socrates." He does not speak the name of such love, but seeks to clear Socrates of a want of "temperance" and does so indignantly (*Two Unpublished Essays,* ed. by Edward Everett Hale, 1896, pp. 21-23). Emerson's explicit sexual world is comprised of straight sex, aiming for marriage, and then, despite aversions, maintaining it. Nevertheless, implicit in his view is the thought that if sexual desire is dependent on the mutual need of contrasting selves (or half-selves) for each other, then the hermaphroditic soul, being more complete, will be less psychologically needy, not more sexually adventurous. In Walt Whitman, however, a link between the hermaphroditic and the bisexual is intimated.

*   *   *

⌐I have already said that Emerson varies his sentiment on the distance between people who are close. He advocates more distance than is customary; he also regrets the increased distance that democratic individuality has created, and he considers distance a permanent fact that must be honestly acknowledged. This variation appears in his discussion of married love as it does in his discussion of friendship that was never sexual. As with friendship, so with married love, it is possible to see Emerson above all as an advocate of distance.⌐

In the case of married love, the advocacy of distance has mixed sources. On the one hand, he says that after the early days of sexual infatuation, things change: insecurity, displeasure, pain enter the relationship. What, after all, could be expected when "two persons, a man and a woman, so variously and correlatively gifted, are shut up in one house to spend in the nuptial society forty or fifty years?" ("Love," p. 337). Surely, a new relationship must grow out of the old one if some relationship is to be preserved. Emerson never mentions divorce; so, permanent marriage frames his discussion of sexual love. If society were starting from scratch, perhaps the institution of marriage would be replaced ("Religion," *English Traits,* p. 883). But it is here: make the best of it; make something really fine out of it—finer even than the early days of infatuation. Let it grow into the worthiest friendship, which is partly defined by distance. On the other hand, Emerson is committed to the belief that the highest relationship cannot be to persons, but to the world. Yet he allows that the best preparation for becoming attached to the world, for praising and affirming it, for beholding it as beautiful, is to be attached first in a relationship of sexual love. With Emerson, then, the much greater reason for advocating distance is philosophical yearning, not the "incongruities, defects and disproportion" he says that one will find in the spouse ("Love," p. 336). Even if infatuation could last, it exists to be superseded. Let distance come, and with effort it will not be the distance of dissatisfaction, but the proper distance, the distance of sympathetic detachment.

Emerson's famous poem "Give All to Love" actually suggests the thought that though love, a god, deserves the lover's complete self-giving, the lover should not give all to love. The lover acts properly when he honors the emotional freedom of the beloved:

> Cling with life to the maid;
> But when the surprise,
> First vague shadow of surmise
> Flits across her bosom young,
> Of a joy apart from thee,
> Free be she, fancy free

What is good for one is good for the other:

> Though thou loved her as thyself,
> As a self of purer clay,
> Though her parting dims the day,
> Stealing grace from all alive;
> Heartily know,
> When half-gods go,
> The gods arrive. (*Works, 9,* p. 92)

Persons are only half-gods; they are partly material. Love is only one of the gods. The greatest gods are truths. The gods arrive when the truth about the imperfections of sexual love are faced. The distance that lovers should need is not literal separation; rather it comes from an unpossessive attitude that only time may grant and with it, the gift of philosophical freedom.

In the lecture, "Home" (1838), Emerson speaks his most fervid words on the excellence of distance between people who are closest:

> I have said that a true Culture goes to make man a citizen of the world . . . at home in nature. It is the effect of this domestication in the All to estrange the man in the particular. Having learned to know the depth of peace which belongs to a home in the Soul, he becomes impatient and a stranger in whatsoever relation or place is not like it eternal. He who has learned by happy inspiration that his home and country are so wide that not possibly can he go forth out of it, immediately comes back to view his old private haunts, once so familiar as to seem part and parcel of himself, under an altered aspect. They look strange and foreign. Now that he has learned to range and associate himself by affinities and not by custom he finds himself a stranger under his own roof. (*Early Lectures, 3,* p. 31)

The aim of glad estrangement is to come to know that not only are those whom one loves infinitely beautiful, but all persons are such to those who love them. Everyone loves arbitrarily, but because everyone does, there is no injustice. But the limits intrinsic to personal love must be overcome. Love can aspire to impartiality. We cannot love the world as we love what we know close to hand and is ours, but we can develop the imagination of love and take to heart the fact that anyone known well can be loved well. Everyone deserves to know and to be known well. "Love," he says, "shows me the opulence of nature, by disclosing to me in my friend a hidden wealth, and I infer an equal depth of good in every other direction" ("Nominalist and Realist," p. 585). Distance between persons whose relationship began in sexual infatuation can enable the best perception of the lovely world, the love-worthy world that houses infinitely more, infinitely more love, than their special love. If, then, Emerson is cold about sex, he has a passionate reason. His entire conception of personal love is determined by his wish to see it serve the end for which mental self-reliance exists: reception of the world, especially other human beings. He gives exclusive love a telos beyond itself, rather than making it the highest condition of life.

In the essay "Love" Emerson says that "even love, which is the deification of persons, must become more impersonal every day" (p. 335). Married love puts the couple "in training for a love which knows not sex, nor person, nor partiality" (p. 337). In one paragraph he reworks the idea of love's ascent in the *Symposium,* but gives less to beautiful bodies than Plato does. (Another version of love's ascent is found in his poem "Initial, Daemonic and Celestial Love.") He thinks that the body is "unable to fulfill the promise which beauty holds out," and continues to say:

> if, accepting the hint of these visions and suggestions which beauty makes to his mind, the soul passes through the body and falls to admire strokes of character, and the lovers contemplate one another in their discourses and their actions, then they pass to the true palace of beauty, more and more inflame their love of it, and by this love extinguishing the base affection, as the sun puts out fire by shining on the hearth, they become pure and hallowed. (pp. 333-334)

We notice that Emerson ingeniously inserts a trope from Plato's parable of the cave in the *Republic* into his super-Platonized picture of the metamorphoses of sexual love. Then he suggests that the lover ideally passes from the beauty of the good character of the beloved to an appreciation of the good character of all persons:

> so is the one beautiful soul only the door through which he enters to the society of all true and pure souls . . . And in beholding in many souls the traits of the divine beauty, and separating in each soul that which is divine from the taint which it has contracted in the world, the lover ascends to the highest beauty, to love and knowledge of Divinity, by steps on this ladder of created souls. (p. 334)

Emerson is carried away; rather he is impersonating the lover and thus magnifies the phenomenon of love. Though his ladder of love reaches beyond persons to "Divinity," Emerson is intensely concerned to show the continuity between love of one person and love of all persons—not love between one person and love of what is other than or more than persons. Of course, even the continuity between love of one and love of all must seem implausible or unwanted to anyone who thinks that being in love with a person is thoroughly discontinuous with any other kind of love, because no one or nothing exists like the beloved or is as good. Emerson is radical in affirming the continuity; he means it, but not quite as Socrates's Diotima urges it when she insists that sexual love of one person should lead to sexual desire toward all. For Emerson, it is only the illusion of love that blinds lovers to the fact that love of any one person is a love of qualities or attributes shared with other persons. One unknowingly loves the type through a single person, the essence through an accident. The beloved is actually an imperfect realization of a complex ideal, whether imagined or vaguely remembered, that can never in truth be perfectly realized. The lover should try to climb to a love of the ideal itself and descend again to a particular love, but now enlightened by an understanding of the nature of love.

Emerson may doubt he will ever be believed. He may have his own doubts. For that reason, the praise of unsexual friendship may be more sincerely congenial to him than praise of love. But he must praise personal love, and what induces the strain of ecstasy in his voice is the possibility that such love can provide the surest access to knowledge of reality, to truth about the world. I think when Emerson says that "Divinity" is the ultimate reality, the place where the ladder of love ends, his best sense is that this place is not love of a theist substitution for Plato's metaphysical absolute beauty, but love of the world. Love of the world, however, is not continuous with or like sexual (or unsexual) love of persons. The beauty of the human and nonhuman world is not like the beauty of persons. The world is not in the image of a person. Friendship, is a relation which, thanks to love, whether sexual or not, brings to birth and nurtures impressions of truth about the world and its beauty. If Emerson, on one occasion, can locate the root of the desire for beauty in a child's bewitchment by a scarlet stain, the love of persons is obviously not a mere bewitchment by surface. Correspondingly, the passage of love leading persons to love of the world is not direct. Emerson's Platonism is revisionary and incomplete. He says:

> whilst every thing is permitted to love, whilst man cannot serve man too far, whilst he may well and nobly die for his friend, yet are there higher experiences in his soul than any of friendship or love,—the revelations of

impersonal love, the broodings of the spirit, there is nothing at last but God only. ("Prospects," 1842, *Early Lectures, 3,* p. 381)

Mental self-reliance begins and may very well end in solitude, but its point, which is love of the world, gathers indispensable help from the friendship in sexual love as well as the love in unsexual friendship.

5

Individuality and Identity

Having discussed Emerson's views on friendship and love from the perspective of *mental* self-reliance, and claimed that no other human relations or engagements contribute directly to it, we must now turn to *active* self-reliance.

There is more to society than love and friendship, and there is more to self-reliance than mental self-reliance. That is to say, there is more to life than life at its best. Necessities, practicalities, and urgencies must be faced and met. Pleasures and opportunities can be seized. Things must be done, tasks performed, relations and associations entered. Life must be lived, much of it on the lower levels, and spent in doing and acting, rather than in thinking and watching, or being joined in friendship and love. And, in any case, doing and acting do not take place for the sake of the perception, contemplation or retrospection that elicit or impose on them their meaning or beauty or worth, but exist for their own reasons, or for many extrinsic reasons, or for no reasons at all. Activity is not merely the raw material for thinking; thinking is better off if doing and acting are done for all the reasons or lack of reasons for which they are done. We can keep an eye on ourselves as we act, but such an attitude of what Thoreau not unfavorably calls "doubleness" is not characteristically Emersonian. Nor is Whitman's great and happy idea of being "Both in and out of the game, and watching and wondering at it" ("Song of Myself," *Whitman, Poetry and Prose,* p. 30). There are distinctively Emersonian ideas about activity. Emerson continuously insists that self-reliance can be shown in activity. Active self-reliance is, independent activity is, possible. But it is lesser than mental self-reliance, as I have tried to suggest, for three main reasons: first, self-reliant thinking is an impersonal embrace of contrast and contradiction, while action (except in the usually abstentionist forms of acceptance and toleration) must choose and exclude; second, even self-reliant activity is dependent on disengaged and retrospective thinking to elicit its worth and meaning; and third, the nature of things seems to obstruct anyone's effort by acting, no matter how self-reliantly, to achieve a feeling that one has experienced and been experienced. Immersion in activity may also be a huge distraction from the life of the mind. Emerson never failed to regret the time he spent publicly opposing slavery—a duty that he would not shirk, especially after 1850. Emerson's work lowers hope for self-reliant activity, while also lowering the dignity of activity in comparison to self-reliant thinking. Yet he does not desert self-reliant activity. To the contrary, he urges it onward. Activity there must and will be. It may show self-reliance, some kind of independence, some daring or initiative or unusual tenacity. It can be inventive. And though self-reliant activity, still bound by the requirements of practical purpose, is guided by thinking that is not freed for reception and affirmation, such thinking can still be one's own. Activity can be the activity of individuals, of people who act as individuals.

What does it mean to act as an individual? We have already mentioned Emerson's use of the rose as an image of living in the present and hence timelessly. The image suggests that a truly individual person will be at one with himself or herself, self-sufficient and self-contained; that its acting will be indistinguishable from its being; that its being will naturally attain its perfection; and that its being is an unintentional blessing on whatever is around it or happens to come its way. This picture, meant to be magnificient, is a gesture on Emerson's part. As I have said, I do not think that it is a success. What matters is that his writing is full of thought about self-reliant activity that is not enthralled by the image of the rose, even though he never altogether abandons the aspiration packed into the image. It adheres faintly to some of his elaborations.

So, if we put the rose to one side, we are then free to explore Emerson's theory of what it means to act as an individual. The theory contains several contrasting notions. I think that he resolves their contention not by eliminating any of them, but by ranking them. These various notions do have, however, a common substantive element: all self-reliant activity is a service or a contribution to others. I do not mean to be paradoxical. In his fierce attack on the slaveholders' contempt for work, Emerson says:

> Use, labor of each for all, is the health and virtue of all beings. *Ich dien,* I serve, is a truly royal motto . . . God is God because he is the servant of all. ("American Civilization," *Miscellanies,* p. 297)

The plain fact is that Emerson's conceptualization of individualism—his philosophy of self-reliance—is always concerned to connect the individual to the world, but only in ways suitable for the individuality of all persons. And just as the higher self-reliance, which is mental, is finally vindicated by the almost indiscriminate appreciation and affirmation of the world to which it should lead, so the lesser self-reliance, which is active, is praiseworthy to the extent that it serves or contributes to those who are mostly unknown to the actor. Emersonian self-reliance is a *democratic* individuality.

A society of individuals is a society made up of individuals serving or contributing to other individuals. Each person is one self; each person gives and receives as oneself. To give under compulsion and to receive too gratefully; to give or to receive because one's role requires it; to give anything that strengthens people in their sense as members or parts of a collectivity and hence as parties to a fiction or abstraction, or to receive anything in that spirit—all these tendencies are ruled out by Emerson's theorization of self-reliant activity.

Although Emerson's emphasis is on service or contribution, his notion of active self-reliance has a complex relation to morality. Emerson does not, with single-minded devotion, yoke self-reliant activity exhaustively to the moral good. More precisely, self-reliant activity will be framed by moral limits, but Emerson does not theorize it as morally motivated, except belatedly when he countenances conscientious resistance to laws that directly implicate all citizens in the maintenance of slavery. Insofar as moral purposes are achieved by self-reliant activity, they should be achieved, for the most part, indirectly. Emerson praises moral conduct insistently, almost obsessively, but his theorization of self-reliant activity is not morally driven. Its core is not moral duty. The core of positive individuality is not moral duty. He says in "Uses of Great Men" that "indirect service" is the best service. Two passages in this essay especially reveal Emerson's strategy:

> Gift is contrary to the law of the universe. Serving others is serving us. I must absolve me to myself. "Mind thy affair," says the spirit:—"coxcomb, would you meddle with the skies, or with other people?" Indirect service is left. (pp. 617-618)

He then gives a general characterization of indirect service and its rationale:

> Men are helpful through the intellect and the affections. Other help, I find a false appearance. If you affect to give me bread and fire, I perceive that I pay for it the full price, and at last it leaves me as it found me, neither better nor worse: but all mental and moral force is a positive good. It goes out from you, whether you will or not, and profits me whom you never thought of. I cannot even hear of personal vigor of any kind, great power of performance, without fresh resolution. (p. 620)

Direct service, whether charity or paternalism, tends to degrade the recipient. Mutual but indirect service is the norm of self-reliant equals. So tenacious is Emerson on this point that he interprets apparent selfless devotion not as a wish to serve but as a commitment to one's own integrity. Such a commitment is not self-love in the ordinary sense, and it is really intrinsic to love of others:

> That all governments are defective instantly appears in the loss of truth and power that befals one who leaves working for himself to work for another. Absolutely speaking, I can only work for myself. When moved by love a man teaches his child or joins with his neighbor in any act of common benefit or spends himself for his friend, or does at an immense personal sacrifice that touches limit and life somewhat public and self-immolating like the fight of Leonidas or the hemlock of Socrates or the cross of Christ it is not done for others but to fulfil a high necessity of this proper character; the benefit to others is merely contingent, is not contemplated by the doer. ("Politics," *Early Lectures, 3,* pp. 246-247)

In self-reliant *mental* activity—whether perception or contemplation or retrospection of the world or anything in it—the *direct* aim is to find reason to love or admire or appreciate. The direct aim is, as it were, benevolent or charitable; it is to bless. I have already said, however, that it is possible only with great difficulty, if it is possible at all, to infer a principle of action from self-reliant mental activity, philosophical self-reliance. We are now dealing with practical self-reliant activity that is unconnected to the highest kinds of mental self-reliance. And in regard to such activity, we can say that, for Emerson, its charity is best when indirect. Of course one does one's duties, and sometimes more than what is required, but self-reliant activity, except in cases of conscientious noncompliance and refusal, is not essentially moral in purpose. We individualize ourselves innocently; ordinarily we do not individualize ourselves for the sake of becoming better auxiliaries of the moral law. The better service is unintentional and is rendered by force of example.

Great men are great inspirations. They are not to be imitated. Rather, they inspire in us the courage to try, especially to try to be not them, and instead, to move along our own paths. Emerson says, "All vigor is contagious, and when we see creation we also begin to create" ("Progress of Culture," *Letters,* p. 229). Greatness would dwarf us if it were admired for its direct service. The ultimate courage that great persons inspire in each of us is to "be what you are" ("Illusions," *The Conduct of Life,* p. 1122). (This Pindaresque phrase looks forward to Nietzsche's precept that one should become who or what one is.) Properly received, the self-reliance of one can help elicit the self-reliance of another. Active self-reliance can stand to have no justification, not even a moral one, outside itself. How do you justify being you? But the effects of being yourself, we are supposed to infer, are benign. The greatest effect of anyone's active self-reliance is to multiply itself contagiously. We all need to be stimulated if we are to be what we are. There is nothing inevitable or irrepressible about it.

The equality of the idea consists in "rotation": not only does one great person check the influence of another, but anyone can serve as an example to someone else in some way ("Uses of Great Men," p. 630). Emerson says that " . . . society is a Pestalozzian school: all are teachers and pupils in turn" (p. 629). He professes that "As to what we call the masses, and common men;—there are no common men" (p. 630). He knows that the very phrase "great men" is "injurious" and that every effort must be made to deflate the cult of heroes (p. 629). "Every hero becomes a bore at last" (p. 627). To repeat, his theory of self-reliance, whether mental or active, is (or strains to be) a theory of democratic individuality.

Emerson's underlying premise, therefore, is that if we strive to be what we are, the world will be better off and all the better without the deliberate attempt to make it better. It will be better because it will be more moral, but also more human. It will be more human because the world will be made up of individuals rather than masses, of individuals, not dependents and recipients, not instruments and followers. The whole hope is for a society where no one is what Emerson calls a "pensioner" or a "permitted person," but rather "an adult, self-searching soul, brave to assist or resist a world" ("Speech" [Free Religious Association], *Miscellanies,* p. 487).

Let us now look at the varieties of active self-reliance found in Emerson's writings and at the way he appears to rank them, while preserving them all.

Following immediately from the sentiment that no one should live as a "permitted person" is the idea of self-reliance as self-help. In its mildest version, the idea of self-help is in the assertion that "He is no whole man until he knows how to earn a blameless livelihood. Society is barbarous until every industrious man can get his living without dishonest customs" ("Wealth," *The Conduct of Life,* p. 989). This idea appears more vividly when Emerson, reflecting on war and on heroism, assimilates these phenomena to a person's securing his subsistence in society. There is, for him, an intimate connection between the readiness to fight and the insistence on making one's own way economically. We can call these traits of self-help *primitive* self-reliance. This is the lowest or preliminary level of active self-reliance.

Emerson always respects a bellicose engagement with the world. Lest this attitude prejudice one against him, it is best to say at once that he typically characterizes bellicosity (whether in war or trade) as defensive and self-preservative, not as predatory. He is eager to redirect the spirit of bellicosity (in its strictly martial form) and put it in the service of either a conscientious ideal or the cause of peace itself. But there is also no doubt that Emerson is enchanted by the whole idea of self-help because he feels, and knows that the world feels, admiration for the will to struggle, whatever the goal; just as it admires physical courage, whatever the purpose; just as it admires physical grace and beauty, no matter how wicked the creature or person.

Before sublimating the will to struggle, Emerson renders it sympathetically in regard to war and to economic independence. His essay, "War"
(1838), is especially rich in formulations on what he rather distantly calls
the "charm" of war, the charm of the masculinity that war calls forth and
enlists. He asks what war signifies, and answers that all the wars throughout history embody and express a principle:

> What is that principle?—it is self-help. Nature implants with life the
> instinct of self-help, perpetual struggle to be, to resist opposition, to attain
> to freedom, to attain to a mastery and the security of a permanent,
> self-defended being; and to each creature these objects are made so dear
> that it risks its life continually in the struggle for these ends. (*Miscellanies,*
> p. 155)

He also asks what makes the attractiveness of the heroes from "that
romantic style of living which is the material of the thousand plays and
romances, from Shakespeare to Scott." It is the "absolute self-dependence"
of the nobles and warriors (pp. 172, 173). The charm of war, then, is the
"self-subsistency" it displays. To be is to have to struggle in order to be;
but really to be is to be disposed to struggle, to look on one's existence
as perpetual struggle, and one's identity as defined by the capacity to
struggle. As Emerson allows himself to say in "Self-Reliance":

> Power is, in nature, the essential measure of right. Nature suffers nothing
> to remain in her kingdoms which cannot help itself. (p. 272)

And then as if to retreat from the potential barbarism of such a sentiment,
he immediately goes on to say:

> The genesis and maturation of a planet, its poise and orbit, the bended tree
> recovering itself from the strong wind, the vital resources of every animal
> and vegetable, are demonstrations of the self-sufficing and therefore
> self-relying soul. (p. 272)

The illustrations are not barbarous but attractive even to unwarlike dispositions.

Yet there is an undeniable and absolutely essential virtue at the bottom
of the waste and slaughter of war. Emerson goes so far as to say in a

proto-Nietzschean passage that I do not think Nietzsche knew, a passage that also sounds Hegelian, that people's attraction to war shows that they are disposed to believe that

> a man should be himself responsible, with goods, health and life, for his behavior; that he should not ask of the state protection; should ask nothing of the state; should be himself a kingdom and a state; fearing no man; quite willing to use the opportunities and advantages that good government throw in his way, but nothing daunted, and not really the poorer if government, law and order went by the board; because in himself reside infinite resources; because he is sure of himself, and never needs to ask another what in any crisis it behooves him to do. ("War," pp. 171-172)

(In the background of his thought is the way in which order preserved itself without established authority in America in the midst of the Revolution ["Speech" to the Kansas Relief Meeting, *Miscellanies,* pp. 261-262].)

As I have said, Emerson's notion of self-help as primitive self-reliance is illustrated not only by the war of survival but also by economic endeavor. Indeed his words sometimes conflate the two sorts of activity. His respect for individual self-sufficiency in the economic sphere is concentrated in a passage from the chapter "Wealth" in *The Conduct of Life* (1860):

> The Saxons are the merchants of the world: now, for a thousand years, the leading race, and by nothing more than their quality of personal independence, and, in its special modification, pecuniary independence. No reliance for bread and games on the government, no clanship, no patriarchal style of living by the revenues of a chief, no marrying-on,—no system of clientship suits them; but every man must pay his scot. The English are prosperous and peaceable, with their habit of considering that every man must take care of himself, and has himself to thank, if he does not maintain and improve his position in society. (pp. 991-992)

I grant that a certain smugness and coldness infect these words. The historical record of the English and Americans is sanitized, while economic talent is falsely attributed only to them.

Reservations about Emerson's notion of economic self-help grow when we come across a passage later in "Wealth," which deals with the tide of immigration from Britain, France, and Germany to the United States in the wake of the Napoleonic wars, dated by Emerson as 1800 to 1812. Notice that he is not speaking here of the later Irish and German immigration.

The wars gave the United States a near world monopoly of the carrying trade. This made the country "rich and great." But, says Emerson, "the pay-day comes round." That is, the universal law of compensation in its grimmest aspect operated, as it must always operate. Every present gain is a future loss. American profits impoverished Britain, France, and Germany; they then sent their poor to America, first by the thousands, then by the millions. Low wages led to stoppages; stoppages to firings; firings to increased expenditure on the relief of poverty. The workers "go into the poor rates, and, though we refuse wages, we must now pay the same amount in the form of taxes." The foreign poor committed most of the crimes, and their crimes added to the burden of taxation. Their children had to be educated at public expense. An exasperated Emerson concludes:

> It is vain to refuse this payment. We cannot get rid of these people, and we cannot get rid of their will to be supported. That has become an inevitable element of our politics; and, for their votes, each of the dominant parties courts and assists them to get it executed. Moreover, we have to pay, not what would have contented them at home, but what they have learned to think necessary here; so that opinion, fancy, and all manner of moral considerations complicate the problem. ("Wealth," pp. 1001-1002)

What stands out is Emerson's expressed dislike of the will to be supported. He fully acknowledges the chain of events that led to the problem. He is not urging that miserable people be ignored or further punished. But clearly he thinks that something crucial has gone wrong: the spirit of economic dependence has spread.

There are mitigations in Emerson's handling of economic self-help. He is attentive to the futility of having to live in such a way as to spend all one's time trying to earn enough to stay alive. In the course of impersonating the idea that race is a fatality, a principal determinant of an individual's nature—a diseased idea which, epidemic in the 19th century, he elsewhere attacks severely, but perhaps never quite completely abandons—he says:

The German and Irish millions, like the Negro, have a great deal of guano in their destiny. They are ferried over the Atlantic, and carted over America, to ditch and to drudge, to make corn cheap, and then to lie down prematurely to make a spot of green grass on the prairie. ("Fate," *The Conduct of Life,* p. 950)

These masses exhaust themselves to work the earth and make it green, but their dead bodies also make it green. They are dead when alive and alive when dead. There is, I suppose, some pity here. The most important mitigation appears in a lecture called "The Fortune of the Republic," given in 1863 and published with changes in 1878. In it he says:

> The genius of the country has marked out our true policy. Opportunity of civil rights, of education, of personal power, and not less of wealth; doors wide open. If I could have it,—free trade with all the world without toll or custom-houses, invitation as we now make to every nation, to every race and skin, white men, red men, yellow men, black men; hospitality of fair field and equal laws to all. Let them compete, and success to the strongest, the wisest and the best. The land is wide enough, the soil has bread for all. (*Miscellanies,* p. 541)

Emerson thus assumes that in the United States poverty is self-correcting. Temporary dependence can give way to self-help.

In the same lecture, he strikes another note, without any feeling of inconsistency:

> Humanity asks that government shall not be ashamed to be tender and paternal, but that democratic institutions shall be more thoughtful for the interests of women, for the training of children, and for the welfare of sick and unable persons, and serious care of criminals, than was ever any the best government of the Old World. (p. 541)

Furthermore, his marvelous book, *English Traits* (1856), published earlier than "Wealth," contains some powerful remarks on the way in which unbridled English capitalism had engendered, along with the greatest wealth in the world, some of its most appalling poverty. There is also moral sweetness in Emerson's passing comment, "I have read some where, that none is accomplished, so long as any are incomplete; that the happiness of one cannot consist with the misery of another" ("Worship,"

The Conduct of Life, p. 1070). Fittingly, this remark is made in the course of impersonating the idea of worship.

The fact remains, however, that despite these mitigations, Emerson does not advocate the end of the economic system that harbors endemic poverty. He looks to amelioration of the worst effects, but genuinely regrets the need for such amelioration to be administered. He is not prepared to reconcile economic dependence, whether on government or on private charity, with self-help. State socialism is altogether incompatible with every aspect of Emerson's thought. Cooperative socialism is not wholly foreign to Emerson, and he pays it tribute by saying:

> The socialism of our day has done good service in setting men on thinking how certain civilizing benefits, now only enjoyed by the opulent, can be enjoyed by all. ("Wealth," p. 995)

But the best socialism must leave Emerson half-hearted. The contributions that people would make to one another under its system are too direct. The benevolence would be too studied, too relentless. There would be no innocence in indifference. The sense of being an individual would become attenuated, even if productivity could be unselfishly maintained.

It is true that Emerson is solicitous of productivity. For that reason the security of private property occupies a major place in his reflections on the purposes of government. Property is one of the "two objects for whose protection government exists." The other object is persons. Although all human beings must have, for the sake of being persons, equal rights "in virtue of being identical in nature . . . in virtue of their access to reason," ("Politics," p. 560) the right of property is the right to unequal amounts of it. What is the moral basis of unequal property?

> One man owns his clothes, and another owns a county. This accident, depending primarily on the skill and virtues of the parties, of which there is every degree, and secondarily on patrimony, falls unequally, and its rights of course are unequal. (p. 560)

This sentence seems straightforwardly Lockean, but it contains one curiosity. The drastically unequal distribution of property, sanctified as a matter of right, is quietly referred to as an "accident." Emerson does not say what the accident is. I suppose that he means luck, good or bad: the large role of luck in being virtuous or deficient, not just in being born an heir or pauper. There is no other explanation for Emerson's use of "accident" in such a strategic sentence. He means to reduce the claim he is defending; he blurs the line between what seems deserved and what seems gratuitous.

In a brief space in "Politics," Emerson discusses the claim that those with more property should have greater political power. He does not find it easy "to settle the equity of this question." On the one hand, the power of property allows "the rich to encroach on the poor, and to keep them poor." Even worse, "the whole constitution of property, on its present tenures, is injurious, and its influence on persons deteriorating and degrading." Perhaps "the only interest for the consideration of the State is persons" (p. 561). On the other hand,

> Things have their laws, as well as men; and things refuse to be trifled with. Property will be protected. Corn will not grow unless it is planted and manured; but the farmer will not plant or hoe it unless the chances are a hundred to one that he will cut and harvest it . . . The law may in a mad freak say that all shall have power except the owners of property; they shall have no vote. Nevertheless, by a higher law, the property will, year after year, write every statute that respects property. (pp. 562-563)

The nub of the matter is that the security of unequal property is a matter both of right and expediency, while wealth's political power must be extensive but should be checked democratically by the power of numbers. The setting of primitive economic self-reliance (and hence of all active self-reliance) is, then, the system of private property.

In order that a more important kind of active self-reliance ensue, primitive self-reliance in the form of economic self-help must first exist and then remain established. I am not saying that Emerson thinks that self-help must mean being self-employed. It does mean making one's way in the world, making it on one's own by an expenditure of one's effort. The key point is that because self-reliance in every one of its active forms is conceptualized by Emerson as necessarily making a contribution to others, or serving them, the self-reliant individual cannot be dependent on the contributions or service of others to such an extent as to be unable to reciprocate. The needy cannot seem to render service, direct or indirect. There must be moral equality, otherwise there would not be democratic individuality—there would not be the active self-reliance appropriate for a democratic society. We must also acknowledge that when Emerson speaks of self-help in both forms—the martial and the economic—he has men in mind. His thought can of course be revised to include both sexes, but certainly there would have to be revision, even if not a great deal of it.

Beyond the will to be economically self-supporting there is inevitably the will to get rich. Emerson sees it everywhere he looks in the Atlantic world of North America and Europe. He never praises it without lamenting it. He knows that the practices of self-help automatically produce in many circumstances the craving for great wealth. The source of his lamentation is not only the way in which the system of wealth creates poverty, but perhaps more important, because less curable, is the moral and spiritual impoverishment that he sees as partly inspiring and as always accompanying and issuing from the desire to accumulate wealth. Yet with Emerson, a story is never simple. He does really praise what he laments.

The first thing to see is that Emerson does not rule out that there may be a conceptual connection between the pursuit of wealth and active self-reliance. I have already quoted the passage from "Wealth" in *The Conduct of Life* in which he says that pecuniary independence—the wish to be self-supporting—is a "special modification" of personal independence (p. 991). But, of course, self-support is distinct from the pursuit of greater wealth or of as much wealth as possible. Is the pursuit of wealth a proper manifestation of active self-reliance? He more or less says that it is.

The pursuit of wealth, like the pursuit of high rank and political and social power and influence, is a display of what Emerson disapprovingly calls "egotism" or "selfism" or "self-love" ("Culture," *The Conduct of Life,* pp. 1016-1017). I here extend to the specific pursuit of wealth the characterization that Emerson makes of any intensely self-absorbed worldly ambition. Naturally the very word *ego* would seem to place us in the realm of individualism. How, therefore, could any variant of egotism not be individualistic? Is Emerson disowning his own offspring? Well, my aim all along has been to show that in its highest form, self-reliance (as mental self-reliance) aspires to impersonality: that is Emerson's teaching. In regard to the lower form, active self-reliance, he persistently rejects egotism as definitive of individualism and refers more than once to the "goitre of egotism," as if to say that the ego is by its nature helplessly inflamed, whereas the self-reliant individual is to be understood otherwise. An even more severe judgment on egotism occurs later, in *Society and Solitude.* Emerson says:

> We [Americans] are great by exclusion, grasping, and egotism. Our success takes from all what it gives to one. 'Tis a haggard, malignant, careworn running for luck. Egotism is a kind of buckram that gives momentary strength and concentration to men, and seems to be much used in nature for fabrics in which local and spasmodic energy is required. ("Success," p. 289)

His condemnation of egotism is most succinct when he says of Shakespeare that, "He dwarfs all writers without a solitary exception. No egotism" ("Shakespeare," *Miscellanies,* p. 451). Is he nevertheless willing to look on self-absorption, especially of any worldly sort, as properly individualist? I suppose he does, but just barely. Here is a good expression of Emerson's ambivalence toward self-assertion, when shown in the pursuit of worldly prizes:

> I know it is a nice point to discriminate this self-trust, which is the pledge of all mental vigor and performance, from the disease to which it is allied,—the exaggeration of the part which we can play;—yet they are two things. ("Success," *Society and Solitude,* p. 295)

The good side of the pursuit of wealth, like other worldly pursuits, is that it is a personal project and calls forth talents that a person may regard as essential to his or her being. I do not think that I violate Emerson's sense when I see the following words as applying to the pursuit of wealth as well as to other ambitions:

> So egotism has its root in the cardinal necessity by which each individual persists to be what he is. This individuality is not only not inconsistent with culture, but is the basis of it. Every valuable nature is there in its own right . . . ("Culture," *The Conduct of Life,* p. 1016)

The work of what Emerson calls "culture" is refine and thereby draw value from egotism, but not to try to kill it. Culture is the lessening of exaggerated self-importance. But some degree of egotism is entwined with any acceptable way of life. "Nature," he says, "has secured individualism by giving the private person a high conceit of his weight in the system" (p. 1015). But he knows that different societies can thwart nature. Hence a partly indulged egotism is indissociable from any society in which individuals rather than masses or mere members are to exist, and in which most people are not instrumentalized by state or caste.

The age of trade or commerce is one that is marked, Emerson says, "by the immense creation of property and so by the increase of the political importance of individuals everywhere, or the steady progress of the democratical element" ("The Present Age," *Early Lectures, 2,* p. 160). These words appear in a lecture of 1837. They are perfectly consonant with Emerson's published work, from start to finish. He cannot reject the pursuit of wealth or the spirit of commerce if he is to be consistently attentive to the necessary preconditions or inevitable accompaniments of a society of individuals. In a slightly later lecture, 1839, he sees commerce as a fruit, though not the only one, of "the new habit of thought." That habit he calls "analysis," which expels religion and all traditional sentiments. Analysis is the secular spirit of modern life. It goes with severance and detachment and hence with freedom. It sustains the culture of commerce. "Commerce removes from nature that mystery and dread which in the infancy of society defend man from profanation before yet his prudence and his conscience are enlightened" (Introductory, *The Present Age, Early Lectures, 3,* pp. 188, 190).

Of course, Emerson is of more than one mind on these tendencies. He conveys powerfully the force lodged in the commercial spirit to dissolve the old structures of reverence, the old feelings that inspired immense creativity and beauty. He goes so far as to say:

> There is nothing more important in the culture of man than to resist the dangers of Commerce. An admirable servant, it has become the hard master. It seems to realize to the senses the sovereignty which the Soul claims . . . The end, *to be rich,* infects the whole world . . . ("Introductory," *The Present Age, Early Lectures, 3,* p. 191)

But greater possibilities are disclosed by the reign of commerce. Emerson's ambivalence concerning the spread of the secular spirit generally covers, I think, the specific matter of commerce: "Analysis is the understanding taking a step forward of the soul; and so it has the freedom of an evil spirit" (p. 190).

It is noteworthy that just as Emerson traces sexual love to something prior to that love, so he traces, here and there, the love of wealth to some passion lying deeper—but not to abstract greed or transgressive covetousness. At one point in *Society and Solitude*, he posits a commendable passion at the basis of the love of wealth. He says:

> And indeed the love of wealth seems to grow chiefly out of the root of the love of the Beautiful. The desire of gold is not for gold. It is not the love of much wheat and wool and house-hold-stuff. It is the means of freedom and benefit ("Domestic Life," *Society and Solitude,* pp. 113-114).

That the sense of beauty is sometimes too coarse does not damage the point that people want wealth because they crave beauty.

In other writings, he produces other individualist interpretations of the love of wealth. The most important ones are related but somewhat distinct. I will first discuss Emerson's assimilation of the love of wealth to a love of power and then take up his vision of the pursuit of wealth as commendable because it is a display of energy. That is, Emerson thinks that many people who love wealth actually love power, not, say, leisure and consumption; second, he is prepared to render the pursuit of wealth as a phenomenon worthy of contemplation because to the abstract eye it appears as the action of energetic people who refuse idleness and passivity, or who refuse even a stable and well-ordered life, whatever their actual motives may be. The love of power and the eagerness to display energy are commendable enough to elevate pursuit of wealth and other worldly ambitions above self-help in the scale of active self-reliance. Worldly activities also have more glamour, more fascination, and may therefore incite self-reliant activity in other and better directions. Let me add that Emerson does not always distinguish between power and energy and sometimes uses the words interchangeably.

I take up first the theme of power. The second chapter of *The Conduct of Life* is called "Power." It amazingly resembles some of Nietzsche's thoughts about the will to power. In fact, Nietzsche read *The Conduct of Life* in German translation. I believe Emerson's influence on Nietzsche's formulations is direct and profound. In any case, Emerson is prepared to say tentative good words about the pursuit of wealth, just because he thinks that it is a primary form that the love of power takes and he is willing to endorse the love of power before he qualifies himself. Emerson says, "Life is a search after power" (p. 971). What is power? "All power is of one kind, a sharing of the nature of the world" (p. 972). The point is to "Enter cordially into the game, and whirl with the whirling world," rather than remaining bystanders whose hands are cold (p. 972). "Health is good,—power, life, that resists disease, poison, and all enemies, and is conservative, as well as creative" (p. 974). Power is a personal quality, "an affirmative force," "a strong pulse," a "*plus* health" (pp. 973, 975); but it is also an aim, a goal. Specifically in reference to the pursuit of wealth as a form of desire for power, more power, Emerson says that human beings are "born to be rich" ("Wealth," pp. 991, 996). But to be rich does not mean to be surrounded by objects, but to be enabled to subdue and remake nature. He goes on to say:

> It is of no use to argue the wants down: the philosophers have laid the greatness of man in making his wants few; but will a man content himself with a hut and a handful of dried pease? He is born to be rich. He is thoroughly related; and is tempted out by his appetites and fancies to the conquest of this and that piece of nature, until he finds his well-being in the use of his planet, and of more planets than his own . . . . Society in large towns is babyish, and wealth is made a toy . . . But, if this were the main use of surplus capital, it would bring us to barricades, burned towns, and tomahawks presently. Men of sense esteem wealth to be the assimilation of nature to themselves, the converting of the sap and juices of the planet to the incarnation and nutriment of their design. Power is what they want,—not candy;—power to execute their design, power to give legs and feet, form and actuality, to their thought, which, to a clear-sighted man, appears the end for which the universe exists, and all its resources might be well applied. (pp. 990-991, 993)

Of course, Emerson is impersonating a human tendency; he proceeds to question the aspirations he eloquently presents. Yet Emerson is sincerely attracted and receptive. Wealthy persons are figures of power; they are enlarged individuals. To be sure they are ferocious; some of their side effects are ruinous. But they can inspire or incite others. They give examples of the extent to which apparently unaided human beings can dare. In this way, they serve others, even though they usually do not intend to. The indeliberateness, the indirection, is all the better. It goes with acting as an individual, acting as and for oneself, rather than having to accommodate one's being to the discipline of others or to the being of others. There is an unenforced or inadvertent cooperation allowing others, despite the benefits received, to escape personal gratitude, which, flowing in only one direction, is often the wrong kind of dependence.

The search for wealth is not only a search for power, it is an impulse of power. That means it is also a display of energy—a display that the philosophical observer can see as a display, even though those who display it are not interested necessarily in offering themselves as a spectacle. The creatures of energy are too busy to watch themselves or convert themselves into the raw material of their own contemplation or retrospection. But Emerson observes and encourages all of us to do so. His writings throughout his life contain tributes to the entrepreneurial energies of the Americans and the English. It is fitting that one of his tributes is found in the chapter, "Success," in *Society and Solitude*:

> Our American people cannot be found taxed with slowness in performance
> or in praising their performance. The earth is shaken by our engineries.
> We are feeling our youth and nerve and bone. We have the power of
> territory and of sea-coast, and know the use of these. (p. 289)

That he says that Americans are not slow in praising their own perform-ance is a sly word of satire. Still, Emerson admires. What I think he admires, above all, is the sense of indefinite yearning and reaching that is conveyed by a wealth-seeking society so extravagant and wasteful in its worldly motions. Hence Emerson finds that recklessness, not prudence, is often at the root of the search for wealth, and that self-expenditure is not for the sake of future economic expenditure but for the sake of self-testing and self-discovery, or, more likely, self-forgetting.

An individual's pursuit of wealth is a kind of indefinite outward reaching. Emerson admires the trait, and praises it as part of what is best in the human race. He praises it even when it seems driven by obscure purposes or by unmastered currents of thought:

> What is all history but the work of ideas, a record of the incomputable
> energy which his infinite aspirations infuse into man? Has any thing grand
> and lasting been done? Who did it? Plainly not any man, but all men: it
> was the prevalence and inundation of an idea. What brought the pilgrims
> here? One man says, civil liberty; another, the desire of founding a church;

and a third, discovers that the motive force was plantation and trade. But if the Puritans could rise from the dust, they could not answer. ("The Method of Nature," p. 129)

So far, then, we find in Emerson's thought about active self-reliance a defense of primitive self-reliance primarily as economic self-help and a qualified admiration of the self-reliance that shows itself in the pursuit of wealth—a pursuit he traces to various passions, all of them commendable to a certain degree, but none wholly admirable in itself. His general implication is that the pursuit of any main worldly prize—like power, position or fame—can be a form of active self-reliance, even though in a commercial democracy, the preponderant overt pursuit is the pursuit of wealth. Yet Emerson has a keen sense of the inadequacy of worldliness. The self-reliance shown is not reliance on the best self, the aspects of the acting self that most deserve display. Worldliness, to Emerson, is too entwined with selfishness or egotism to be wholly commendable. The deeper trouble is that the ego on display when wordly prizes are pursued is often not really the ego, but its simulacrum, an imitation of egotism. To be worldly is to want what others want because they want it and to exult in success because others have succeeded or failed. Or it is to take unconscious satisfaction in playing one's part in a game or drama; keeping the whole thing going becomes one's interest. One is owned by the world and as it were selflessly obeys its commands by accepting and acting on its definition of what is worthwhile. In being worldly, one does not break away; one does not break one's neck by turning around; one does not think oneself into a position where one can ask oneself why one is pursuing the things one is; one looks at one's life as something obvious and hence does not *look* at one's life at all; one does not try to live from point zero. One knows how to play the games, but not why they exist or why one should play them. Worldliness is conformity, but conformity cannot be self-reliance. Conformity is the main antithesis to self-reliance.

But even if not a duped selflessness but a pure egotism motivates worldly pursuits, Emerson suggests that after a certain near point, an inverse relation exists between egotism and self-reliance, and hence between the self-assertion and self-expression of worldly pursuits and true active self-reliance. Nevertheless, Emerson adores expressiveness and he is willing to admire self-assertiveness. He is not merely prepared to make concessions to inevitable active egotism. He favors it. But he wants the search for power and the desire to display energy to find better channels than those already established in the world, established by and for the world, established by society understood as an unself-examining organization of power ("Society," *Early Lectures, 2*, p. 105). Emerson wants individuals to look at their lives from the perspective of power and energy, but to cut their own channels.

What does this mean? Two principal conceptions emerge as we try to think about Emerson's philosophy of active self-reliance as a whole. They can both be seen, at least provisionally, as conceptions of personal identity, of being in the world. One is the idea that a person's movement through life should be restless, unfixed, an unceasing creation and abandonment of channels and positions. One's identity should be fluid, not easily defined by others or by oneself. The other idea is that one should do one's work in a certain unegotistical spirit. After finding one's vocation, one should do the work that one does best—indeed, work that one was born to do. Obviously there is dissonance between these two ideas. A life of restless movement is a life of perpetual self-finding and self-loss. A life of vocation is willing one thing, a life of perfect adherence to one commitment, even if such adherence is not static, but rather something more like a process of what Emerson calls "unfolding" ("Uses of Great Men," p. 617). I believe that he ranks vocation above movement. Vocation is, as far as I can see, the highest form of active self-reliance in Emerson's philosophy. Before turning to it, I will explore his views on the excellence of a life spent in movement, in restless searching and finding, losing and searching. This, too, is a kind of unfolding. The good life, by this account, is the life of growth or change.

The basic text in which Emerson impersonates self-reliance as the self-trust permitting a person to undergo frequent change is "Circles," in *Essays: First Series*. By common consent, this is one of his greatest essays. In recent days, it has called forth some splendid commentary from Stanley Cavell. I would like only to say a few things in order to continue sketching the kinds of active self-reliance that I find in Emerson. The first matter to notice is that the essay does not specify activities or pursuits that are appropriate to the self-reliant individual. Rather what is at stake is perhaps one's identity, understood as the spirit in which one undertakes to live a life of actions and relations. The active pursuit of identity surpasses worldly pursuits—pursuits of tangible results—provided that it is done in a spirit attempting to emulate the nature of things, which is interpreted quite selectively in "Circles" as indefinite mutability, and expressed in the answer Emerson has nature make to those who complain about its shortcomings: "I grow" ("The Method of Nature," p. 121). Emerson's deeper sense of the nature of things—that the world is comprised of permanent and antagonistic forces—is therefore suspended for the occasion:

> There are no fixtures in nature. The universe is fluid and volatile. Permanence is but a word of degrees . . . Everything looks permanent until its secret is known. ("Circles," pp. 403-404)

Change is the law of life, and we consequently obey the law if we choose to live a life of change, to live life as welcomed change. He says:

> Valor consists in the power of self-recovery, so that a man cannot have his flank turned, cannot be out-generalled, but put him where you will, he stands. (p. 407)

Unless we outflank ourselves, circumstances will outflank us. Our motion is, in part, preemptive. The implication is that only conformists try to be fixed, and that in a democratic society, where change is allowed as a matter of principle, only conformists crave fixity. Thinking that they can conform to democracy, they betray it. Thus the self-reliant personal identity is not really an identity but something more like an unlimited repertory. "The only sin is limitation" (p. 406).

The complication in Emerson's account is that living a life of change is not simply going from one thing to another, accumulating heterogeneous experiences and thereby putting a life together by means of unpurposive addition. Ideally, one aims to draw a circle around oneself, succeeds in drawing it, but then draws another circle around the previous one. Drawing circles signifies the effort to attain completion—that is, perfection. One aspires to an admirable fixedness of identity, and one is also disposed to grow bored with what seems fixed. But change is genuine only if it is not sought for itself, but is accepted for the sake of an idea of completeness or perfection. New courage arises from new dissatisfaction, but it is a courage that dares to try to achieve satisfaction. The memory of failure must become a source of energy; hope for success must be sincere. One must try to acquire a rounded identity and persist in the effort, and although one must always fail, perhaps one will ascend into a higher state, which is itself fluid. One spirals. The very energy that goes into the effort to achieve perfection is an indication that the results of the effort will eventually be found unsatisfactory. Emerson says, "That which is made instructs how to make better" (p. 412). A self- reliant individual is disposed to see around himself or herself, to glimpse a new possibility of experience, and to jump out of the self-enclosure. "Nature, a mountain walk, always gives us to suspect the poverty of life, and we believe that we have run along only one thread of experience out of millions of varied threads which we were competent to combine with that single-string of ours" (*Journals, 8,* p. 419).

The point is not to outlive hope. "People wish to be settled; only so far as they are unsettled is there any hope for them" ("Circles," p. 413). The only security lies in transition: "the coming only is sacred" (p. 413). The attributes one is most proud of in oneself must be discarded, because the "terror of reform is the discovery that we must cast away our virtues" (p. 411). The mere fact that I am loved or admired means that a mistake has been made. "She was heaven whilst he pursued her as a star: she cannot be heaven, if she stoops to such a one as he" ("Nature," p. 553). In a cruel passage Emerson says:

> The sweet of nature is love; yet if I have a friend I am tormented by my imperfections. The love of me accuses the other party. If he were high enough to slight me, then could I love him, and rise by my affection to new heights. ("Circles," p. 406)

The thought of living by the code compressed in these words is dizzying. One must outgrow the love that has enabled one to grow. "A man's growth is seen in the successive choirs of his friends" (p. 406). It would seem that I can grow only by being loved, but it would also seem that I can love only what disdains me. I also helplessly disdain what loves me:

> When much intercourse with a friend has supplied us with a standard of excellence, and has increased our respect for the resources of God who

thus sends a real person to outgo our ideal; when he has, moreover, become an object of thought, and, whilst his character retains all its unconscious effect, is converted in the mind into solid and sweet wisdom,—it is a sign to us that his office is closing, and he is commonly withdrawn from our sight in a short time. (*Nature,* p. 31)

A brief, grim conclusion follows from a tremendous buildup in the prose, just as in the pattern of life that is urged. One can barely hear Emerson's later claim that "Welfare requires one or two companions of intelligence, probity, and grace, to wear out life with . . . these we are always in search of" ("Social Aims," *Letters,* p. 89). Life is a process of shucking off and putting on. "The way of life is wonderful; it is by abandonment," he says in one of his most famous sentences ("Circles," p. 414).

I grow by being loved, but perhaps even more by being rejected:

Dear to us are those who love us . . . they enlarge our life; but dearer are those who reject us as unworthy, for they add another life: they build a heaven before us whereof we had not dreamed, and thereby supply to us new powers out of the recesses of the spirit, and urge us to new and unattempted performances. ("New England Reformers," p. 604)

I must convert my being rejected into—not exactly my opportunity to reject, but into, say, mutual abandonment.

The irony is that by the abandonments we initiate or exploit we more nearly approach ourselves. The more we change, the more coherent we become, despite appearances. In talking about the advantages of calamity, Emerson says:

The changes which break up at short intervals the prosperity of men are advertisements of a nature whose law is growth . . . In proportion to the vigor of the individual these revolutions are frequent, until in some happier mind they are incessant and all worldly relations hang very loosely about him, becoming as it were a transparent fluid membrane through which the living form is seen, and not, as in most men, an indurated heterogeneous fabric of many dates and no settled character, in which the man is imprisoned. ("Compensation," pp. 301-302)

Growth means voluntarily discarding the less voluntarily or involuntarily acquired crust of custom. What is left? Perhaps nothing more than an ever greater appetite to be undefined. The goal is to solidify the sense that:

Man was made for conflict, not for rest. In action is his power; not in his goals but in his transitions man is great. Instantly he is dwarfed by self-indulgence. The truest state of mind rested in becomes false. ("Natural History of Intellect," *Natural History,* p. 60)

Emerson's tone is Faustian; Goethe's *Faust* is a book he respected.

Where is the end in sight? No end is in sight because our life is only an apprenticeship. It is "an apprenticeship to the truth that around every circle another can be drawn" ("Circles," p. 403). For a self-reliant individual the only rest from apprenticeship is in attaining not mastery but death. Until then, life is learning and forgetting and learning again the truth of incessantly available possibility that is lodged in one's storage of power.

The only motive at all commensurate with his force, is the ambition to discover *by exercising* his latent power . . . The true culture is a discipline so universal as to demonstrate that no part of a man was made in vain. ("Introductory," *Human Culture, Early Lectures, 2,* p. 215)

In a passage that sounds like Whitman before Whitman got started, Emerson says:

I am not careful to justify myself . . . But lest I should mislead any when I have my own head and obey my whims, let me remind the reader that I am only an experimenter . . . I unsettle all things. No facts are to me sacred; none are profane; I simply experiment, an endless seeker with no past at my back. ("Circles," pp. 411-412)

Writing essays is here merged with living a life. Emerson uncharacteristically breaks into the apparently sincere confessional mode because he anticipates that some reader will accuse him of Pyrrhonism, "an equivalence and indifference of all actions" and will impute to him the unpleasant thought that even out of crimes "we shall construct the temple of the true God." Emerson answers that reader with the word "experimenter" (pp. 411-412). It is not easy to say whether he hides from his implications or is underlining them. But the passage is stirring, and its effect is not blunted when Emerson invokes a principle of "fixture or stability in the soul." For what is the soul? It is the eternal generator; its "central life" is superior to all it generates and it "contains all circles" (p. 412). The self is larger than anything it creates. No creation excels the power that created it or can satisfy the fixed soul in which the power of movement is lodged. But dissatisfied with not creating, the soul creates, and then it is also dissatisfied with what it creates, and so it creates anew, again and again. What Emerson says about great works of art is also what he would have us feel about all works, all deeds, all states of being: "They create a want they do not gratify. They instantly point us to somewhat better than themselves" ("Introductory," *Human Culture, Early Lectures, 2*, p. 217). The great philosopher of affirmation is concurrently the great teacher of dissatisfaction, even disappointment. In each of us, the energies of hope should make room for the emotion of philosophical acceptance of the world as it must be.

I think that the life sketched in "Circles" provides the most benign version of the surmise that we exist to realize a will to power. It is benign because it is free of praise for a situation in which self-reliant individuals define themselves as competitors who must take joy in the defeat of their rivals, or desire to see themselves as collaborators in a common project of subduing and exploiting outsiders who are less courageous and who therefore allow themselves to be victimized. The Emersonian image of the will to power posits, instead, a world in which the circles made by a person intersect those of other persons only with their consent. Otherwise, one's experiments are carried out not so much in isolation as in the interstices of social forms, or in one's little world, or on the road, or on the edge.

No doubt Emerson is keenly aware that the will to power, even (or especially) in the most unexpressed persons, can be limitless in its intentions or fantasies, which is why he hopes that all people will be encouraged in it:

> For nature wishes every thing to remain itself; and whilst every individual strives to grow and exclude, and to exclude and grow, to the extremities of the universe, and to impose the law of its being on every other creature, Nature steadily aims to protect each against every other. Each is self-defended. ("Uses of Great Men," p. 628)

One of the horrors of slavery is that it allows the master "the voluptuousness of holding a human being in his absolute control." The "love of power" is the "bitter element" in the institution of slavery ("Address: Emancipation in the British West Indies," *Miscellanies,* p. 118).

I do not find in Emerson theoretical praise for a person who acts out of character in a radical sense, who acts against his grain or takes sides against himself, or who changes because of a strong conviction that he has been in serious error. These phenomena seem contrary to unfolding. To think self-reliantly is to think against oneself, but one cannot expect or be expected to act that way. Emerson did act against himself when he took up the abolitionist duties of citizenship in the 1850s. But interrupting the arc of one's circle is not what Emerson praises. The life of movement is nevertheless a life of risk. Experimentation is life as an adventure; being the hero of one's life means taking on the world, not merely as something that needs resistance, but as something that needs definition as one's own, one's rightful place. And in the process, the contribution to others that experimenters make is the inspiration they give by their exemplary courageous self-reliance. They invite the more timid to live more.

If, however, Emerson is a theorist of active self-reliance as the search for power and the display of energy, he is also a theorist of compensation. This is a complex idea in Emerson's version. The most relevant aspect of it for the way of life projected in "Circles" is compensation as the fate that must be endured by an actively self-reliant individual prone to repeated efforts of ever more ample self-definition. The net result of the law of compensation is that the adventurous or experimental person is eventually "outflanked." He or she is encircled, hemmed in, limited, thrown back. From one perspective, there is no progress, no ascendant movement, no breaking out. At the start of "Circles," Emerson says that the form of the circle is read by us all our lives. The moral drawn from that fact in this essay is that "every action admits of being outdone" (p. 403). But a different and adversarial moral can be drawn from "the circular or compensatory character of every human action" (p. 403). If what is circular is compensatory, it is not progressive. In "Compensation" (*Essays: First Series*); in "Uriel," a poem from the mid-1840s; in *The Conduct of Life* and elsewhere, Emerson struggles to put forth the moral idea of compensation. Its preponderant effect is a qualification of his exuberance, even though it also attempts to convert despair into hope.

In the poem, it is said of Uriel, one of the young gods, that he:

Gave his sentiment divine
Against the being of a line.
'Line in nature is not found;
Unit and universe are round;
In vain produced, all rays return;
Evil will bless, and ice will burn.' (*Works, 9,* p. 14)

Uriel is speaking to his fellows in Paradise, among the Pleiads. The scene is dreamlike; the population is a mixture of gods and devils, seraphs and war gods; it is as if heaven, hell, paradise, imagination, and dreaming are all interchangeable, as are the good and bad superhuman forces. These equivalences—not exactly Pyrrhonist, but actually more radical than any Pyrrhonism—already imply the principle of compensation, because everything contains or tends to turn into its opposite. This must mean, to begin with, that "the first lesson of history is the good of evil" ("Considerations by the Way," *The Conduct of Life,* p. 1083). Evil helplessly turns good. Emerson says:

> Nature is upheld by antagonism. We acquire the strength we have overcome . . . The sun were insipid, if the universe were not opaque. And the glory of character is in affronting the horrors of depravity, to draw thence new nobilities of power . . . And evermore in the world is this marvellous balance of beauty and disgust, magnificence and rats. (p. 1084)

So far, then, we have the Emerson who tries to unmask suffering and evil in order to reveal their helpfulness—a project he executes with a faultless power of impersonation, or, if you will, with a chilling literal-mindedness, in the lecture from 1844 on "The Tragic."

But there must be some reason that, in the poem on Uriel, the teaching of Uriel withers his beauty, and his words cause a shudder to run around the sky, and a "forgetting wind" passes over the celestial beings, inducing them to be conveniently oblivious of his words. Compensation is the hardest teaching. Why? The poem ends by suggesting that gods are not willing to admit "the good of evil born." Nevertheless, this truth offends only moralists. And Emerson compensates for this offense to the moralists by including within the theory of compensation the reassurance that every wrong done is paid for, just as every good effort is rewarded, and every unlucky disadvantage has a corresponding strength. The world is a compensatory economy of inflexible justice. "Justice is not postponed. A perfect equity adjusts its balance in all parts of life" ("Compensation," p. 289). Retribution is scarcely distinguishable from being. "There is a crack in every thing God has made" (p. 292). Yet at the same time, there is "the deep remedial force that underlies all facts" (p. 302). Emerson brings his point home in the language of business when he speaks of "the subtle and inextricable compensation that attaches to property":

> Every thing God hath made has the two faces. Every cent in a dollar covers its worth and also covers its evil . . . if so much property, then so much risk; if so much power, then so much danger; if so much revenue, then so much tax . . . All property must and will pay its tax. If it come not by fair means, then it comes by foul. ("Politics," *Early Lectures, 2,* p. 79)

The more pressing truth, the devastating truth, however, is that "line in nature is not found." Good turns into evil, or every gain is a loss. "Eternal compensation" means that every good thing has a "dark side" ("Literature," *Early Lectures, 2,* p. 68). The nature of things is that

> the varieties of condition tend to equalize themselves. There is always some leveling circumstance that puts down the overbearing, the strong, the rich, the fortunate, substantially on the same ground with all others. ("Compensation," p. 288)

This is a teaching of futility, or almost is. The futility here is not that which Emerson takes up in "Experience"—namely the frustration involved in attempting to touch and be touched, reach and be reached, experience and be experienced. Rather the effort to surpass oneself constantly, the effort to discover always new powers in oneself and to remain unpredictable to oneself, may lead one into self-repetition. Seemingly progressive indefiniteness may only be a lifelong recurrence of the same, of going around in a circle. Defeat awaits every exertion, because every exertion has something inaccurate, excessive, in it. "Every excess causes a defect; every defect an excess" (p. 287). The circle of defect and excess seems closed. Audacity is born to fail. Experimentation tends to the presumptuous because it is entwined with self-ignorance. The failure lies not only in natural impermanence but in irresistible self-condemnation. Really, the will to succeed encloses a will to fail, and not only because one grows impatient with success. Even in "Circles," Emerson points to the underside of the will to succeed:

> The great moments of history are the facilitator of performance through the strength of ideas, as the works of genius and religion. "A man," said Oliver Cromwell, "never rises so high as when he knows not whither he is going." Dreams and drunkenness, the use of opium and alcohol are the semblance and counterfeit of this oracular genius, and hence their dangerous attraction for men. For the like reason they ask the aid of wild passions, as in gaming and war, to ape in some manner these flames and generosities of the heart. (p. 414)

These words come right after the great sentence on abandonment and conclude the essay. But I find that they almost cancel the preceding celebration. The line between inspired abandonment and mere delirium is made faint. The "levelling circumstance" to which Emerson points in order to explain the setbacks of exceptional exertion may finally be as much inside the person as in the constitution of the universe. Anyway, experimentation can become exhausting. Indefiniteness may be too great a burden, or the wrong kind of burden, for the actively self-reliant individual to carry. The likely result, much more often than not, would be to find oneself lost in semblances and counterfeits of enlarging movement, with wild passions only aping the sincerity of self-pursuit. Why make your self the work of your life? Why not make work the life of your self? These questions are forced on us by Emerson's theory of compensation, but may not be answered by it.

No matter what one may say, however, about the precariousness of Emerson's commitment to the idea of active self-reliance as indefinite motion outwards, as change in the boundaries of identity, it is not rejected. An individual's life should have periods or moods of abandonment. Abandonment is best when fitful—then one is truly overcome. But Emerson has yet another idea of active self-reliance that I think he ranks higher than this one—in fact, ranks as the highest one of all in his writings: the idea of active self-reliance as finding and doing one's work. To "be what you are" is to pursue not an endless experiment but your vocation. In pursuing one's vocation, one most certainly acts as an individual, as oneself, and also makes the greatest contribution to others, even if not always or not even usually mindful of one's work as a contribution, but rather thinking that in caring for one's work, one is caring for oneself as an object worthy of care, and caring for oneself nonegotistically. Let it be said that Emerson lived life as vocation: he remained as true to his vocation as anyone could desire while refusing experiments in living.

One's work comes out of a purposive (not experimental or adventurous) unfolding of one's powers. "By doing his own work he unfolds himself" ("Spiritual Laws," p. 310). Powers should be concentrated in the work one does. One stays with one's work; one does not abandon it after finding it, though abandonment *to* it is essential to performance. In doing one's work, one goes some way toward uniting what is most deeply present in oneself with what is most resistantly present in the world, while constantly being aware of the difference and the distance between oneself and the world. The world is inchoate until one works on it; human exertion is needed to make the world known; the world responds to the effort; and unless work were necessary, human beings would never know their powers or limits ("Trades and Professions," *Early Lectures, 2,* p. 113). One's work is one's double, not as a friend or lover is or may be, but as a deliberate externalization.

"The common experience," says Emerson,

> is that the man fits himself as well as he can to the customary details of that work or trade he falls into, and tends it as a dog turns a spit. Then is he a part of the machine he moves; the man is lost. Until he can manage to communicate himself to others in his full stature and proportion, he does not yet find his vocation. ("Spiritual Laws," pp. 310-311)

Self-reliant individuals cannot be moved by their machine. They must be self-moved, and thus move in their own direction until they find their work to do. Society may set up constraints to self-choice in occupations, and then be, for a while, insensitive to the results of one's efforts. The shame is that the world is full of involuntary work and hence waste and routine ("Doctrine of the Hands," *Early Lectures, 2,* p. 236). But some are lucky and face the difficulties of vocation. By "doing his work he makes the need felt which he can supply, and creates the taste by which he is enjoyed" ("Spiritual Laws," p. 310). Persistence is necessary. Emerson is aware that temporary defections from one's work are likely. In a general formulation that appears in his discussion of vocation, he says:

We side with the hero, as well read or paint, against the coward and the robber; but we have been ourselves that coward and robber, and shall be again—not in the low circumstance, but in comparison with the grandeurs possible to the soul. ("Spiritual Laws," p. 309)

If determination is needed to find one's vocation and remain with it, the rewards are immense. One both discovers and defines oneself. One shares the attribute of what Emerson calls the Supreme Cause—namely, self-existence. No one is literally self-authored. Rather one comes closest to creating oneself if and when one apprehends, and not too late, the work that is one's own, and then does it. One's being is transmitted, returning to oneself as oneself, even though no result, perhaps, is ever good enough in itself or adequate to express the mere fact of the ability to do work and create what did not exist before. Emerson says:

Self-existence is the attribute of the Supreme Cause, and it constitutes the measure of good by the degree in which it enters into all lower forms. All things real are so by so much virtue as they contain. Commerce, husbandry, hunting, whaling, war, eloquence, personal weight, are somewhat, and engage my respect as examples of its presence and impure action. ("Self-Reliance," p. 272)

Emerson blends divinity and humanity, divine creation and human works, celebration and discontent, in a few lines. Thus, as with God, an individual's performance never ideally represents the performer. Yet if Emerson is to satisfy himself that self-reliance can show itself in enactment, then vocation, though apparently always "impure action," is the best way.

A person's vocation is the work that one can do well or do better than others can, or it is the work that no one else can do. Emerson's formulations vary. "There is one direction to every man in which unlimited space is open to him . . . He finds obstruction on all sides but one" ("Ethics," *Early Lectures, 2,* p. 147). At the same time, he seems insistent that there is something to do that best suits each of us. What is best for us is therefore best for our work. "Society can never prosper," Emerson says, "but must always be bankrupt, until every man does that which he was created to do" ("Wealth," *The Conduct of Life,* p. 1003). And neither can the individual prosper. Unless one does the right work one would not attain the human status. Persons must have a conscious feeling of their necessity if their existence is to be justified in their own eyes. Again, it is not that they must feel useful to others. That sentiment would only make them into instruments. Nor is it the case that their work must directly contribute to the world's welfare. But it must be work free of triviality. "Whatever games are played with us, we must play no games with ourselves" ("Illusions," *The Conduct of Life,* p. 1122).

One must not let one's forces be scattered. By concentration one becomes distinctive. If the doctrine of "Circles" is that the only sin is limitation, then the superior doctrine, the doctrine of vocation, entails that "narrowness" is necessarily involved in concentration, and that concentration surpasses continuous experimentation. Concentration is the best transmutation of one's incurable limitedness of sensibility and capacity to experience. "If you ask what compensation is made for the inevitable narrowness, why, this, that in learning one thing well you learn all things" ("Natural History of Intellect," *Natural History,* p. 51). Though each person is "a partialist" in doing what he or she does through a "self-conceit," every person is also justified in such individuality because each is of an immense nature. " . . . and now I add," Emerson says, "That every man is a universe also":

> as our earth, whilst it spins on its own axis, spins all the time around the sun through the celestial spaces, so the least of its rational children, the most dedicated to his private affair, works out, though as it were under a disguise, the universal problem. ("Nominalist and Realist," pp. 585, 586)

No account of Emerson's idea of vocation can, however, omit mention of the striking reflection on the division of labor in "The American Scholar." It is not so much a counterweight to the idea of vocation as a reminder that, after all, contrary to the reassurances given, narrowness is narrowness. Emerson admires versatility because the division of labor has become so special that "if anything gets out of order," the workman is "helpless to repair it" (*Journals, 14,* p. 400). "Now that the machine is so perfect, the engineer is nobody" ("Works and Days," *Society and Solitude,* pp. 165). An ancient fable instructs us, he says, that originally there was Man, not men, but the gods divided Man into men so that "he might be more helpful to himself." Now "you must take the whole society to find the whole man" ("The American Scholar," pp. 53-54).

> The state of society is one in which the members have suffered amputation from the trunk, and strut about so many walking monsters,—a good finger, a neck, a stomach, an elbow, but never a man. Man is thus metamorphosed into a thing, into many things . . . The priest becomes a form; the attorney a statute book; the mechanic, a machine; the sailor, a rope of a ship. ("The American Scholar," pp. 53-54)

How does each one of us become whole again, become Man doing this or that, rather than remain an embodied function? Emerson has no everyday answer. Only when each of us is thinking is each of us Man. To be a professional thinker, however, is not the same as having the vocation of thinking. If we press Emerson for an everyday answer, all he can offer is the hope that a worker in the world will, by an act of reconception, give "an ideal worth to his work" and not be "ridden by the routine of his craft" or allow his soul to be "subject to dollars" (p. 54).

The narrowness of one's work, in any case, reflects the fact that a person's very uniqueness or genius ("the peculiar quality that differences him from every other") is "a selecting principle." Emerson refers to "that mysterious emphasis" that each person places on all events and situations and hence on his memory, and that "quite without any effort of his will" determines the choices of his life ("The School," *Early Lectures, 3,* pp. 36-37).

Thus mindful of inevitable and profitable limitation, one does one's work, which must give an example of powers and talents under the control of a life-shaping commitment. One's work becomes one's self. Emerson says:

> Life is hardly respectable,—is it? if it has no generous, guaranteeing task, no duties or affections, that constitute a necessity of existing. Every man's task is his life-preserver. The conviction that his work is dear to God and cannot be spared, defends him. ("Worship," *The Conduct of Life,* p. 1071)

Notice that the work is dear to God, which can be another way of saying that the standard of usefulness is not directly social or even moral. The work contributes to preserving the sense of the world's possibilities, and it is a manifestation of what any one human being is capable of. Beyond that lies the simple, individualistic and not quite egotistical notion that from doing work for its own sake one will derive a supreme pleasure. Emerson makes his point in two rhetorical questions:

Is there no loving of knowledge, and of art, and of our design, for itself alone? Cannot we please ourselves with performing our work, or gaining truth and power, without being praised for it? ("Success," *Society and Solitude, Works, 7,* p. 294)

The basis of Emerson's view of vocation, as already indicated, is that every individual is unique. It is one's uniqueness that makes one indispensable to others, and irreplaceable, simultaneously allowing one to live properly with oneself. From one's uniqueness as an individual flows the uniqueness of one's work. Emerson's idea of individual uniqueness is centered in the idea that Hannah Arendt later calls "natality": the world is new to each of us, and each of us is new in it. Out of this encounter comes the ability to say or do what has never appeared before. Emerson formulates our newness in this way:

> every man, with whatever family resemblances, has a new countenance, new manner, new voice, new thoughts, and new character. Whilst he shares with all mankind the gift of reason, and the moral sentiment, there is a teaching for him from within, which is leading him in a new path, and, the more it is trusted, separates and signalizes him, while it makes him more important and necessary to society. We call this specialty the *bias* of each individual. And none of us will ever accomplish anything excellent or commanding except when he listens to this whisper which is heard by him alone. ("Greatness," *Letters,* pp. 306-307)

(In "Natural History of Intellect," [*Natural History,* p. 10] Emerson calls this "bias" each person's "angle of vision," and equates one's life with that angle.) "The divine," Emerson says, "resides in the new." That is why infancy is, as he calls it, "the perpetual messiah" (*Nature,* p. 46). "The wise man ever finds himself conscious of knowing nothing but being just ready to begin to know. He is as if just born and ready to ask the first questions" ("Modern Aspects of Letters," *Early Lectures, 3,* p. 383).

It is only when we persist in our work that we disclose our originality:

> But there remains the indefeasible persistency of the individual to be himself . . . Every mind is different; and the more it is unfolded, the more pronounced is that difference . . . And what is originality? It is being, being one's self, and reporting accurately what we see and are. ("Quotation and Originality," *Letters,* pp. 200-201)

Emerson is trying to democratize genius, or greatness.

> Greatness,—what is it? Is there not some injury to us, some insult in the
> word? What we commonly call greatness is only such in our barbarous or
> infant experience. ("Greatness," *Letters,* p. 302)

The truly great are not the famous warriors. Greatness is faith in one's
uniqueness; such faith is self-respect. "Self-respect is the early form in
which greatness appears" (p. 303). If one has self-respect, one "learns to
be at home with himself" (p. 307). I must point out that whereas mental
self-reliance requires only being "a guest" in one's own thought, active
self-reliance in the form of vocation requires one to be "at home" with
oneself. This difference of imperatives is another indication of the superiority of mental to active self-reliance.

Emerson says in "Spiritual Laws" that "Every man has this call of
power to do somewhat unique, and no man has any other call" (p. 310).
He tries to persuade his audience that each of us has something to do that
is worth doing, and that if we do not do it, we die. Doing one's work until
the end is the only linear forward movement; it is an audacity unravaged
by the laws of compensation, unlike the audacities of "immeasurable
credulity" inherent in always trying to draw a greater circle than the last
one ("Nominalist and Realist," p. 586). "There is no tax on the good of
virtue" ("Compensation," p. 300). The immense cost of doing one's own
work counts for nothing because no price can be placed on being oneself.

The idea of vocation is therefore the highest form of practical self-
reliant activity. Work is one's work, but one's work is also work on the
self. Work exceeds the play, if you will, magnificently urged in "Circles."
And it is free of the contaminations of egotism or its simulacrum that
afflict the projects of pursuing wealth and political power and social
standing. I do acknowledge, however, that Emerson sometimes depicts
these wordly pursuits also as vocations. But his characterizations of one's
vocation as the work that emerges out of one's uniqueness do not typically
correspond to worldly exertions, which are impure or low, or ruled by the
world's discipline. What then are the best vocations?

It is hard to infer Emerson's meaning. "The soul," he says, "strives
amain to live and work through all things. It would be the only fact"
("Compensation," p. 290). At the limit, this means that one transforms the

world by one's activity in it. One remakes it in one's image. Who has come
closest to doing so? Emerson's answer seems to be Jesus, though he does
not name him in this context. About the life of Jesus, he says, "This great
defeat is hitherto our highest fact." But Emerson contends that "the mind
requires a victory to the senses" ("Character," *Essays: Second Series,*
p. 508). Force of character would convert "judge, jury, soldier and king."
But such strength not even Jesus had. What then? Emerson gives the prize
to Jesus, nevertheless:

> when that love which is all-suffering, all-abstaining, all-inspiring, which
> has vowed to itself that it will be a wretch and also a fool in this world
> sooner than soil its white hands by any compliances, comes into our streets
> and houses—only the pure and aspiring can know its face, and the only
> compliment they can pay it is to own it. (p. 509)

Jesus is the model of faithfulness in vocation, but he is hardly a model
any of us can expect to follow, not because he is divine but because he is
humanly perfect, not all-too-human. That aspect, too, is part of his defeat.
Perhaps Emerson's teaching is that defeat is the inescapable destiny of
activity in the world? No, that is not what he wants us to take as his final
meaning, though it may be what he feels. He says:

> My work may be of none, but I must not think it of none, or I shall not do
> it with impunity. In like manner, there is throughout nature something
> mocking, something that leads us on and on, but arrives nowhere, keeps
> no faith with us. All promise outruns the performance. ("Nature," pp.
> 551-552)

The height of Emerson's chagrin at the insufficiency of action, even in
the form of vocation, to display the fullness of anyone's character comes
out in a passage from the essay "Politics":

> The gladiators in the lists of power feel, through all their frocks of force
> and simulation, the presence of worth. I think the very strife of trade and
> ambition is confession of this divinity; and successes in those fields are
> the poor amends, the fig-leaf with which the shamed soul attempts to hide
> its nakedness. I find the like unwilling homage in all quarters. It is because
> we know how much is due from us that we are impatient to show some
> petty talent as a substitute for worth. We are haunted by a conscience of

this right to grandeur of character, and are false to it. But each of us has some talent, can do somewhat useful, or graceful or formidable, or amusing or lucrative. That we do as an apology to others and to ourselves for not reaching the mark of a good and equal life. But it does not satisfy *us.* . . . . Most persons of ability meet in society with a kind of tacit appeal. Each seems to say, "I am not all here." . . . Surely nobody would be a charlatan who could afford to be sincere. (pp. 568-569)

It is hard to say what Emerson leaves for self-reliant work, given this radical dissatisfaction. What does it mean for a person to be "all here"? Is it just like being a rose?

The trouble is that his descriptions of vocation usually seem to make the most sense when they are read as referring to mental activity, which was Emerson's own vocation. Individual uniqueness is one's special power to see and to say; it is a power of observation and distillation. It is as if true expressiveness could only be mental, and what one expresses is not oneself but the world in which one finds oneself. We exist to produce the best possible sentences, to say the world as unegotisically or impersonally as possible; yet inevitably, and desirably, each one of us says something different because each one of us is new and meets the new. What we express comes out as a perspective. Each one of us has "some incommunicable sagacity" ("Natural History of Intellect," *Natural History,* p. 32). The incommunicable must inform the communicated.

I know that it may be exasperating to keep returning to mental activity as the only real domain of self-reliance. But I think that this is the point Emerson always makes, although he comes at it, or comes upon it, in many different ways. Everyone's vocation is to philosophize. Nothing is like it. The gulf between success in thinking and success in doing is vast because the world is too hard for self-reliance to be shown with much success in anything but mental activity; yet the world is, of course, inconceivably wondrous and hence worth the exertions, which self-reliant mental activity makes, to receive and affirm it, and to do so being aware of its uncorrectable imperfections. But I do not intend to efface the significance for Emerson of active self-reliance. The temptation to efface it must be resisted by us just as strenuously as Emerson tries to resist it (but not more strenuously than he). Many kinds of engagement with the world certainly do show traces and more than traces of the qualities he thinks proper to self-reliant individuals. And the best activities will be those that the more

they are pursued as vocations the more gratifying they become. They are
the most real to the self and help to make the self feel most real.

*   *   *

I propose that mental self-reliance—thinking one's thoughts and thinking them through in the modes of perception, contemplation, and retrospection—is the *model* of active self-reliance. Acting self-reliantly is
analogous to thinking self-reliantly. The link comes from the idea that
thinking is close to prayer, is like prayer, though in a secular sense. But
action can also be like prayer. In "Self-Reliance," Emerson says that it is
open to us to see "prayer in all action. The prayer of the farmer kneeling
in his field to weed it, the prayer of the rower kneeling with the stroke of
his oar, are true prayers heard throughout nature, though for cheap ends"
(p. 276). I here make use of this formulation, cited before, to suggest that
any activity, any work, when done like prayer—when done after the
model of concentrated self-reliant thinking—can be a vocation, even if it
has no philosophical thinking in it, even if the thinking it contains is only
practical thinking, even if it is done "for cheap ends." Similarly, any work
can be done poetically. In words to which I have also already referred,
Emerson suggests that any craft or trade can be "handled poetically,"
which means that the worker stands superior to facts and masters them,
rather than apprehending them through a sense of their beauty ("Politics,"
Early Lectures, 3, p. 239). What do these analogies to prayer and poetry
point to? The spirit of vocation would be an unegotistical concern to draw
from oneself the best one has, and to do so for the sake of the work. "This
is the heroism of a calling, to prefer the work to the reward" ("Trades and
Professions," *Early Lectures, 2,* pp. 124-125). Doing one's own work
properly means discovering that one could not imagine oneself, as oneself, doing anything else. Work and self merge. One works on and cares
for oneself just by working for the sake of the work. One's work becomes
oneself.

Finally, perhaps Emerson's suggestion is that one's ideal vocation is to
build one's character and remain true to it for as long as possible. This
work on the self does not proceed by continuous experiment or adventure
(as in "Circles") but by an ever more intense search for integrity. "Be what
you are" is a precept of self-consistency amid tremendous resistances and

obstacles, both in finding oneself and keeping oneself. The precept means that one should try to be "what cannot be skipped, or dissipated, or undermined" ("Illusions," *The Conduct of Life*, p. 1122). If one is oneself and not a socially constructed collage, one's uniqueness is revealed. At the same time, one stands for something. The world always needs examples of integrity. In seeing character as vocation, we avoid excessive intellectualism and we also repel delusions about the chances of an objective, substantive, monumental achievement that is truly one's own. One's character may show itself in any particular activity one wants to do or must do, as well as in the whole range of activities that one chooses or is driven to take up as especially appropriate for one's unfolding in one's specific vocation. Work exists for the self, provided the work is done for its own sake and on its own best terms; but the self exists for more than work. One's character is one's manner of being, one's continuous style. To work on it is to refuse to think that one just exists, like a rose in bloom. One must work to persist as oneself. One neither invites nor declines challenge to one's integrity. Identity is discipline. One takes the world seriously by taking oneself seriously. One wants to be the best one can. One's character is an offering to the world in the sense that an example of self-search and self-finding is being presented. To interpret Emerson I can do no better than quote a passage from an interview Foucault gave a few months before his death:

> Let us take for example Socrates. . . . He is truly the man who cares for others. That is the particular position of the philosopher. But let us say it simply: in the case of the free man, I think that the assumption of all this morality was that the one who cared for himself correctly found himself, by that very fact, in a measure to behave correctly in relationship to others and for others. A city where everyone would be correctly concerned for self would be a city that would be doing well, and it would find therein the ethical principle of its stability. But I don't think that one can say that the Greek who cares for himself should first of all care for others. . . . One must not have the care for others precede the care for the self. The care for self takes moral precedence in the measure that the relationship to self takes ontological precedence. (J. Bernauer and D. Rasmussen, eds., *The Final Foucault*, 1988, p. 7)

Foucault ends where Emerson begins and ends.

6

Self-Reliance, Politics, and Society

A t this point, a reasonable question may arise. What provision does Emerson make for a self-reliant individual to work with others, to cooperate and collaborate? No doubt the very idea of association disturbs self-reliant people when association moves out of a small circle of friends and includes numbers of people, many of them strangers or only acquaintances. When association is extended even more to one's numerous fellow citizens, the condition of self-reliance becomes all the more uncertain. Unfolding one's powers, becoming and staying what one is, living a life that one defines for oneself—all these conceptualizations fit uneasily with associative activity, if they fit at all. Systematic association is a disfigurement, a loss of integrity.

> People wrap themselves up in disguises, and the sincere man is hard to reach. A man is concealed in his nation, concealed in his party, concealed in his fortune, and estate, concealed in his office, in his profession, concealed in his body at last, and it is hard to find out his pure nature and will. They speak and act in each of these relations after the use and wont of those conditions. They talk as Americans, as Republicans . . . each cunningly hiding under these wearisome commonplaces the character and

flavor which is all that can really make him interesting and valuable to us. Of course, he only half acts,—talks with his lips and not his heart. (Notes to "Courage," *Society and Solitude,* p. 431)

At the same time, working with others may mean that each person in the group aims to make a direct contribution to the well-being of the group, oneself included. Yet Emerson is wary of the organized effort to compel or even elicit continuous benevolence from individuals. Both the prudential motive and the moral motive have a necessary place in every individual life and in the psychological economy of every complex society. Nevertheless, active self-reliance, as Emerson conceptualizes it, is not, for the most part, motivated morally or prudentially, though it must be framed by both morality and prudence. The motives of individualism are, so to speak, existential.

There are obstacles, then, to reconciling active self-reliance and working with others. How does Emerson deal with these obstacles?

Before attempting an answer to this question, we should notice that in one essay, "Manners" (*Essays: Second Series*), where Emerson impersonates aspects of the idea of worldliness—fashion, manner, decorum—he makes a fine case for suppressing active self-reliance and, instead, encouraging conformity to codes or styles for the sake of cooperating to maintain the fabric of elegance in being. Emerson eventually allows, even in this essay, the reassertion of creative individuality as sanely disruptive, but for a time he lets the idea of worldliness appear attractively. But I believe this essay is aberrant. The system of exquisite manners has no general significance in Emerson's thought; it is not a model for other activity. In any case, taking part in a system of manners (ordinary politeness is not at issue) is, or should be, more like playing a game by the rules or performing a ritual correctly than living a life. As long as games and rituals are seen for what they are, they bring only a little benefit or a little harm to self-reliance.

A passage from "New England Reformers" (*Essays: Second Series*) contains the gist of Emerson's usual disposition:

These new associations are composed of men and women of superior talents and sentiments; yet it may be easily questioned whether . . . the members will not necessarily be fractions of men, because each finds that he cannot enter it without some compromise. Friendship and association are very fine things, and a grand phalanx of the best of the human race, banded for some catholic object: yes, excellent; but remember that no society can ever be so large as one man. He, in his friendship, in his natural and momentary associations, doubles or multiplies himself; but in the hour in which he mortgages himself to two or ten or twenty, he dwarfs himself below the stature of one. (p. 598)

Emerson passes this judgment in the course of considering small, communal societies started in Massachusetts on the principles of Saint-Simon or Fourier or Robert Owen. (It is surprising that Emerson briefly flirted with the idea of living in the Fourierist Brook Farm community.) He intends to apply what he says about these societies to all associations beyond those of intimate friendship, love, and plain good neighborliness. I think that the key consideration is that by mortgaging or pledging oneself to others, by committing oneself to defer to the preponderant will and judgment of others for the sake of some common purpose, by embarking on the relationship of solidarity, one may dwarf oneself. Movements for reform fall under the same individualist skepticism as experiments in communal living. Emerson insists:

The union is only perfect when all the uniters are isolated. It is the union of friends who live in different streets or towns. Each man, if he attempts to join himself to others, is on all sides cramped and diminished of his proportion; and the stricter the union the smaller and the more pitiful he is. (p. 599)

Emerson preaches "the distrust of numbers" when numbers are zealous to improve society ("Lecture on the Times," p. 162).

It could be asked, Does not the urgency of reform—to leave aside communal experiments—override concern for the individualistic independence of the reformers? Indeed, can't reformers find realization of their individuality, employment for their active self-reliance, in lending—giving—themselves to movements of reform? Can't reformers discover new energies and unsuspected talents in themselves? Emerson gives little to the good effects of reformist participation on the individual's unfolding. He does not find in the average reformer the apparent selflessness that is actually a commitment to his or her own integrity. There is shrinkage into monomania, and then into reaction.

> To every reform, in proportion to its energy, early disgusts are incident, so that the disciple is surprised at the very hour of his first triumphs, with chagrins, and sickness, and a general distrust: so that he shuns his associates, hates the enterprise which lately seemed so fair, and meditates to cast himself into the arms of that society and manner of life which he had newly abandoned with so much pride and hope. ("The Method of Nature," p. 127)

If the reform is to be genuine, the reformer must first be self-reformed. It is not clear, however, that Emerson thinks that a self-reformed person will find it sensible to devote himself or herself to projects of reform, which often appear to be projects for the reform of the character of others as much as for the reform of practices and institutions. The unreformed cannot reform the unreformed; all must reform themselves. He says:

> The criticism and attack on institutions which we have witnessed, has made one thing plain, that society gains nothing whilst a man, not himself renovated, attempts to renovate things around him: he has become tediously good in some particular, but negligent or narrow in the rest; and hypocrisy and vanity are often the disgusting result. ("New England Reformers," p. 596)

Emerson provides the sketch of a sociology of formal associations for reform:

> A society of 20,000 members is formed for the introduction of Christianity into India or the South Sea. This is not the same thing as if twenty thousand persons without formal cooperation, had conceived a vehement desire for the instruction of those foreign parts. In that case, each had turned the whole attention of the Reason, that is, the quite infinite force of one man, to the matter, and sought by what means he, in his place, could work with most avail on this point. ("Society," *Early Lectures, 2,* p. 106)

The end is compromised or lost in regard for the organization.

> But in our formal association, how much machinery! How much friction! The material integument is so much that the spiritual child is overlaid and lost. . . . the least streamlet of the vast contributions of the public trickles down at last to the healing of the evil. (p. 106)

And the pressure exerted by an organization on nonmembers to sign pledges or join up is "using numbers, that is, mobs and bodies, and disusing principles" ("Society," *Early Lectures, 2,* p. 107). Emerson would hate himself for going along: "If I yield to this force, I degrade myself and have only exchanged one vice for another, self-indulgence for fear, which it is to be presumed was not the intention of the society" (p. 106).

But the question persists: Are there not institutions so dreadful that what matters is their reform or abolition, not any other consideration? Emerson pays tribute to the spirit of dissent and to the conscientious protest against the ingrained abuses of American society. "Man the Reformer" (1841) is a powerful indictment of prevailing practices, centered in the maldistribution of property: "Of course, whilst another man has no land, my title to mine, your title to yours, is at once vitiated" (pp. 138-139). But Emerson, throughout the 1840s, looks for remedy to individual exertions, to personal reform or material improvement, to self-help or the practice of "economy" (in the full sense later elaborated by Thoreau) (p. 144). Emerson also tries to establish so great a need of reform as to make efforts to achieve it quixotic. In addressing those who harp on one deficiency, he says:

> Do not be so vain of your one objection. Do you think there is only one? Alas! my good friend, there is no part of society or of life better than any part. All our things are right and wrong together. The wave of evil washes all our institutions alike. ("New England Reformers," p. 596)

The wave of evil does not wash over, it washes.

With the passage of the Fugitive Slave Law of 1850, Emerson embarks on a lengthy episode of agitation for one reform: the containment or abolition of slavery. This spreading evil—this evil which is truly evil, not only apparently so—forces him to change his attitude on the subject of associating for reform. He does his share by speaking his mind and trying to persuade others to a common anti-slavery cause. What is remarkable is not that Emerson frequently makes public speeches against slavery and even campaigns in 1851 for a particular anti-slavery candidate, John Gorham Palfrey. (Even in the denunciation of slavery he can be philosophically respectful of the fateful and as it were helpless enmeshment of slaveowners in their evil.) The aberration is that he urges solidarity—indeed mobilization—on others, and, when the occasion arises, does not shrink from advocating violence in the effort to destroy slavery. That profound change is a deviation from his theory of self-reliance, not its transformation. Or, we can say that Emerson accepts the sacrifices of every sort—including the abandonment of aspirations of free persons to self-reliance—which are needed to give all Americans, not just some, the chance for self reliance. Perhaps a society has no self-reliance anywhere in it if there are slaves anywhere in it. But before this change in, or suspension of, Emerson's teaching takes place, he discountenances association as solidarity.

There must be association, but proper terms are needed so that no dwarfing results and practical self-reliance remains intact. Are proper terms ever really possible? I would concentrate my discussion of this question by exploring Emerson's thinking about citizenship and political life. I will then return to the issue of slavery.

Can you be politically active and still be self-reliant? Citizenship is enacted in a political system or in defiance of it. Emerson's acts of citizenship as well as his reflections on the meaning of citizenship take place in and are framed by American democracy. That the democracy is radically incomplete, that it is stained by slavery, exclusions, and territorial rapacity, is precisely what leads Emerson to produce most of his political writings. But protest is not the totality of his political thought. He also thinks about what an unstained democracy would be, and does so as an adherent. He may not say explicitly enough or often enough that his doctrine of self-reliance in all its kinds, mental and active, is a democratically-inspired doctrine, a doctrine unthinkable outside democracy and that also signifies the culmination and the spiritual reason for the being of democracy. But that thought is there, sometimes on the surface of his work, and the rest of the time not far beneath it.

It must be conceded that before the slavery crisis in the 1850s permanently changes Emerson's political sensibility, he can speak with a certain lightness of his commitment to democracy. In "Politics," which is not an impersonation of the dignity of politics, but of the sentiments of anti-politics, he makes democracy into something merely congenial, not something morally imperative:

> In this country, we are very vain of our political institutions, which are singular in this, that they spring, within the memory of living men, from

the character and condition of the people, which they still express with sufficient fidelity,—and we ostentatiously prefer them to any other in history. They are not better, but only fitter for us. We may be wise in asserting the advantage in modern times of the democratic form, but to other states of society, in which religion consecrated the monarchical, that and not this was expedient. Democracy is better for us, because the religious sentiment of the present time accords better with it. Born democrats, we are nowise qualified to judge of monarchy, which, to our fathers living in the monarchical idea, was also relatively right. (p. 563)

These words culminate in the stern reminder that "Every actual State is corrupt. Good men must not obey the laws too well" (p. 563). Corruption, however, does not prevent Emerson from being magnanimous to political parties in their "benign necessity" to represent "some real and lasting relation," but he is harsh to party leaders who "reap the rewards of the docility and zeal of the masses which they direct." The defense of interests is good; the defense of principle much better; but a party is "perpetually corrupted by personality" (p. 564).

Despite his complex bemusement with democratic politics, however, Emerson's work is soaked in democratic spirit. Emerson's guiding sense is that society is a means for the ends of individuals, who are themselves ends. Only modern democracy, among societies, is devoted to this precept. Democracy is the set of political arrangements that provide the protections and encouragements for individuals to become individuals, rather than the servants of society. This is an Emersonian theme. Emerson says:

The modern mind teaches (in extremes) that the nation exists for the individual; for the guardianship and education of every man. The Reformation contained the new thought. The English Revolution is its expansion. The American Declaration of Independence is a formal announcement, though a very limited expression. ("Introductory," *Human Culture, Early Lectures,* 2, pp. 213-214)

The passion in Emerson for democracy is strong, and is made poignant when he adds:

The furious democracy which in this country from the beginning of its history, has shown a wish, as the royal governors complained, to leave out men of mark and send illiterate and low persons as deputies,—a practice not unknown at this day—is only a perverse or yet obstructed operation of the same instinct,—a stammering and stuttering out of impatience to articulate the awful words *I am.* (p. 214)

Democracy is the unfinished rescue of ordinary humanity from ignominy. But does democracy as a practice of citizenship fulfill self-reliant individuals or does it impede their self-reliance? Before I explore this question, I would like to mention how Emerson praises democracy.

Democracy, for Emerson, is emancipation ("Boston," *Natural History,* p. 87). This word appears in his work at the beginning of the Civil War, but its sense dominates his political thinking from the start. Democracy is emancipation from aristocracy, especially. No real aristocracy has ever reflected the natural aristocracy of a society, but has had, instead, an enforced and artificial hierarchy ("Aristocracy," *Lectures and Sketches,* p. 33). In England and elsewhere, the aristocracy "incorporated by law and education, degrades life for the unprivileged classes" ("The Young American," 1844, *Nature, Addresses and Lectures,* ed. by R. Spiller and A. Ferguson, p. 243). In the same lecture Emerson says:

> The unsupportable burdens under which Europe staggers, and almost every month mutters "A Revolution! a Revolution!" we have escaped from as by one bound. No thanks to us; but in the blessed course of events it did happen that this country was not open to the Puritans until they had felt the burden of the feudal system, and until the commercial era in modern Europe had dawned, so that without knowing what they did, they left the whole curse behind, and put the storms of the Atlantic between them and this antiquity. (p. 242)

It is a matter of luck that America has been spared aristocratic degradation, but it is the kind of luck that has been commendably exploited. In his lecture about the city of Boston, Emerson says:

> European critics regret the detachment of the Puritans to this country without aristocracy; which a little reminds one of the pity of the Swiss mountaineers when shown a handsome Englishman: "What a pity he has no goitre!" The future historian will regard the detachment of the Puritans without aristocracy the supreme fortune of the colony; as great a gain to mankind as the opening of this continent. ("Boston," *Natural History,* p. 201)

"We began well," Emerson says, because "America was opened after the feudal mischief was spent and so the people made a good start" ("The Fortune of the Republic," *Miscellanies,* p. 528).

For Emerson, democracy is a gamble, but it is one worth taking:

> We wish to put the ideal rules into practice, to offer liberty instead of chains, and see whether liberty will not disclose its proper checks; believing that a free press will prove safer than the censorship; to ordain free trade, and believe that it will not bankrupt us; universal suffrage, believing that it will not carry us to mobs, or back to kings again. I believe that the checks are as sure as the springs. ("Progress of Culture," *Letters,* p. 231)

More positively, Emerson affirms democracy because it is the only political system that pays homage to the idea that all human beings, just by the fact that they are human beings, are morally equal, morally identical; they share "radical identity." In the most important respects, one is "more like and not less like other men" ("The Over-Soul," p. 396). Monarchy is a romantic system because, like romantic art, it is full of chance and caprice; democracy is classic, and like classic art, it grows out of necessity and is organic ("Art and Criticism," *Natural History,* p. 304). In 1863, in the middle of a terrible and uncertain war, Emerson writes:

> There is in this country this immense difference from Europe, that, whereas all their systems of government and society are historical, our politics are almost ideal. We wish to treat man as man, without regard to rank, wealth, race, color, or caste, simply as human souls. We lie near to nature, we are pensioners on Nature, draw on inexhaustible resources, and we interfere the least possible with individual freedom. ("The Fortune of the Republic," Notes, *Miscellanies,* p. 644)

Democracy is a moral system; it is the only moral political system. In the American democracy, the only democracy in the world at that time, the human race is "poured out over the continent to do itself justice" by hard work. The poor climb out of poverty and into a dignified equality. The country is constantly full of "exclamations of impatience and indignation at what is short-coming or is unbecoming in the government,—at the want of humanity, of morality." American protest is universalist, not driven by narrow class feeling. This fact, Emerson says, demonstrates that the United States is "a nation of individuals" ("The Fortune of the Republic," pp. 526, 529). After the Civil War, he offers this judgment: "I will not say that American institutions have given a new enlargement to our idea of a finished man, but they have added important features to the sketch" ("Progress of Culture," *Letters*, p. 208).

Respect for democracy as an ideal is Emerson's positive political theory. Let us now return to the question of whether the practice of citizenship can be an expression of active self-reliance. Emerson's fullest answer comes out in an address he gave in 1835, before he began publishing those books that established his reputation. The "Historical Discourse" was occasioned by the 200th anniversary of the incorporation of the town of Concord. Emerson reflects on the character of New England, and the essence of the address lies in the way the people of the various towns created a society by agreement and maintained it through constant attention and involvement. He fixes his attention also on the Massachusetts Bay colony and praises the consensual relation that tied the overall political authority and the people. Boston did not monopolize power, but left the towns to govern themselves in most respects. Power was tolerable because it was decentralized, and in each lesser unit—that is, in each town—popular self-government existed in the form of the town meeting. Emerson says:

> In a town-meeting, the great secret of political science was uncovered, and the problem solved, how to give every individual his fair weight in the government, without any disorder from numbers. In a town-meeting, the roots of society were reached. Here the rich gave counsel, but the poor also; and moreover, the just and the unjust. (*Miscellanies,* pp. 46-47)

The right to speak and hence exercise some power was given to all as God makes rain to fall on the just and the unjust. Such is primary democracy.

Emerson builds a picture of a band of individuals working together for a common purpose, and that purpose often a directly moral one. Where is the individual in all this? Did he submerge himself in a unitary cause, or was he conscripted into making a moral contribution? If so, then the town meeting can be praised as true group self-government, but group self-government is not the same as an individual's active self-reliance. Can the latter be politically expressed? Does Emerson avoid the theoretical move made by

Rousseau, by which social uniformity effaces the distinction between the individual and the general, and one's will ideally tends to the general will? The proposition that I obey myself by obeying the same law everybody else does, and which we have made together to bind us all, is not truly individualist. Emerson does not reach for it. To be sure, self-reliant individuals demand popular self-government, and each demands inclusion for himself ("The Fortune of the Republic," *Miscellanies,* p. 528). But Emerson's approach is not Rousseau's.

If, from one perspective, the town meeting is collaboration and cooperation, from another and equally valid perspective, it is an opportunity for individuals to speak their minds, and just by doing that, remain individuals. Their wills are to be bound by the laws and decisions that no one individual can make for oneself. But before the will is bound, the mind of each may disclose itself. Indeed, active self-reliance sublimates itself into mental activity by becoming speech for the sake of speech. The content, of course, is practical, not philosophical. Still, equal citizenship provides an excellent opportunity for everyone's practical sense to be used in a group without compromising anyone's self-reliance. The politics of the cooperation of equals is also the politics of individual self-expression. And self-expression occurs in conditions of unembarrassed and indeed encouraged frankness. Democracy becomes, in its political process, the register of diversity, of *individual* diversity, perhaps even of individual uniqueness. Emerson makes it clear that without diversity of voice, of speech, of articulated attitude, there is no democracy. He finds that both the humdrum and the urgent lend themselves as subjects that can elicit the self in its political appearances. He says:

> In these assemblies, the public weal, the call of interest, duty, religion, were heard; and every local feeling, every private grudge, every suggestion of petulance and ignorance, were not less faithfully produced. Wrath and love came up to town-meeting in company. ("Historical Discourse," *Miscellanies,* p. 47)

Emerson mixes moral motives together with nonmoral and even immoral or impure ones, and indulges the articulation of the latter sorts and even their influence. For him, unlike Rousseau, the jury is not the best model of deliberative politics. His extraordinarily democratic inclusiveness shows more wisdom than any theorist of civic virtue can ever hope to show:

> I shall be excused for confessing that I have set a value upon any symptom of meanness and private pique which I have met with in these antique books [the Town Records], as proof that justice was done; that if the results of our history are approved as wise and good, it was yet a free strife; if the good counsel prevailed, the sneaking counsel did not fail to be suggested; freedom and virtue, if they triumphed, triumphed in a fair field. (pp. 48-49)

In Emerson's hands, the town meeting becomes a miniature world in which the observer can take the sort of high pleasure that he or she can take in the contrasting and antagonistic elements of the whole world. As for the participants, they show the proper spirit when they see themselves as individuals joined in a common enterprise of speech that thrives to the extent that they remain individuals. They uphold the structure that is rooted in everyday necessities, but that needs them to be or become individuals. The better each person speaks, the better the life: "an example of a perfect society is in the effect of eloquence" ("Society," *Early Lectures, 2,* p. 109). Primary democracy is the best worldliness.

Where politics is speech, and the choir of voices is disputatious, then Emerson is prepared to square citizenship and active self-reliance. Even at the national level he has the same sympathy. He approvingly calls Congress "a standing insurrection" ("The Fortune of the Republic," *Miscellanies,* p. 529). Are there other occasions than deliberative ones that Emerson sees as individualist exercises of citizenship? There is, first, the politics of individual resistance. He is initially unattracted by the refusals of Alcott and Thoreau to pay taxes as protest against war, and slavery, and religious establishment, but passage of the Fugitive Slave Law in 1850 changed his mind. In his speech of 1851 on the law, he says:

> An immoral law makes it a man's duty to break it, at every hazard. For virtue is the very self of every man. It is therefore a principle of law that an immoral contract is void. For, as laws do not make right, and are simply declarative of a right which already existed, it is not to be presumed that they can so stultify themselves as to command injustice. . . . If our resistance to this law is not right, there is no right. (*Miscellanies,* pp. 186-187)

His journals record his horror at the thought of enlisting people in the legal duty to help catch and return runaway slaves. He lent himself to one or another attempt to help runaways; he quietly broke the law, I suppose. But it is really Thoreau who, before the Fugitive Slave Law and after, best epitomizes Emerson's defense of individualist politics as resistance in behalf of others. It may not be inconsistent for Emerson to speak twice in admiration of John Brown, but the advocacy of violence *is* inconsistent with the theory of self-reliant activity.

Emerson's own characteristic citizenship was giving speeches at meetings or writing public letters rather than claiming a part in the give-and-take of debate in assembly. He lectured on many occasions, especially about slavery. This was the only public matter that ever really engaged him, except for the displacement of the Cherokee Indians, on which he wrote a passionate public letter of protest to President Martin van Buren in 1838.

In another way Emerson pays tribute to the self-reliant possibilities of political involvement. These possibilities, however, pertain to the eminent man, the one whose political self-reliance is shown in creative initiative and in command. The primary example is Napoleon, about whom Emerson writes an ambivalent essay in *Representative Men*. What Emerson admires about Napoleon was his uncanny ability to match means with ends and thus effect his will. The events of Europe became the effluence of Napoleon's genius. But Emerson does not admire merely; in fact, by the time the essay ends, Emerson expresses disgust and horror at the costs of Napoleon's individualism, among them the destruction of the individuality of thousands who obeyed him or lent him their force.

> And what was the result of this vast talent and power, of these immense armies, burned cities, squandered treasures, immolated millions of men, of this demoralized Europe? It came to no result . . . this exorbitant egotist narrowed, impoverished, and absorbed the power and existence of those who served him. (pp. 744-745)

Emerson also came to revere Lincoln, whom he speaks about movingly after the assassination. But the war leader does not fit into the conceptualization of active self-reliance in a democratic society.

Given Emerson's individualist political ideas, what follows when co-operation is desperately needed? Slavery energizes Emerson's own citizenship, but the truth is that evil, this evil, cannot be handled by his theorization of what counts as admirable in political life. Even his appreciation of the virtues that war can inspire and employ only goes so far. In war he sees barbarism above all, while a barbarous war was needed to abolish slavery. The institution that denied every hope for millions of people that they could ever aspire to self-reliance had to be destroyed by the ready abandonment or self-reliance through mobilization, military discipline, obedience, and eventually by a conscripted self-sacrifice. The potential individualism of black slaves required the suspension of the individualism of free Northern whites. The politics and then the war of abolition became all-devouring. The Fugitive Slave Law of 1850 leads Emerson to a wholly uncharacteristic praise of mobilized human beings. He finds it delicious to act with great masses to great aims. "We shall one day bring the States shoulder to shoulder and the citizens man to man to exterminate slavery" ("The Fugitive Slave Law," 1851, *Miscellanies,* p. 208). At another point he says in his journal:

> 'Tis high time the people came together. I know the objections commonly urged by the best against popular meetings. . . . This has ceased to be a Representative Government. . . . nothing remains but to begin at the beginning to call every man in America to counsel, Representatives do not represent, we must (now) take new order and see how to make representatives represent us. (*Journals, 14,* pp. 420, 421, 423)

A stupendous moral emergency existed beyond the reach of self-reliance. But, of course, slavery and the Civil War shattered all conceptual frameworks, not only Emerson's, and replaced a positive idealism with the negative one of abolishing evil.

In the decade before the Civil War, Emerson repeatedly expresses a sense of the desperation which slavery created on all sides. A committed abolitionist, he develops no settled opinion on the policies needed to contain, weaken, or end slavery. His only counsel is noncompliance with the Fugitive Slave Law. His fondest hope is for a compensated emancipation:

> Why not end this dangerous dispute on some ground of fair compensation on one side, and satisfaction on the other to the conscience of free states?

. . . I say buy,—never conceding the right of the planter to own, but that we may acknowledge the calamity of his position, and bear a country-man's share in relieving him; and because it is the only practicable course and is innocent. ("The Fugitive Slave Law," 1851, *Miscellanies*, p. 208)

He estimates the cost at $2 billion (*Journals, 14,* p. 400). But he never indicates that compensated emancipation has much of a chance. He does not demonize slaveholders: he knows how easy it is to persist in custom, whatever conscience says. What, if not the universal persistence in cus-tom, has irritated him into his philosophy of self-reliance? He only knows that if slavery is not wrong, nothing is wrong. "The case is so bad, that all the right is on one side" (*Journals, 14,* p. 385). His capacity to embrace phenomena that go against his grain simply will not allow itself to be enlisted by slavery. At moments his sorrow is bitter:

If by opposing slavery I undermine institutions, I own I do not wish to live in a nation where slavery exists. The life of this world has but a limited worth in my eyes, and really is not worth such a price as the toleration of slavery. (*Journals, 14,* p. 383)

Emerson does not flinch. He suspends his theory, just as the war against slavery suspended many positive projects. Emerson urges the war on. "America, the most prosperous country in the Universe, has the greatest calamity in the Universe, negro slavery" ("The Fugitive Slave Law," 1851, *Miscellanies*, p. 186). The lesser calamity of war must be endured to end the greater calamity. Emerson's moral commitments silence his existential passions. Just after the war ends, he addresses a Harvard commemoration, and accepts for himself a thought he had attributed to John Brown on the eve of the war:

We see—we thank you for it—a new era, worth to mankind all the treasure and all the lives it has cost; yes, worth to the world the lives of all this gener-ation of American men, if they had been demanded. (*Miscellanies*, p. 345)

What Emerson hates most about politics—its violent suppression and destruction of individuals—he now confesses he had eagerly accepted. That the occasion demanded a certain rhetoric does not reduce the shock that the rhetoric is Emerson's.

Slavery causes a tremendous strain in Emerson's thinking, which was far advanced along its own lines before he felt he had to worry about slavery. The strain shows itself as a clash between Emerson's passionate desire to end slavery by all means, on the one hand, and his characteristically low view of most politics, on the other hand. This point emerges more starkly when we consider his hatred of slavery against the background of his general political teaching in the essay of 1844, "Politics" (*Essays: Second Series*), published before he allowed the issue of slavery to dominate him.

We have seen that he admires the primary democracy of the town meeting, but admiration is ungrudging only because his emphasis is on the talk that goes on. I do not deny that he has an eye for the good decisions that sometimes were made and hence the projects of common good that the people themselves authorized and benefitted from ("Historical Discourse," *Miscellanies,* p. 49). But when politics leaves the face-to-face situation, Emerson finds abstractness, alienation, unreality; he also finds gross distortions of the political person's character that indicate various kinds of egotistical self-loss. Further, enterprises of power are often wicked. If he does not define self-reliant activity as morally driven, he certainly insists that it be morally enclosed. The regular immorality of political life—even when democratic—appalls him. The inveterate nature of political life—even when democratic—appalls him. As Emerson says in his speech of 1856 on the troubles in Kansas:

> I own I have little esteem for governments. I esteem them only good in the moment when they are established. I set the private man first. He only who is able to stand alone is qualified to be a citizen. Next to the private man, I value the primary assembly, met to watch the government and to correct it. That is the theory of the American State, that it exists to execute the will of the citizens, is always responsible to them, and is always to be changed when it does not. First, the private citizen, then the primary assembly, and the government last. (*Miscellanies,* p. 258)

These words distill Emerson's political sense and they obviously suspect the grandeur of politics and locate its individualist excellence in talk, but not in command or administration or discretionary judgment or in heroic initiative that subordinates large numbers of people. The unfortunate essence of government is the executive power, and the democratic assembly scarcely restrains it from becoming dictatorial, and often does not restrain it at all, but encourages it.

Emerson would be an anarchist if he could. "The appearance of character makes the state unnecessary" ("Politics," p. 568). In an earlier and perhaps better formulation he says: "The appearance of character rebukes the state. It makes the state unnecessary" ("Politics," *Early Lectures, 2,* p. 243). As the Federal Union is close to breaking up, Emerson says:

> I am glad to see that the terror at disunion and anarchy is disappearing. Massachusetts, in its heroic day, had no government—was an anarchy. Every man stood on his own feet, was his own governor; and there was no breach of peace from Cape Cod to Mount Hoosac. ("Speech" [Kansas Relief Meeting], *Miscellanies,* pp. 261-262)

Emerson goes on to talk about the unadministered justice of California in its gold rush days, and even attributes to "Saxon man" a natural social tendency very much like that of harmoniously ungoverned social insects. This expression of mood is interesting only because it tells us that Emerson is sincere when he records, as he regularly does, his aversion to political life. Town meetings are marginal, almost merely incidental.

Politics is a machine that exists to create "friction" ("Politics," *Early Lectures, 2,* p. 69). The search for power corrupts character, and so does its exercise. The association of politics with force and violence, and with deceit and charlatanry, is incurable and dismaying. Of all worldly pursuits, politics is the most likely to be immoral, and that is in part the case because it joins the most real means to the most unreal ends. Equally important, the very idea of political order—namely, that each of us is to be bound by innumerable political enactments—is offensive. Political discussion is a lovely thing, but no matter how lovely, discussion has an upshot: regulation. I am being told what I must do, well beyond the minimum of respecting the claims of others. Even though I may be a participant in the assembly that makes a decision, I revert to the status of subject insofar as I now must obey. But more typically, politics is not all deciding for each, but some deciding for others, when it would be better if no decision were made. And when the law commands me to do what I know I must do without being told, the insult is deep. What Emerson thinks Jesus perceived about the law of Moses is present also in Emerson's opinion about the state's codification of the moral minimum: "Having seen that the law in us is commanding, he would not suffer it to be commanded" ("Address," Harvard Divinity School, p. 80).

Emerson is faithful to the original democratic idea as recorded by Aristotle (whom he read but does not cite). According to Aristotle, democrats want to live as they like, which is the source of the "claim of men to be ruled by none, if possible" (*The Politics,* [B. Jowett, Trans.], Bk. 6, ch. 2, 1317b). The alternative principle that all should take turns in ruling and being ruled is only second-best and should be put into practice if nonrule is impossible. As Thoreau puts the Athenian and Emersonian point in "Civil Disobedience": "For government is an expedient by which men would fain succeed in letting one another alone" (*Thoreau: The Major Essays,* p. 107). For Emerson, it is a horror that democracy should be continuously active, even if it were a primary democracy. Democracy is a device to limit rule, to neutralize legislation as well as to chasten administration. To think otherwise is to attribute individuality to a fictitious entity, whether it be a people or a society or a state, and proceed to find the value of group expressiveness or group self-realization in its activity. Emerson is ill-disposed to such abstractness. In "Politics," he says:

> This undertaking for another is the blunder which stands in colossal ugliness in the governments of the world. It is the same thing in numbers, as in a pair, only not quite so intelligible. I can see well enough a great difference between my setting myself down to a self-control, and my going to make somebody else act after my views; but when a quarter of the human race assume to tell me what I must do, I may be too much disturbed by the circumstances to see so clearly the absurdity of their command. Therefore all public ends look vague and quixotic beside private ones. . . . A man who cannot be acquainted with me, taxes me; looking from afar at me ordains that a part of my labor shall go to this or that whimsical end—not as I, but as he happens to fancy. . . . Hence the less government we have the better—the fewer laws, and the less confided power. (p. 567)

The machine of politics, however, must and will find work to do. It will induce dependence on it. At the same time, the growth in scale, numbers, and wealth of American society makes the state ever more important and hence ever more distant. Emerson is keenly aware that the old American days of semianarchy are gone forever:

But now, vast property, gigantic interests, family connections, webs of party, cover the land with a network that immensely multiplies the dangers of war. ("Speech" [Kansas Relief Meeting], *Miscellanies*, p. 263)

Thus the grim fatality by which a more complex politics interweaves itself with a more complex society threatens to undo Emerson's thinking on the possibilities of all forms of active self-reliance, not only primary citizenship.

* * *

The evil of expanding slavery and the lesser evil of violent mobilization in order to end it shake the theory of self-reliance. But there is the problem of the growth of society, and this problem will outlive slavery and civil war. In Emerson's view, the combination of social underdevelopment and intellectual refinement that was once definitive of America was receding. The urgency with which Emerson teaches the doctrine of the individual does not increase with time. It was urgent at the beginning. Society itself, whatever its size or complexity, is the inevitable adversary of active self-reliance because it is the indispensable setting. But the "massification" of society, if I may call it that, can make the defense of self-reliance more interesting or more poignant. Of course it may turn out that the only self-reliance possible in a huge society is mental self-reliance in the manner of the late Stoics living in the Roman empire, with practical activity subjected to disciplines and constraints that render it less and less self-reliant. But it would be wrong to think that Emerson ever gives up on self-reliant activity.

In the lecture, "The Individual," 1837, he says:

All philosophy, all theory, all hope are defeated when applied to society. There is in it an incontrovertible brute force and it is not for the society of any actual present moment that is now or ever shall be, that we can hope or argue well. Progress is not for society. Progress belongs to the Individual. (*Early Lectures, 2*, p. 176)

He puts his point more mildly later in "Self-Reliance":

Society never advances. It recedes as fast on one side as it gains on the other. (p. 279)

But his real passion is in the first statement. It is consoling that in a few societies the very idea of the individual does get started. Emerson knows that fact well. The trouble is that individuality—perhaps more in the form of active self-reliance than mental self-reliance—is an easily blocked aspiration. We have already explored his concern with conformity and lack of courage: they account for both "the brute force" that is in society, that *is* society, and the reluctance to controvert it. The sense of this force increases in Emerson with the sense of massification. I now want to take up some of Emerson's thoughts about masses, about the growth of society, and the relation to the possibilities of active self-reliance.

Emerson hates the word "masses," but uses it, especially in the work published in 1860, *The Conduct of Life* (his last great book and a book as great as any he wrote). Masses are large crowds of undifferentiated people. They seem to resist individualization. Emerson tries to avoid adopting the reactionary perspective from which large numbers of people simply look like a mass and therefore must be a mass. He tries to judge honestly. He finds that at all times people lend themselves to being massed, heaped up:

> Why are the masses, from the dawn of history down, food for knives and powder? The idea [of the hero] dignifies a few leaders, who have sentiment, opinion, love, self-devotion; and they make war and death sacred;— but what for the wretches whom they hire and kill. The cheapness of man's life is every day's tragedy. It is as real a loss that others should be low, as that we should be low; for we must have society. ("Uses of Great Men," p. 629)

Common susceptibility to social illusions makes people into masses waiting for a sacrificial use. A use will always be found. He reports Plutarch's judgment without taking exception to it:

> He thinks that the inhabitants of Asia came to be vassals to one, only for not having been able to pronounce one syllable; which is No. ("Plutarch," *Lectures and Sketches*, 314)

The struggle for self-reliance is a struggle against being used. But the struggle is frequently a failure. It is easier to be silent than to say No.

Emerson articulates one of the main sentiments which dispose the few to use the many, especially in the modern age. In "Fate," the first section of *The Conduct of Life,* he says:

The opinion of the million was the terror of the world, and it was attempted, either to dissipate it, by amusing nations, or to pile it over with strata of society . . . The Fultons and Watts of politics, believing in unity, saw that it was a power, and, by satisfying it (as justice satisfies everybody), through a different disposition of society—grouping it on a level, instead of piling it into a mountain—they have contrived to make of this terror the most harmless and energetic form of a State. (pp. 959-960)

Emerson seems to be saying, and without regret, that modern democracy is the regime of docility. He seems to dislike people when they are numerous. His misanthropy thrives amid multitudes. "If I see nothing to admire in the unit, shall I admire a million units?" ("The Method of Nature," p. 116). The charity present in the passage on the sacrificial susceptibilities of people that benefit the one or the few tends to be occasionally compromised. For example, Emerson says, in a passage reminiscent of the darkest page of Plato's *Gorgias*:

A person seldom falls sick, but the bystanders are animated with a faint hope that he will die:—quantities of poor lives; of distressing invalids; of cases for a gun. ("Considerations by the Way," *The Conduct of Life*, pp. 1080-1081)

(In *Gorgias*, the ship's pilot "knows enough to reason that it's not clear which passengers he has benefitted by not letting them drown, and which ones he has harmed" [T. Irwin, Trans., 511e-512a]). Emerson here looks at humanity with an unsparing sense of beauty, a sense that seeks not to uncover beauty but to condemn ugliness, a sense that is undemocratized aestheticism. He can say:

The man is physically as well as metaphysically a thing of shreds and patches, borrowed unequally from good and bad ancestors, and a misfit from the start. ("Beauty," p. 1108)

"The man" is anyone at all. But masses darken Emerson's vision even more. And toward the end of *The Conduct of Life*, when he is impersonating the thesis that life is sustained and saturated with illusions, he gives words on the failure to become individual that sound all the more harsh when massification is present to mind:

> Like sick men in hospitals, we change only from bed to bed, from one folly to another; and it cannot signify much what becomes of such castaways,—wailing, stupid, comatose creatures,—lifted from bed to bed, from the nothing of life to the nothing of death. ("Illusions," p. 1122)

But Emerson does not yield to despair or to his misanthropy. It is of course characteristic of him that he tries not to allow his most disturbing thoughts merely to disturb. Masses are one of his hardest tests. In one passage on "hypocritical prating about the masses," there is a strenuous mixture of anger and hope:

> Masses are rude, lame, unmade, pernicious in their demands and influ-ence, and need not to be flattered but to be schooled. I wish not to concede anything to them, but to tamp, drill, divide, and break them up, and draw individuals out of them. The worst of charity is, that the lives you are asked to preserve are not worth preserving. Masses! the calamity is the masses. I do not wish any mass at all, but honest men only, sweet, accomplished women only, and no shovel-handed, arrow-brained, gin-drinking million stockingers or lazzaroni at all. If government knew how, I should like to see it check, not multiply, the population. When it reaches its true law of action, every man that is born will be hailed as essential. ("Considerations by the Way," p. 1081)

It is as if the mere presense of numbers, apart from any human suscepti-bility to invite being used, is intrinsically degrading. But Emerson wants hope to triumph; he wants to give hope. He therefore abates his anger:

> Meantime, this spawning productivity is not noxious or needless. You would say, this rabble of nations might be spared. But no, they are all counted and depended on. Fate keeps everything alive so long as the smallest thread of public necessity holds it on the tree. The coxcomb and bully and thief class are allowed as proletaries, every one of their vices being the excess or acridity of a virtue. . . . The rule is, we are used as brute atoms, until we think: then we use all the rest. . . . To say then, the majority are wicked means no malice, no bad heart in the observer, but, simply, that the majority are unripe, and have not yet come to themselves, do not yet know their opinion. (pp. 1082-1083)

Emerson, then, will try to break up the mass, break up the masses, by both the method of his perception and the substance of his teaching, thus teasing out individuals. He desires to discredit a condition in which "Most men and most women are merely one couple more" ("Fate," p. 947).

His final insistence is that not by means of politics and not in spite of politics will people become self-reliant individuals, at least some of the time and to some degree, both philosophically and practically. In a paragraph in which he grants that public necessity may be a standard of judgment, he once again affirms the ultimacy of the individual:

> No sane man at last distrusts himself. His existence is a perfect answer to all sentimental cavils. If he is, he is wanted, and has the precise properties that are required. That we are here, is proof we ought to be here. We have as good right, and the same sort of right to be here, as Cape Cod or Sandy Hook have to be there. ("Considerations by the Way," p. 1082)

Every person must be inspired to have moments when he or she passes outside society in thought and deed. Emerson says, "Speak as you think, be what you are, pay your debts of all kinds" ("Illusions," p. 1122). He endorses the view he attributes to the Hindus: "the beatitude of man they hold to lie in being freed from fascination" (p. 1123). That is to say, the only affirmation of life that is defensible comes from an opening to reality and is as unillusioned as possible. What elevates democracy above aristocracy, after all, is the possibility that individuals may take themselves seriously as separate beings. Individualism must battle massification, more and more.

$$* \quad * \quad *$$

More than 20 years before his death, Emerson produces his valedictory in the words that close *The Conduct of Life*. He tells a parable of a young mortal who suddenly finds himself in the company of the gods. On this creature "fall snow-storms of illusion." But illusions can be resisted, provided one holds to oneself—against oneself, against the state, against society, against masses, against the gods. The aim is to heal oneself. Emerson ends his parable in this way:

> He fancies himself in a vast crowd which sways this way and that, and whose movement and doings he must obey: he fancies himself poor,

orphaned, insignificant. The mad crowd drives hither and thither, now furiously commanding this thing to be done, now that. What is he that he should resist their will, and think and act for himself? Every moment, new changes, and new showers of deceptions, to baffle and distract him. And when, by-and-by, for an instant, the air clears, and the cloud lifts a little, there are the gods still sitting around him on their thrones,—they alone with him alone. ("Illusions," pp. 1123-1124)

Alone, one is like a god because only when one is withdrawn can reality present itself by presenting itself as beauty. This life of illusions is transformed by self-reliance into the sublime spectacle of appearances.

7

Conclusion

Emerson is the American Shakespeare. His power of articulation is so great, so uninhibited, that he gives voice to almost all the general thoughts and recurrent sentiments that have since arisen in American culture. Not only does he wield his great influence, whether admitted or not, he also and perhaps more importantly has the uncanny ability to be the supreme representative man. He is always present. He not only codifies all that is radical in his inheritance, he pursues its intimations to a very far distance. And he anticipates what will be said and felt. He helps to map the mind of the American democracy. Emerson's formulations and general method of intellectual self-reliance can inspire a renovation of outlook, while his theorization of active self-reliance can give clues to the meaning of living and acting as oneself. Emerson is the founder of the philosophy of democratic individuality.

But are the claims I am making inflated—perhaps grossly so? Grant that in his time and place Emerson played a needed role, awakening longings and a sense of life that justified his (radical) eloquence. But is his work still usable? Is it relevant now? Has it actually been relevant for a century or more? Did the failure of the Emersonian theory of self-reliance in the face of the crisis over slavery and the Civil War portend that theory's general inapplicability to ever more dire or complex social circumstances? We have referred to Emerson's growing preoccupation with masses. But let us say that his theory supplies guidance in the effort to break up masses and that masses do not crush his theory. The very fact of numbers, of immense populousness need not preclude even active self-reliance, let alone mental self-reliance. We can even add that the work of Walt Whitman shows how enormous is the digestive capacity of a theorization of democratic individuality that is closely related to Emersonian self-reliance in both its mental and active meanings. Whitman plants democratic individuality firmly in the city, and the theory emerges, if anything, enhanced. What then may be the undoing of Emersonian self-reliance?

I would suggest that the great obstacle to finding self-reliance a genuine ideal is the chance that innocence is no longer possible, no longer defensible. I do not say that Emerson's theory is inherently innocent, innocent at birth, hopelessly innocent even in its own time. I wonder rather whether it has become innocent. What I mean is that if slavery was an exceptional phenomenon, an aberrant system of atrocity, the political events of this century—beginning with World War I—have established atrocity as the norm. There has been deliberate infliction of suffering on a large scale and as a matter of policy and there is a quantity of material misery that is scarcely imaginable even to us today—leave aside what Emerson or people in his times could have conceived. On the one hand, mass wars, extermination camps, the gulag; on the other hand, millions and millions of human beings living in inhuman conditions. The extent of capitalist misery, the sort that enraged and incited Marx and others, is dwarfed by the misery of the immensely overpopulated globe of the twentieth century. How, in the face of these horrors, can Emerson's vision of life be compelling?

We have seen that Emerson interprets life in such a way as to find in its antagonisms and diversity the very reason to affirm life. To the unorthodox eye, the world is helplessly and unintentionally a glorious spectacle. Mental self-reliance gains from the world a constant impression of beauty. Such beauty carries the self-reliant person through the days and years, leaving that person with the sense that perceptual justice has been done to the world and its phenomena. But if many of the phenomena cannot possibly be beautiful, if they are terrible beyond the most deter-mined will to transform them into objects worthy of generous interpreta-tion and steady contemplation, what happens to the point—as we have called it—of mental self-reliance? When life shows so much evil, how can life be affirmed in good conscience? Must not life be essentially innocent if the self-reliant mind is to affirm it innocently? Yet if we affirm life, as Emerson affirms it and asks us to affirm it, may it be that our supposed innocence is merely silliness or superficiality?

It may be said that there was a time when the amount of deliberate evil and unplanned misery in the world were considerable but not so immense as to be overwhelming. The world could look innocent, or almost inno-cent, and be innocently affirmed. No doubt Emerson looks on the world as preponderantly benign; he can, therefore, look upon all of it as beauti-ful. He is assisted in the endeavor by a disposition to regard human beings not as innocent in their motives and designs but rather as restrained, often enough, in their displays of power and energy. The self-reliant mind can make play out of seriousness; it can see life governed by illusions and bewitchment, not by depravity or moral blankness. Fate itself constrains, but not with a relentless accumulation of unintended effects that staggers the conscience. In Emerson's time, one could affirm inexhaustible life despite suffering and wrongdoing with some plausible hope that one was not a coward or a cruel aesthete. But in this century, is this hope tolerable? The possible consequence of maintaining Emerson's conception of men-tal self-reliance is to turn oneself into a late Roman Stoic for whom mental self-reliance becomes escape and self-consolation, and, more, a self-enclosure that aspires to make the dismal world unreal. Alternatively, one pervertedly finds beauty in the horror.

The preponderance of evils threatens to change mental self-reliance into bad play, into fooling around. The very same evils also threaten to undermine the innocence that permeates Emerson's conceptualization of active self-reliance. We have seen that once confronted with public moral imperatives, Emerson does not hesitate to urge the claims of duty. Of course, he does not say that he suspends his doctrine of self-reliance for the sake of duty. It is not easy to decide whether he is aware that his sense of morality is being allowed to overcome his advocacy of active inno-cence, either in the pursuit of indefiniteness (as in "Circles") or in the steady but inspired completion of vocation. He certainly complains to himself in his journal that political speeches take him away from the matters he would rather think about. But he does not ponder the cost of moral urgency for the enactment of self-reliance. He does not ask what happens to active self-reliance when the moral motive overrides all else and when therefore persons are supposed to devote themselves to the direct achievement of moral good, even to the point of self-sacrifice. If we can say that individual acts of conscientious refusal and participation in town meetings (or in something similar and similarly episodic like voluntary associations) are genuine vehicles of active self-reliance, we cannot say the same about voluntary or compulsory enlistment in a mobilized and full-time cause.

Yet some people now say that the crises facing humanity are so great that one must place oneself in a permanent state of mobilization. Failing to do so, one's innocence becomes culpable. A moral person must be morally motivated continually and judge one's every act and whole life by reference to the effort to combat or prevent gross evils, whether political or environmental or some other kind. A sense of impending calamity is the only realism. One must offer oneself to a cause and accept its discipline. The world is too crowded and dangerous and miserable for a person with a good conscience to pursue indefiniteness or aim to practice his or her unique vocation. To insist on acting as oneself, as the individual that one is, means that one will become merely self-seeking, not truly innocent but culpably indifferent. Such insistence should be impossible to defend to oneself.

The prevalence of evil, then, denies the self-reliant mind permission to absolve and affirm the world, and for that very reason demands that the person act in order, at the least, to make things a little less terrible or to prevent even worse from happening. Self-reliance is only a guilty luxury when innocence is no longer possible.

It may be that there is no answer to this line of argument. Or rather it may be that only in unhelpful exaggeration can one say that the world's condition is largely evil. If the world can be accurately described otherwise, then self-reliance remains a compelling ideal because innocence is not now, or not yet, absolutely culpable. I would naturally like to give the latter alternative and give it the benefit of the doubt.

To speak first of active self-reliance. When I observe that most people, including myself, live life as they please, I give myself a reprieve. I am restored—but not completely—to the persuasion that the postulate of innocence is not (or not merely) self-serving and culpable. The pattern of interrupted self-reliance emerging from a study of Emerson's philosophy and involvements may be the right one after all. A good person will give himself or herself for some part of the time to a suspension of individuality. Undeniably, even the acceptance of organizational discipline—if one could only find the right organization—can be an enlightening experience. Isn't experience—within very broad limits—a good in itself, even when not fully free? Periods of turning one's back on oneself may even help one find oneself. The finding may be all the better for being unexpected. But given the condition of the world, the most important hypothesis, in any case, is that one may be obliged to endure voluntary mobilization, just as one is obliged to resist an enforced mobilization for evil purposes.

In regard to mental self-reliance, we may have to qualify Emerson's will to absolve and affirm. Although he certainly pays attention to the worst evil in his society, he may also avert his sight from evils elsewhere or the evils that have figured so prominently throughout human history. Emerson may be said to limit the scope of his attention in order to allow himself to affirm life; he may deliberately make it easy on himself to absolve. Be that as it may, we cannot, as students and admirers of Emerson, pretend that the evils of the twentieth century did not occur and are not occurring. Given the amount of terrible evils in the world, what we can do is ask ourselves whether we would wish that human existence cease. I cannot think that anyone would have the right to countenance such a prospect. If that is the case, then we are led to the effort not merely to tolerate humanity's continued existence, but to want it. Without suppressing our knowledge of evil, we may open our thinking to the pervasiveness of beauty and the chance occurrence of sublimity in the human and nonhuman world. (I distinguish between beauty and sublimity, even is though Emerson usually does not.) Not beauty, not sublimity even, is sufficient either to affirm or to absolve the world. But each supplies some part of the reason we could give in saying why we have no right to countenance the end of human existence as the reward for its perpetration of evil. Humanity elicits beauty or sublimity from nature and produces both of them in itself and in its works and days. As Emerson portrays mental self-reliance, it may go too far in the direction of heedlessness. We can revise it without crippling it by staying honest about the extent of evil.

But instructed by Emerson we can learn to behold the world's beauty and sublimity and also learn to find them where we had not been expecting them—in antagonism and contrast. Driven to ask whether and why we want human existence to go on, we put on a more experienced innocence.

There is one last and less grand consideration. The truth is that if we close off the possibility of innocence altogether, we call into question the legitimacy of democracy. The doctrine of self-reliance, mental and active, must be retained if our commitment to democracy is to be anything more than a grudging acceptance of it as merely the least bad form of government, acceptable to us but with no special place in human life and unimplicated in enhancing human nature. Self-reliance is the soil and fruit and flower of modern democracy. If self-reliance is discredited, democracy is reduced. The status of Emerson is tied to the status of democracy.

Bibliography

List of Selected Writings on Emerson

Allen, Gay Wilson. (1981). *Waldo Emerson: A Biography.* New York: Viking.

Anderson, Quentin. (1971). *The Imperial Self.* New York: Knopf.

Anderson, Quentin. (1992). *Making Americans.* New York: Harcourt Brace Jovanovich.

Bercovitch, Sacvan. (1993). *The Rites of Assent.* New York: Routledge.

Bishop, Jonathan. (1964). *Emerson on the Soul.* Cambridge: Harvard University Press.

Bloom, Harold. (1976). *Poetry and Repression.* New Haven: Yale University Press.

Bloom, Harold. (1982). *Agon.* New York: Oxford University Press.

Bromwich, David. (1989). *A Choice of Inheritance.* Cambridge: Harvard University Press.

Buell, Lawrence. (1973). *Literary Transcendentalism.* Ithaca: Cornell University Press.

Cabot, James Elliot. (1887). *A Memoir of Ralph Waldo Emerson.* (Vols. 1-2). Boston: Houghton Mifflin.

Cadava, Eduardo. (1993). "The Nature of War in Emerson's 'Boston Hymn.' " *Arizona Quarterly, 49,* 21-58.

Cavell, Stanley. (1981). *The Senses of Walden.* (Expanded ed.) San Francisco: North Point.

Cavell, Stanley. (1988). *In Quest of the Ordinary.* Chicago: University of Chicago Press.

Cavell, Stanley. (1989). *This New Yet Unapproachable America.* Albuquerque, NM: Living Batch.

Cavell, Stanley. (1990). *Conditions Handsome and Unhandsome.* Chicago: University of Chicago Press.

Chai, Leon. (1987). *The Romantic Foundations of the American Renaissance.* Ithaca: Cornell University Press.

Donadio, Stephen. (1978). *Nietzsche, Henry James, and the Artistic Will.* New York: Oxford University Press.

Donadio, Stephen, Stephen Railton & Ormond Seavey (Eds.). (1986). *Emerson and His Legacy.* Carbondale: Southern Illinois University Press.

Gugeon, Len. (1990). *Virtue's Hero.* Athens: University of Georgia Press.

Howe, Irving. (1986). *The Anerican Newness.* Cambridge: Harvard University Press.

James, Henry, Sr. (1885). *The Literary Remains.* Boston: Osgood.

James, Henry. (1984). *Literary Criticism.* New York: The Library of America.

James, William. (1987). *Writings 1902-1910.* New York: The Library of America.

Levin, David. (Ed.). (1975). *Emerson: Prophecy, Metamorphosis, and Influence.* New York: Columbia University Press.

Marx, Leo. (1964). *The Machine in the Garden.* New York: Oxford University Press.

Matthiessen, F. O. (1941). *American Renaissance.* New York: Oxford University Press.

Miller, Perry. (1940). "From Edwards to Emerson." *New England Quarterly, 13,* 587-617.

Packer, B. L. (1982). *Emerson's Fall.* New York: Continuum.

Paul, Sherman. (1952). *Emerson's Angle of Vision.* Cambridge: Harvard University Press.

Poirier, Richard. (1966). *A World Elsewhere.* New York: Oxford University Press.

Poirier, Richard. (1987). *The Renewal of Literature.* New York: Random House.

Poirier, Richard. (1990). Introduction. *The Oxford Authors: Ralph Waldo Emerson.* New York: Oxford University Press.

Poirier, Richard. (1992). *Poetry and Pragmatism.* Cambridge: Harvard University Press.

Porte, Joel. (1979). *Representative Man.* New York: Oxford University Press.

Santayana, George. (1989). *Interpretations of Poetry and Religion.* Cambridge: MIT Press.

Sattelmeyer, Robert. (1989). " 'When He Became My Enemy': Emerson and Thoreau, 1848-49." *New England Quarterly, 62,* 187-204.

Shklar, Judith. (1990, November). Emerson and the Inhibitions of Democracy. *Political Theory, 18,* 601-614.

Stack, George. (1992). *Nietzsche and Emerson.* Athens: Ohio University Press.

Teichgraeber, Richard. (forthcoming). *"Sublime Thoughts" and "Penny Wisdom": Emerson, Thoreau and the Market.* Baltimore: Johns Hopkins University Press.

Urbinati, Nadia. (1991, November). "John Stuart Mill on Androgyny and Ideal Marriage." *Political Theory, 19,* 626-648.

Van Leer, David. (1986). *Emerson's Epistemology.* New York: Cambridge University Press.

West, Cornel. (1989). *The American Evasion of Philosophy.* Madison: University of Wisconsin Press.

Whicher, Stephen. (1953). *Freedom and Fate.* Philadelphia: University of Pennsylvania Press.

Whicher, Stephen. (1957). *Selections From Ralph Waldo Emerson.* Boston: Houghton Mifflin.

Whitman, Walt. (1982). *Complete Poetry and Collected Prose.* New York: The Library of America.
Ziff, Larzer. (1981). *Literary Democracy.* New York: Viking.

List of Related Works Quoted in the Text

Aeschylus. (1953). *Agamemnon.* (R. Lattimore, Trans.). In D. Grene and R. Lattimore (Eds.), *The Complete Greek Tragedies.* (Vol. 1). Chicago: University of Chicago Press.
Arendt, Hannah. (1978). *The Life of the Mind: Vol. 1. Thinking.* New York: Harcourt Brace Jovanovich, 1978.
Aristotle. (1988). *The Politics.* (B. Jowett, Trans). New York: Cambridge University Press.
Bernauer, James, & David Rasmussen (Eds.). (1988). *The Final Foucault.* Cambridge: MIT Press.
Blake, William. (1977). *The Marriage of Heaven and Hell.* In Alfred Kazin (Ed.), *The Portable Blake.* New York: Viking.
Frost, Robert. (1979). *The Poetry of Robert Frost.* Edward Connery Lathem (Ed.). New York: Holt, Rinehart and Winston.
Hamlyn, D. W. (1980). *Schopenhauer.* London: Routledge and Kegan Paul.
Hartman, Geoffrey. (1954). *The Unmediated Vision.* New Haven, CT: Yale University Press.
Keats, John. (1970). *Letters.* Robert Gittings (Ed.). New York: Oxford University Press.
Lacan, Jacques. (1974). *Television.* In John Rajchman. (1991). *Truth and Eros.* New York: Routledge.
Mill, John. Stuart. (1984). *The Subjection of Women.* In *Collected Works* (Vol. 21). Toronto: University of Toronto Press.
Montaigne, Michel de. (1958). *The Complete Essays* (Donald Frame, Trans.). Stanford: Stanford University Press.
Nietzsche, Friedrich. (1954). *Twilight of the Idols* and *The Anti-Christ. The Portable Nietzsche* (William Kaufmann, Trans.). New York: Viking.
Nietzsche, Friedrich. (1962). *Philosophy in the Tragic Age of the Greeks* (Marianne Cowan, Trans.). Chicago: Regnery.
Nietzsche, Friedrich. (1968). *The Birth of Tragedy, On the Genealogy of Morals, Ecco Homo.* In William Kaufmann (Ed. and Trans.), *Basic Writings of Nietzsche.* New York: Modern Library.
Nietzsche, F. (1974). *The Gay Science* (William Kaufmann, Trans.). New York: Vintage.
Plato. (1979). *Gorgias.* (Terence Irwin, Trans.). Oxford: Clarendon.
Plotinus. (1991). *The Enneads* (Stephen MacKenna, Trans.). New York: Penguin.
Rilke, Rainer Maria. (1939). *Duino Elegies* (J. B. Leishman & S. Spender, Trans.). New York: Norton.
Schopenhauer, Arthur. (1966). *The World as Will and Representation* (Vols. 1-2, E.F.J. Payne, Trans.). New York: Dover.
Stevens, Wallace. (1982). *The Collected Poems.* New York: Vintage.
Thoreau, Henry David. (1972). *Thoreau: The Major Essays.* New York: Dutton.

Index

About the Author

George Kateb teaches political theory at Princeton University. His earlier books include *Utopia and Its Enemies* (1963, 1972), *Hannah Arendt: Politics, Conscience, Evil* (1984), and *The Inner Ocean* (1992). He is Consulting Editor of *Political Theory*.